W9-BAS-232

WITHDRAWN
NDSU

THE PHILOSOPHY OF FICTION

THE PHILOSOPHY OF FICTION

by

Grant Overton

46521

D. APPLETON & COMPANY
New York :: London :: Mcmxxviii

COPYRIGHT — 1928 — BY
D. APPLETON AND COMPANY
PRINTED IN THE UNITED STATES OF AMERICA

PN
3331
O8

ACKNOWLEDGMENT

The author wishes to express his thanks to the following publishers for permission, so graciously granted, to include in this volume selections and quotations from the following works, issued under their imprint:

The Century Company, for quotations from *The Great Hunger,* by Johan Bojer; Cosmopolitan Book Corporation, for quotations from *The Unearthly,* by Robert Hichens; The Dial Press, for quotations from the preface by John Galsworthy to *The Spanish Farm,* by R. H. Mottram; Doubleday, Doran and Company, for quotations from *Hildegarde,* by Kathleen Norris (copyright, 1926), from Joseph Conrad's *Youth* (copyright, 1903), *Nostromo* (copyright, 1904 and 1921), and *A Personal Record* (copyright, 1912), from Arnold Bennett's *Clayhanger* (copyright, 1910) and *Riceyman Steps* (copyright, 1923) and *The Old Wives' Tale* (copyright, 1911), and from *A Manual of the Art of Fiction,* by Clayton Hamilton (copyright, 1918); Harcourt, Brace and Company, Inc., for quotations from *A Passage to India* and *Aspects of the Novel,* by E. M. Forster, and from *Black Stream,* by Nathalie Sedgwick Colby; Harper and Brothers, for quotations from *Tess of the D'Urbervilles,* by Thomas Hardy; Henry Holt and Company, for quotations from *Euripides and His Age,* by Gilbert Murray, from *Swann's Way,* by Marcel Proust, and from *Some Modern Novelists,* by Helen Thomas Follett and Wilson Follett; Houghton Mifflin Company, for quotations from *The Heart of Emerson's Journals,* edited by Bliss Perry, and from Anne Douglas Sedgwick's *Tante* and *Franklin Winslow Kane;* Alfred A. Knopf, Inc., for quotations from *Death Comes for the Archbishop, The Professor's House* and *A Lost Lady,* by and with permission of Willa Cather, and from the preface by Burton Rascoe to *Manon Lescaut,* and from *Mornings in Mexico,* by D. H. Lawrence, and from *The Decline of the West,* by Oswald Spengler, reprinted by and with permission and special arrangement with Alfred A. Knopf, Inc., authorized publishers; The Macmillan Company, for quotations from *Shantung,* by Vachel Lindsay, and from *English Literature During the Last Half-Century,* by J. W. Cunliffe; Charles Scribner's Sons, for quotations from *The Craft of Fiction,* by Percy Lubbock, and from the poem by George Santayana.

PREFACE

When I read a good book, say, one which opens a literary question, I wish that life were 3000 years long.

EMERSON, *Journals*

This book is the work of one who has spent twenty years with writing, his own and other people's; whose published work includes five novels; and whose duties have included the judgment of fiction both for book and magazine publication. In the activity described it was seldom possible to sit back and formulate the principles of the craft, or to try to think out the sources of fiction's appeal. One saw the effects, yes; one saw or guessed the means by which they were secured. But *why,* was a more difficult question.

In spite of the acute and sound investigations in Percy Lubbock's *The Craft of Fiction* and the exciting quality of E. M. Forster's *Aspects of the Novel,* there seemed to be a field for a book which should trace the *historical idea* in fiction, more specifically in the novel, although it was necessary to go far behind the birth of the novel to show how the novel came to be.

In spite of the existence of numerous books on how to write fiction—chiefly the short story—there seemed to be a field for a book which should *deal genetically with novel-writing* by exhibiting the raw material, showing how the mind works upon it, discussing and settling the interior subject and the method, and covering most of the ground that must be traversed before pen scratches on paper the heading "Chapter I."

And finally, although there exist many works of criticism, there appeared to be room for a book in which some of the best novels should be reanalyzed with the essential history of fiction in the immediate background and on the threshold of a serious attempt to design a novel of that particular stamp.

This book does not attempt to teach directly how to write fiction. In the experience and judgment of the author, the ability to write, especially to write well, is mainly self-taught. If there is to be any form of direct teaching it requires, for real success, to be oral. This does not mean that books may not assist. It does mean that no book can help the beginner who is halfway through a story and finds his construction at fault, without knowing where or why. It means that a book is bound to offer rules, or at the least, generalizations, that will be innocently misapplied. There is real and constant danger of this kind where the object is to write salable short stories; fiction for book publication is a much freer domain. The object in this work has been to trace principles, not to offer rules; to venture generalizations with care; and *to give as much help as is safe,* but not to mislead with overflowing advice.

Every one should attempt to write fiction, not with the idea that it is his destiny, not for the happy reward of a possible sale, but because it is one of the great resources of the human spirit. The production of fiction *as a writer* usually turns out to be on a strictly professional basis; it is not an occupation for a dilettante, nor something to be casually dropped and as casually returned to. One must work at it very hard and with a good deal of consistency. But that has nothing to do with the general practice of writing a little fiction, or attempting to write it—an exercise of the greatest benefit if only because it develops better readers of good fiction.

We cannot expect the fiction of the next twenty-five years to resemble that of the first quarter of our century. It is doubtful if, in our hearts, we really would want it to do so. It is probable that the novel, in the nineteenth century, reached a fruition in certain directions, as philosophy may be said to have reached a particular climax in the eighteenth century. If the morphological view of history and cultures, so impressively advanced by the German, Spengler, be well-founded, we stand at the beginning of a civilization-epoch such as the world has seen several times before and which is defined, in one of the tables appended to the first volume of his *The Decline of the West,* as possessing these characteristics: "Existence without inner form. Megalopolitan art as a commonplace: luxury, sport, nerve-excitement: rapidly-changing fashions in art (revivals, arbitrary discoveries, borrowings)." One does not have to look far among the novels of the hour to find work which shows these traits. Some of it is popular, much of it is interesting; as yet, not a great deal of it is convincing; its day, quite possibly, may be just ahead of us, but its day is not yet.

Meanwhile it may help us to know just what the human

spirit has done with fiction, since fiction first began. That is the story this book endeavors to give—and it may be simply a fiction about fiction, who knows? It has been an inspiring story to trace, and is offered in the hope that it may carry some inspiration to those who read it.

G. O.

CONTENTS

PAGE

ACKNOWLEDGMENT v

PREFACE vii

CHAPTER

I. FICTION AND TRUTH 1

II. A SHORT HISTORY OF FICTION 32

III. THE MATERIAL OF FICTION; OR, THE MIND OF THE READER 90

IV. FIRST STUDY IN METHOD. NOVEL OF CHARACTER . 136

V. SECOND STUDY IN METHOD. PLOT, ANCIENT STYLE 226

VI. THIRD STUDY IN METHOD. TRANSCENDENTAL REALISM, OR "PROPHECY" 282

VII. CRITICISM: MORALITY: TASTE: ART 345

INDEX 361

"Pure reason" denies all possibilities that are outside itself. Here strict thought and great art are eternally in conflict. The one keeps its feet, and the other lets itself go. A man like Kant must always feel himself as superior to a Beethoven as the adult is to the child, but this will not prevent a Beethoven from regarding the "Critique of Pure Reason" as a pitiable sort of philosophy.

SPENGLER, *The Decline of the West*

CHAPTER I

FICTION AND TRUTH

I

FICTION is older than truth. We must start our quest with these two undefined terms—undefined, because undefinable. Nobody knows what truth is. It is the thing that seems so. Nobody knows what fiction is. It is the thing that is not "true."

The scientist seeks facts, that is, appearances. More or less dependable. But the mathematician and philosopher are not slow to point out the merely apparent character of what the scientist finds. And what the scientist discovers next year may confute the findings of to-day.

The fictioner also seeks facts, but of a different order, not necessarily related to appearances at all. Indeed, if his exploration merely confirms externals he is bored. He is a curious miner who can suffer defeat only if he uncovers the expected. Perhaps the surface indication is lead and he turns up gold; but if gold is indicated and he comes upon lead his mood is one of equal satisfaction.

We must dwell a little, considering fiction and truth, and how the two are often indistinguishable. All the great religions of the earth set themselves up as true, yet all include acknowledged fictions and probably not a few unacknowledged ones. A thoughtful mind might conclude that some fiction was indispensable if truth is to stand—mortar to weld bricks and make a firm wall. It seems so.

"The truth shall set you free"—but there is a freedom men do not want, that they will not have at any price. It is freedom from the things they want to believe in and it leaves them in a spiritual loneliness that appalls them worse than death.

There is, then, at the bottom of our natures a wish to believe, even where the will to believe is weakened or gone. This wish is the oldest thing in thought, and nearly the oldest thing in the world. It began before thought, probably as a mere nervous reflex, perhaps from simple muscular activity. First the expansion and retraction of a strip of flesh, then a filament in that flesh to direct the blind movement, then a nervous center, and lastly a brain. But the brain is very recent, a new toy; we are delighted with it, overwork it, and may end by tearing it in pieces—the child's choo-choo in tin fragments.

The ascidian put out his feelers. He wanted to believe in this world in which he so surprisingly found himself. He made up a fable to account for the things he found; so do we. That fable, in man, is his science, or knowingness. But sometimes the ascidian did not find the thing. This caused no trouble until the development of an inconvenience known to us as memory. The animals had this thrust upon them, particularly the elephant, in whom memory attains the proportions of a social error. But to find the thing and then not to find it! That was horribly disconcerting. Was the thing or wasn't it? Life proceeds by affirmations only, and so, once detected, the thing had being, whether there the next time or not. Yet when it wasn't there, memory was poor comfort.

So began the wish to believe.

The thing was somewhere else.

At any rate, the thing *was*.

As thousands of years passed, humility was born and with it a Thought:

Perhaps the thing not only is, but is there, although I do not perceive it.

II

The wish to believe never bothered itself as to what was fiction and what was "true."

Always very busy assembling, relating, and reconciling the data furnished to it by the senses, it had the elastic conscience of a good newspaper reporter. Like him, it had to have a story.

It sought only to serve its creature, man, more capably.

Man was its child, raised a little higher than the other animals because the wish to believe had been able to anticipate his needs before he could exactly define them to himself.

Man found that he agreed with his fellows that the sky was blue; he called this "true," and as soon as he had called it that it ceased to interest him.

But as he looked up at this blueness, it gave him a peculiar tingle. The tingle was much more real to him than the lovely color that apparently caused the thrill.

He at once communicated this perception. But from his neighbor no tingle was reported.

This was even more exciting. Like being in love and

encountering some one who has never been in love; and making him understand what love is. . . .

"Ho!" from your neighbor. "There was no tingle."

"But I felt it. It was like this—"

Much explanation and close listening. At length:

"I believe," peering at the wash of color between the tops of the trees, "I do feel a—a kind of——"

"An emotion," firmly. "Let's call it that, because it's something that goes out from you to meet the sky. Now when you were looking at——did you ever feel——"

"Of course! Always!"

The wish to believe sat back for a contented moment. It had taken an eyeless cell that contracted and expanded blindly and had made of it Man, with something in him that went out to meet the sky—that would always go out to meet the sky.

III

Fiction sprang from the attempt to communicate emotion. It is, therefore, one of the arts, like painting, sculpture, or music.

Its truth is its own, and lies in what it makes you feel. Its value is in direct ratio to the intensity of emotion.

It uses words, for the most part deprived of the aids of face, voice, and gesture. The sounds of the words upon the mental ear must take the place of voice. The words, flowing, must alter like a face, gesture like a body.

The bright stream flashed in sunshine, fell into a layer of white crawling smoke and vanished on the black surface of coal. Steam ascended, mingling with the smoke. We poured salt water as into a barrel without a bottom. It was our fate to pump in that ship, to pump out of her, to pump into her; and after keeping water out of her to save ourselves from being drowned, we frantically poured water into her to save ourselves from being burnt.

And she crawled on, do or die, in the serene weather. The sky was a miracle of purity, a miracle of azure. The sea was polished, was blue, was pellucid, was sparkling like a precious stone, extending on all sides, all round to the horizon—as if the whole terrestial globe had been one jewel, one colossal sapphire, a single gem fashioned into a planet.[1]

Since fiction is an art, there are no rules of exact procedure. Certain practices are generally followed, certain methods have been found generally to produce particular effects. But any one is at liberty to experiment and innovation is constant.

The philosophy of fiction is the body of secure wisdom as well as we can assemble and extract it in our day; but more especially it is the relation this chunk of wisdom bears to the wisdom of our whole life and thought, actual as well as fictional.

Those who write fiction and those who read it are too often unable to extract the fullest enjoyment from what they do. In the exercise of a vocation or the satisfaction of an appetite they do not sit back for the indispensable moment of savoring. They should imitate Bishop Latour.

Father Joseph lifted the cover and ladled the soup into the plates, a dark onion soup with croutons. The Bishop tasted it critically and smiled at his companion. After the spoon

---

[1] From *Youth: A Narrative,* by Joseph Conrad.

had travelled to his lips a few times, he put it down and leaning back in his chair remarked,

"Think of it, *Blanchet;* in all this vast country between the Mississippi and the Pacific Ocean, there is probably not another human being who could make a soup like this."

"Not unless he is a Frenchman," said Father Joseph. He had tucked a napkin over the front of his cassock and was losing no time in reflection.

"I am not deprecating your individual talent, Joseph," the Bishop continued, "but, when one thinks of it a soup like this is not the work of one man. It is the result of a constantly refined tradition. There are nearly a thousand years of history in this soup."

Father Joseph frowned intently at the earthen pot in the middle of the table. His pale, near-sighted eyes had always the look of peering into distance. *"C'est ça, c'est vrai,"* he murmured.[2]

Many more than a thousand years of history are in a novel of an excellence like that of Father Joseph's soup.

Physical sensation, emotion, the communication of emotion—these were stages of the great climb, the prehistory of the arts. This or that mode of communicating emotion was developed into an art. In the case of sculpture we have deliberately sacrificed the appeal to the sense of touch, leaving only the appeal to the eye. Yet sometimes we may look at a piece of sculpture even now; as Rodin's "The Age of Bronze," the green figure in the Metropolitan Museum of Art in New York City, and feel a nearly irresistible desire to trace the clean curves with our fingers, to caress the limbs.

---

[2] From *Death Comes for the Archbishop,* by Willa Cather.

In the great art that alone appeals to the sense of taste, the preparation of food and drink, we have never really developed emotion as a race. We have been content on the whole with physical sensation. Here, with individual exceptions, we remain animals.

The sense of smell has led to the creation of lovely essences and perfumes; but this subtlest of the senses is perhaps too subtle for our skill as artists. We can do almost nothing with the great natural fragrances—the smell of piñon in the flood of golden light on the New Mexico mountains, the waft of English meadows after spring rains, or musky scent of ripening grapes in a terraced vineyard on the Italian hillsides. It may be also that the sense of smell cannot be controlled as an art; and it is certainly true that the appeal to it, even though removed and attenuated, arouses in some natures a curious emotion of shame. There is the famous instance of Mark Twain's wife, who three separate times objected to his mentioning the "stink" of Asiatic harbors; "stench" she found little better.[3] Kipling was more fortunate.

The eye has been overworked, of course. The other senses are appealed to only occasionally; but except when we are asleep we are seeing something all the time. We have, in fact, grown to the condition where we demand to see something; and this is a matter that the writer neglects at his extreme peril. His words must incessantly make little pictures for the reader. The effect of the overuse of the eye has been, in painting, to develop a visual art that is frequently too far removed from ordinary powers of emotional response—that is, as we say, too esoteric

[3] *The Ordeal of Mark Twain,* by Van Wyck Brooks.

or too precious; too much the art of a few. Painting as a whole moves fewer people than any of the arts, although it moves them perhaps more intensely.

The art of appealing to the ear has developed most satisfactorily of all the arts appealing directly to a sense. Music, which has here and there become as esoteric as painting, never has lost touch with the ordinary man and woman. Alone among the arts we have been recapitulating, music offers a smooth progression from the uttermost simplicities of emotional statement to the most complex and acutely refined appeal. One may actually begin with "Home, Sweet Home" and "Yankee Doodle" and attain to the comprehensive enjoyment of Johann Scbastian Bach.

All these arts are fiction, properly speaking. The godlike Hermes of Praxiteles is a fiction, a French chef's endive salad, an American wife's fresh cocoanut cake, are fictions; and so is attar of roses. Every Rembrandt is a fiction—and it now appears that a great many are especially fictitious. Fiction—and at last we may approach a definition—is what man does with the truths of his world by way of adapting them to his physical and emotional needs. Art is the means he uses and also the degree of his success.

But we have names for all these exercises of our nature, and so fiction has been narrowed down, as a designation, to the written word. Since the appeal of the written word is only indirect, it must carefully conserve and cultivate its appeal to every sense. Writing must not only convey the intonations of speech, alter like the face of one speaking, gesture like a body, it must make the reader touch, taste, and smell; must make him hear the shock of battle, see the scene in the London concert hall when the great artist acknowledges applause.

> The hush that had fallen was like the hush that falls on Alpine watchers in the moment before sunrise, and, with the great musician's slow emerging from below, it was as if the sun had risen.
>
> She came, with her indolent step, the thunder of hands and voices greeting her: and those who gazed at her from the platform saw the pearl-wreathed hair and opulent white shoulders, and those who gazed at her from beneath saw the strange and musing face. . . . Her dress was strange; it had folds and amplitudes and dim disks of silver broideries at breast and knee that made it like the dress of some Venetian lady, drawn at random from an ancestral marriage coffer and put on dreamily with no thought of aptness. Her hair was strange; no other woman's hair was massed and folded as was hers, hair dark as night and intertwined and looped with twisted strands of pearl and diamond. Her face was strange, that crowning face, known to all the world. Disparate racial elements mingled in the long Southern oval and the Slavonic modelling of brow and cheek-bone. The lips, serene and passionate, deeply sunken at the corners and shadowed with a pencilling of down, were the lips of Spain; all the mystery of the South was in the grave and tragic eyes. Yet the eyes were cold; and touches of wild ancestral suffering, like the sudden clash of spurs in the languors of a Polonaise, marked the wide nostrils and the heavy eyelids and the broad, black crooked eye-brows that seemed to stammer a little in the perfect sentence of her face.[4]

Your hand cannot stroke Rodin's man of the Bronze Age, but the figure can be put before you in writing so

[4] From *Tante,* by Anne Douglas Sedgwick.

that you feel its shapeliness under your fingertips, so that the striving forward in that ancestral brain finds an echo in your own. The purpose of writing is to communicate emotion, but the means is by constant appeal to all the senses. None must be ignored, because it is only writing which can appeal to all; this, indeed, is its compensation for the loss of direct appeal. How potent is the continual recollection of smells in May Sinclair's *Mary Olivier!* And when Irvin S. Cobb writes about food, you can taste it in your mouth.

Can the appeal, since it is always indirect, be overdone? Yes, just as easily as it can be underdone. One recalls the rather frivolously-minded elderly lady who picked up a copy of *Three Soldiers*, by John Dos Passos, remarking: "This is the 'goddam'-est book I ever read." To exhaust the senses is scarcely a way of appealing to them; and one of the most delicate problems of art is to discover the limits which a particular appeal must observe. Unfortunately, in an organized society, it cannot remain a problem of art exclusively, but becomes to a variable extent a problem of morals too.

Emotion is a product of physical sensation, as we have seen; sublime—the psychologist would say, a sublimation; but a by-product, no less. No way has ever been found to create it directly. If Richard tells Harry that he is sad, Harry is but little moved, unless from a strong attachment to Richard or from previous knowledge of the causes of Dick's sadness. But let them be total strangers and the spectacle of Richard, broken, his face a desolation, will move Harry deeply. For then Harry sees. There is no attempt to arouse his emotions directly. They are only appealed to.

There is a faculty of the human mind and heart which we speak of as imagination. But it is much more rare than one would suppose from the free use of the word. To understand it we must go back for a moment to the ascidian reaching out its feelers, drawing them back, extending them again, and so on endlessly through a lifetime.

The ascidian's feeler touches something. That object, it knows, has existence at that moment. This is physical sensation.

Another time the feeler touches nothing. We will endow the little creature with a continuance or renewal of physical sensation. The object has now no existence, but it once existed. This is memory.

After æons we will suppose the ascidian capable of a conjecture. The thing exists, perhaps, but is somewhere else.

More æons. The ascidian has attained to a much more advanced conjecture. The thing exists; perhaps is even there where once I touched it, although I no longer get any physical sensation of its presence.

Æons and æons and æons. The ascidian is now either a poet or a higher mathematician. It says confidently: "That thing existed and probably still exists, maybe in the same place. But that's nothing! I am capable of understanding that many things exist which I have never touched, seen, heard, smelt, or tasted. Or have existed. Or will exist. *And that's not all.* I can . . . get around them. You know, endow them with existence."

Imagination has been born.

IV

Imagination is thus several long strides beyond memory, as memory is a stride beyond physical sensation. All men have physical sensation and memory, and most men have progressed a little beyond into what may be called the early conjectural stage. But there they stop. The wish to believe can at present propel them no further. It has endowed them with emotion, but only to the extent of responding to physical sensation or memory. What they can recognize, that is, what they can re-know, moves them. And only when new knowledge comes in terms of some physical sensation can they be moved by it.

The writer, then, who possesses imagination and appeals to imagination in others, fences off his work from the overwhelming majority of his fellows, however involuntary his choice. William Blake, both in his words and his pictures, is an outstanding example. The American poet, Emily Dickinson, is another. The point must be carefully distinguished. The mere creation of a fanciful country, like the Poictesme of James Branch Cabell's tales, is no exercise of the imagination. Everything about Poictesme and the characters who people it is offered for the reader's recognition as a sly parallel to ourselves and to-day. But when Swift took Gulliver to Lilliput, he was genuinely imaginative, and we must be equally so to respond completely to his story. It is because we are, for the most part, not nearly imaginative enough to do so that we lay such stress on *Gulliver's Travels* as a satire. We yearn to recognize, unable to feel anything much if we can't. Imagination has play in the Caliban and Ariel of Shakespeare's "The Tempest"; and "A Midsummer Night's Dream" is merely fanciful in comparison. And in American literature imagination has never surpassed the monomania of Captain Ahab in Herman Melville's *Moby Dick*. Poe? There is a good deal in Poe that is only dressed up as imagination.

All the high types of religious feeling are imaginative. When imagination reaches a certain point, hardly definable, at which the assistance of physical sensation and memory (that is, "reality") is mostly rejected, the imaginator becomes a mystic. Mysticism often seems to be appealing to physical sensation but the appeal is across a vast gulf, so that to the reader on the hither side, these sights, sounds, smells, contacts, and tastes are merely the names and descriptions of unknown and unknowable things. Emily Dickinson was imaginative, but Blake was a mystic. Shakespeare and Swift were imaginative; Melville bordered on mysticism in *Moby Dick* and became wholly mystic in some later work.

Of all writers living in our time Thomas Hardy is probably the most splendid example of vaulting imagination without a trace of mysticism. To explain his Wessex peasantry his mind found it necessary to re-interpret the universe.[5]

Most mystics are, as we say, a little mad; but it is a madness that has nothing to do with insanity. Wordsworth knew Blake's work and remarked that "there is something in the madness of this man which interests me

[5] The best short account of Hardy, including an exposition of his philosophy, is the chapter on him (Chapter III) in *English Literature During the Last Half-Century*, by J. W. Cunliffe (second edition revised and enlarged, Macmillan, 1923).

more than the sanity of Lord Byron and Walter Scott." Mysticism is absence. Mrs. Blake, whom Swinburne called "about the most perfect wife on record," explained it when she said: "I have very little of Mr. Blake's company; he is always in Paradise."

The greatest philosophers have been equipped with imagination; in particular, Kant, who had the genius to see that time and space are most likely a condition of our knowing, and not actual otherwise. Nothing could better illustrate the way in which imagination ranges beyond the ordinary grasp than Kant's teachings or a good exposition of the fourth dimension.[6]

Imagination, also, is a "fiction." Except as it brings something tangible into the world of physical sensation and memory, like the airplane, or Thomas Hardy's Immanent Will, how can it be "true" to the mass of mankind? But to storm at men for their enslavement by the "true" fetish is to be as stupid as one accuses men of being. The artist accepts the limitations within which he must work, and even rejoices in them. Patiently over and over again he goes back to physical sensation and memory so that what he does may have reality for the many. He brings imagination down from its heights that he may draw men a little way up from the plain. He is mankind's teacher, priest, and prophet; but only by his own form of humble service. Just as much as the workingman of Kipling's poem is he a son of Martha, and not of Mary.

---

[6] For the best accounts of Kant see Josiah Royce's *The Spirit of Modern Philosophy* and Will Durant's *The Story of Philosophy*. Durant's book is the best "popular" account of philosophy as a whole.

It will be perceived how paramount is the necessity for the writer, to the extent of his power, to sow his work thickly with detail familiar to great numbers of readers. For the average man or woman derives from many small and welcome recognitions a delight not, perhaps, strictly comparable with the delights of imagination, but proportionally as great. It is not a matter of pleasantness, but of physical sensation, memory, reality.

Hildegarde slopped seriously in the gray, warm dishwater that was furred with cooling grease. Her fingers were greasy, the plates and lead spoons were greasy, and the damp cloth upon which she wiped them was gray and greasy, too. With the mush pot and spoon she could do nothing, so she abandoned them. The butt of the cigar her father had been smoking at breakfast rose to the surface of the water and floated there, and she scooped it up in a cup, and flung it into the bucket under the sink.

There was a smell of swill in the kitchen, souring, decayed vegetable matter, a smell of ashes and dust and cold coffee grounds, a smell, ammoniac and stifling, of babies' wet bedding, dried too quickly. But Hilda had grown up in this atmosphere, and she did not notice it.[7]

The material of recognition differs greatly for men and for women; between various nationalities and races there are also wide divergences. The sexual differences will be hinted in a later chapter.

V

But it is time we considered with some closeness the exact attitudes of fiction and truth. All this time we have

[7] From *Hildegarde,* by Kathleen Norris.

been saying "truth" and "true" with the ordinary view of both. There is, no doubt, ultimate or final truth, but the philosophers assure us we cannot know it.

It is easy and natural for man to think of two divisions of truth, or perhaps we should rather say, truth in two places. There is the truth of things outside himself, to find which he has the help of science, or religion, or both. There is the truth inside himself, the laws of his being and his nature. What help has he to discover this truth so personal to him and his fellows?

Doctrinal religion, going as far back as history, has always been accessible to him. It proceeds from a theology constructed by generations of highly imaginative men and mystics. Its forms, Christian and non-Christian, are often far apart; its function is always the same: to help man toward the truths of his own nature, to make him spiritually a member of mankind as his body makes him physically a man. For this purpose the imaginators and mystics elaborated splendid dogmas, fictions of the first order appealing constantly to physical sensation and memory, and so made living truths for all men.

That they have not always been so received is no fault of the great and scrupulous artists handling them. Any human attempt to be utterly intelligible must fail. Any human attempt at the uttermost comprehension will fall short somewhere. But the scientist who invites us to humility because we were once ascidians and the religious teacher who is gently patient with us because we are less than gods serve us well.

There is another direction in which man has looked for the truths of his nature. In the last few hundred years the growth of science and the work of philosophy have seemed to many to promise an approach toward inner truth as confident as religion's. This promise has not been fulfilled, but has undoubtedly kept numbers of men from the religious threshold.

A disappointment not yet fully realized, and one that will be hard to bear, lies in this direction. Some future generation must suffer this weight of woe. That may occur in the present century.

Psychology, which began as wisdom of the mind and soul, degenerated into a study of muscular twitchings in frogs. When the dust of sensationalism has settled it will be apparent that the work of Freud has partially rescued the science, by restoring the emphasis on feeling—for Freud is really dealing with emotion, not explaining bad dreams.[8] Philosophy, in the phrase of Durant, has been "kidnaped and well nigh ruined" by epistemology.[9] For aid in the discovery of personal truth, the student of philosophy must either go back to Plato and Spinoza or tread among the cactus growths of Schopenhauer and Nietzsche.

But perhaps some other department of science has led man into the mystery of his nature? None except psychology and philosophy will consent to the task. When

---

[8] *Life and Confessions of a Psychologist,* by G. Stanley Hall. This work, mainly autobiographical, is fairly difficult reading, and perhaps the point may be grasped sufficiently by the chapter on G. Stanley Hall in *Cargoes for Crusoes,* by Grant Overton, especially pp. 153-157.

[9] This long word means the study of how we come to know, the process of knowing, and the worth of knowledge so acquired. In its present development it entirely lacks the definiteness of the little girl who, when asked how she knew God approved of her behavior answered, "I know it with my Know."

they decline it, the path is left clear for charlatans. Doctrinal religion and some philosophical and psychological fragments, then, are the only means open to man to understand his inner truth, aside from fiction in general, that is, the arts, and especially the story arts, the drama and writing.

And at once we notice an important difference between religious and scientific instruction, on the one hand, and the inculcation of truth by fiction, on the other. The first comes frankly as instruction and assumes a greater or less degree of authority. But the arts as a whole merely submit their findings and leave man free to assent if he agrees.

"The most influential books, and the truest in their influence, are works of fiction," said Stevenson. "They do not pin their reader to a dogma, which he must afterward discover to be inexact; they do not teach a lesson, which he must afterward unlearn. They repeat, they rearrange, they clarify the lessons of life." Man has always learned most readily by the process of agreement. Wishing to believe, he desires to choose, or seem to choose, his what, how, when, where, and why.

VI

Man's own nature, the law of his being, is the sole material of the drama and fictional writing. Things outside of him intrude, as they do in his life, but their intrusion cannot exceed that common in life itself; for the general semblance of life is indispensable if physical sensation and memory are to be appealed to and emotion be aroused.

"The general semblance of life." But fiction is not life. In the phrase of Stevenson, it repeats, rearranges, and clarifies. It will occur to us immediately that the repetition and re-arrangement are useless unless clarification is the issue.

Some hundreds of miles westward of the Marabar Hills . . . Professor Narayan Godbole stands in the presence of God. God is not born yet—that will occur at midnight—but He has also been born centuries ago, nor can He ever be born, because He is the Lord of the Universe, who transcends human processes. He is, was not, is not, was. . . .

> *"Tukaram, Tukaram,*
> *Thou art my father and mother and everybody."* . . .

Where was the God Himself . . . ? Indistinguishable in the jumble of His own altar, huddled out of sight amid images of inferior descent, smothered under rose-leaves, overhung by oleographs, outblazed by golden tablets representing the Rajah's ancestors, and entirely obscured, when the wind blew, by the tattered foliage of a banana. . . .

. . . The tiny fragment of Professor Godbole that attended to outside things . . . remembered an old woman he had met in Chandrapore days. Chance brought her into his mind while it was in this heated state, he did not select her, she happened to occur among the throng of soliciting images, a tiny splinter, and he impelled her by his spiritual force to that place where completeness can be found. Completeness, not reconstruction. His senses grew thinner, he remembered a wasp seen he forgot where, perhaps on a stone. He loved the wasp equally, he impelled it likewise, he was imitating God. And the stone where the wasp clung—could he . . . no, he could not, he had been wrong to attempt the stone, logic and conscious effort had seduced, he came back to the strip of red carpet and discovered that he was dancing upon it. Up and down, a third of the way to the altar and back again, clashing his cymbals, his little legs twinkling, his companions dancing with him and each other. Noise, noise, the Europeanized band louder, incense on the altar, sweat, the blaze of lights, wind in the bananas, noise, thunder, eleven-fifty by his wrist-watch, seen as he threw up his hands and detached the tiny reverberation that was his soul. Louder shouts in the crowd. He danced on.[10]

Too many novels are as indiscriminate in their repetition and rearrangement of life as Professor Godbole without justifying their confusion by a similar ecstacy. The rôle of the fictioner is not that of Godbole, if he can help it, but that of the drummer whose rhythms inspire the sacred dance.

There are in existence many books on the art of writing fiction. They use an exact terminology. The difficulty which we are confronting, of the relation of fiction and truth, is neatly handled. No opposition is found between the two; the only antithesis is between fiction and "fact."

What is fact? "A fact is a specific manifestation of a general law: this general law is the truth because of which that fact has come to be. It is a fact that when an apple-tree is shaken by the wind, such apples as may be loosened from their twigs fall to the ground: it is a truth that bodies in space attract each other with a force that varies inversely as the square of the distance between them. Fact is concrete, and is a matter of physical experience:

---

[10] Much condensed from Chapter XXXIII of *A Passage to India*, by E. M. Forster.

truth is abstract, and is a matter of mental theory."[11] It is not the purpose of this book to assail other books occupying more or less the same field; were one to demolish them all it would not erect anything in their place. The work from which we have quoted has many excellencies, but this dogma of fact and truth seems scarcely to be among them. If a fact is a specific manifestation of a general law, then the fictioner can accomplish little or nothing, and fiction would not exist. For let us suppose a man to murder his wife. How often will this fact be repeated, close enough for scrutiny, in the fictioner's lifetime? Will he perhaps be able to study three such facts? And if he is so horribly favored, will he be able safely to induce the general law, the truth behind this variety of crime? The answer is, of course, that, never having been near a fact of the sort, nor known the parties thereto, he will nevertheless portray the deed in utterly convincing fashion. And is there a general law or truth behind the murders of wives by husbands? Instinct tells us there is not, and reason will have a tough time proving that there is.

Very wisely this author chose his illustration of a fact and a truth from the world outside man's self. A falling apple is a fact, but the force of gravity, if it be truth, is a perfect example of truth's irrelevance and unimportance. We duck falling apples and we pick them off the ground to eat; and otherwise they are a vast unconcern to us. If man in his living, or a fictioner in his semblance of life, were to interest himself in the apple it would be by way of delight in its shapeliness, coloring, scent, texture, and

[11] From *A Manual of the Art of Fiction,* by Clayton Hamilton.

taste; gratitude because it quenches his thirst and fills his stomach; wonder at the Providence that could bring a thing so exquisite and desirable into existence and drop it gently at his feet. These would be the truths about the apple, truths as old as Eden; the wisdom of Adam if not of Eve, and a wisdom that Sir Isaac Newton can hardly be felt to have improved upon.

> The history of man [this author continues] is the history of a constant and continuous seeking for the truth. . . . In the earliest centuries of recorded thought the search was unmethodical; truth was apprehended, if at all, by intuition, and announced as dogma; but in modern centuries certain regular methods have been devised to guide the search. The modern scientist begins his work by collecting a large number of apparently related facts [wife murders?] and arranging them in an orderly manner. [The work of the scientist is built upon by the philosopher; then the artist steps in.] Accepting the correlated theoretic truths which the scientist and the philosopher have given him . . . he clothes them in invented facts; he makes them imaginatively perceptible to a mind native and indued to actuality; and thus he gives expression to the truth.
>
> This triple process of the scientific discovery, the philosophic understanding, and the artistic expression of truth has been explained at length, because every great writer of fiction must pass through the entire mental process. The fiction-writer differs from other seekers for the truth, not in the method of his thought, but merely in its subject-matter. His theme is human life. It is some truth of human life [the law of gravity?] that he endeavors to discover, to understand, and to announce; and in order to complete his work, he must apply to human life an attention of thought which is successively scientific, philosophic, and artistic.

This passage, which has been somewhat condensed, offers a great deal for our consideration; there are times when disagreement with a given set of assumptions is the most direct path toward another set, apparently sounder. This is such a time.

"The history of man is the history of a constant and continuous seeking for the truth." But is it? Is not the history of man rather the record of a constant and continuous seeking for *the thing that it has moved him most, at a particular time and in particular circumstances, to believe in?* Fiction is older than truth. We may even resort to one of the scientist's, the truth-seeker's, proofs—which, in our diffidence, we will not assert as proof but merely offer as illustration.

It is a favorite theory of science that children resume the history of the race—that they offer us a highly compressed panorama of prehuman and human development.

We may accept this and apply it to Anne, a girl of six years, who informs her parents that she has a son. From day to day she reports the news of this phenomenal male. Her son has had an accident; he will come to stay with her and his grandparents for a week; he is actually here. And so on.

Parents generally may be invoked to witness that six-year-old Anne is not exceptional.

If children re-live the history of the race, truth, either as a "fact" or as an abstraction, "mental theory," and general law, does not appear to have been man's earliest objective.

It was not, and it is not now. Truth is a stone in the road of man's journey. When he can use it to build a wall he likes it well enough; when he can't, he rolls it out of his way; if he can't do that, he walks around it.

But our author seems to recognize, by his next statement, that there is a flaw in his assertion. "In the earliest centuries of recorded thought the search was unmethodical"—when what he means is that the method has changed. "In modern centuries certain regular methods have been devised"—what are they? By what regular method did Newton discover gravity? or Franklin divine that electricity might be drawn down from the clouds? We may grant at once the value of patient and exhaustive laboratory research for the finding of the properties of matter—or what the physicists used to call matter. But this method, even if it were applicable to fiction, would produce the first novel about the year 3541. In that novel a man, fully supported by scientific data proving conclusively that he could not do otherwise, would murder his wife.

What are the regular methods that have been devised for guiding the search for the truths of human life? Ask Plato, St. Paul, St. Augustine and the Scholastic philosophers; ask Spinoza. But "in modern centuries"? Shall we inquire of Lange and James, who tell us that we do not cry because we are sorry, but are sorry because we cry? Shall we ask H. G. Wells? Shall we address Bernard Shaw or Gilbert K. Chesterton? Each of these men is a fictioner of a high order. What regular method has guided them along their so separate paths except the things it has moved each one most strongly to believe in?

It will be difficult to convince the reader who has not had experience of writing fiction that the triple process of the art, so impressively described ("scientific discovery, philosophic understanding, artistic expression of truth") is not one followed by the fictioner. Yet the attempt must be made. It has been pointed out that a lifetime would not suffice for the scientific method in the first stage. How many Noras did Ibsen see slam the door before he had the material of *A Doll's House?* Perhaps one. But must not the fictioner exhibit philosophic understanding? Honesty compels a negative answer; the fictioner, with truly magnificent rashness, generalizes from his single instance, if any. As for accepting "correlated theoretic truths" and giving them flesh and blood, the novelist who should seriously undertake this—and by more than one aspiring writer it has been essayed—would give us, instead of human beings, either automatons or monsters. And why should any one take a theoretic truth and "clothe it in invented facts" while the world all about him is strewn with tragic, beautiful, and actual facts, and peopled with men and women in all the variety of their hates, loves, hopes, ambitions, strivings, despairs, defeats, and victories?

VII

This author's difficulty is one common to highly-trained minds since the middle of the eighteenth century; he feels that an important human activity must proceed from a rational basis. If perhaps it has elements of irrationality in its source or technique, these elements must be disallowed, and gently but firmly supplanted by the logical and the reasonable. But such an attitude is wrong.

It issues from a mistaken attempt to dignify the human

mind. Not without cause has there come into existence the adjective "high-minded." Not by accident is that word shadowed by the implication "well-meant," which confesses a degree of failure.

What do we mean by reason? We do not mean an enlightened and conscious acceptance of the sort perfected by Santayana, "the happy marriage of impulse and ideation."[12] We mean the rational faculty, so-called, the precariousness of which even the philosophers know. (If they trust it too far, that is their affair.)

The human mind is a recent affair. And the child likes its newest, brightest, most intricate plaything. Mind, materialized chiefly as a brain, is a result of coördination of nervous impulses and a refinement upon the nervous system. There is nothing final about mind. It is a functional rearrangement and may not last. The cells of the body are a militant democracy and they have created this tissue for certain ends. If the ends are not competently served, the brain will atrophy, perhaps be superseded by something else. It is new, comparatively untried, and so far has shown a tendency to break down under stress. Its life to date, compared with cell life, or even with man's life as man, is rather less than the influential period of the

---

[12] George Santayana, perhaps alone among philosophers since Spinoza, has devised a "regular method for guiding the search for the truths of human life." No philosopher ever wrote more beautifully or more lucidly. Born in Spain in 1863, he was brought to the United States at the age of nine. From his twenty-seventh to his fiftieth year he taught at Harvard, in company with Josiah Royce, William James, and Hugo Münsterberg. He now lives in Paris. A brief account of him will be found in *The Story of Philosophy*, by Durant. Santayana's great work is *The Life of Reason*, five volumes. It is best to begin him with a later book, *Scepticism and Animal Faith*.

Electoral College for American Presidents, and its fate may be the same.

The nervous system is far older and far stronger. So-called "nervous breakdowns" are mere derangements, no more to be compared with the mental breakdown of insanity than a disordered liver can be likened to the last stage of tuberculosis.

Not only is the mind recent, the logical faculty is still more recent. It can scarcely be said to have existed, from a present point of view, until mathematics had got well beyond the simpler arithmetical operations. It had no language until the Greeks produced a language with abstract words, like "beauty," in place of the more primitive, sensual images of earlier tongues. And nothing like the use of "reason," in this sense, as distinguished from obedience to emotion, had any more than a phenomenal existence among men until well into historic times. It was the Greeks who taught us how to think, if by thinking we mean some operation of the rational faculty of the mind, as we usually do.

The Greeks thought sanely—more sanely than we have ever been able to think since. But those among them who thought—who, as it were, did the official thinking—were not under some of the difficulties that impede and govern the thinker in our day. Because printing had not been invented, the goal of popular education had not been fixed. Plato was free to constitute his ideal republic without settling how best to make imitation silk purses out of sows' ears. His mature conclusions, communicated to apt pupils by word of mouth or recorded for others equally apt but unfortunate enough to be at a distance, were in little danger of distortion by stupid minds. Lucky Plato not to have to prepare a text suitable for use in high schools and endorsed by leading educators! The time had not come when third- and fourth-rate persons would be able to teach because armed with a textbook; nor the time when an absurd scheme of mass education would compel the mobilization and march of armies of such "teachers." The time was not yet, in those Grecian days, when the ends of thought would be swayed by the requirements of an industrial machine. The time was still to come when a lifetime spent in some slight improvement of technical routine would be esteemed above a life devoted to the question of where routine led. All the multiple pressures developed in an over-civilized society were withheld from these Greeks of the truly spacious days—men who were farmers, soldiers, statesmen, and artists by turns, and to whom most lives of our day would have seemed both bleak and servile.

In them the rational faculty had an early flowering. Badly frost-bitten in the centuries following the conquests of the northern barbarians, it has survived to bear a curiously shrunken and dwarfed fruit. . . .

VIII

We make of our rational faculty a kind of Binet-Simon test, indiscriminately applied. For everything that we do we try to find a "reason." Every impulse must have its logical extenuation. In this we forget that impulse is older than reason, that not his rational power, but his instinct and natural genius brought man up from the dust and slime. A plant perhaps remains only a plant; it has no brain; but it grows. The mind is not an instrumentality for growth but a by-product of it which may yet convert itself into some thing more nearly indispensable. What we have tried to do is to make the mind the unrestricted master of the forces which created it; we back this John Lackland against the barons of genius and will but we do so vainly.

"Is it the mind that controls the bewildered body and points out the way to physical habits uncertain of their affinities?" asks Santayana, and continues: "Or is it not much rather an automatic inward machinery that executes the marvelous work, while the mind catches here and there some glimpse of the operation, now with delight and adhesion, now with impotent rebellion?" And he indicates that thought is properly the theater of pictured experience, the recipient of moral and æsthetic delights.

Because we cannot rush our profoundest feelings and impulses up to the badly organized, overworked little bureau of the brain called the "reason" and get them ok'd in a hurry, it follows forsooth that we are to abandon immense, natural objectives? It does not follow, but we have trained ourselves to do it.

Because we cannot explain the process by which great fiction creates itself, we are to explain it very conclusively as a logical and rational procedure consisting of Steps. But the Steps lead nowhere.

IX

When we are very young we look forward, perhaps, to the time when we shall be in love. We drink in, with indescribable anticipation, the reports of that experience.

We understand then that there is something in it which we cannot grasp. No physical sensation, no memory assists us except with poor, weak analogies.

And then comes the time when we are in love. Our "truth" of anticipation has become a living truth of realization. The two are not the same.

If we are so unfortunate as to live to look back on that time, the truth of it has changed again.

Experience, which is the process of living, is a moving stream. Love is a cascade in that stream. Our "truth" is in the particles of water which collect at the source, flow downward, leap over the cascade and wash on into some sea of which we have no knowing.

Where the little cascade leaves the edge of rock to pour into the pool below the water has a certain shape, fluent but unchanging, a certain color. It catches the light in a particular way and the song of its adventure is upon unvarying notes. But this shape, color, reflection, and music are the merest fiction; they have no existence for the particles of water, which nevertheless give them existence and even conceivably run their course solely to make this magic.

Busy with our truth of experience, it is, no doubt, too much to expect us to understand its purpose, secret music in a hidden place.

X

This is a note to the reader, more important than anything in the chapter it concludes.

The clearest and simplest description of the relation of fiction to truth is communicated—with what not of beauty!

what not of wisdom!—in the Preface appearing in later editions of Joseph Conrad's *The Nigger of the Narcissus.* Any edition subsequent to 1913 will do. It did not appear in the editions published from 1897 to 1913 under the title, *The Children of the Sea.*

CHAPTER II

A SHORT HISTORY OF FICTION

I

PLOT is the oldest thing in fiction, even as fiction is the earliest shaping of knowledge.

There is direct and unbroken descent for the cheapest detective story from the first and most sacred literature. A knowledge of that pedigree does nothing to elevate the cheap story in our esteem, but it can save us from a modern fallacy—that the less plot a story has, the better that story is. Let us aspire to be able to distinguish between the degraded body and the immortal soul.

The earliest fictions of which we now have knowledge were religious. It gave primitive man the greatest satisfaction to believe in Deity. The something in him which went out to meet the sky sought an eternal satisfaction, one that would abide when the heaven became dark and the sun hid, one that would explain a new stir he felt in himself.

He spoke of this stirring to his neighbor. They stood together in a cave in what we now call northern Spain. The neighbor had just finished painting a bison on the ceiling of the cave and was wiping the pigment from his palette, originally a reindeer's shoulder-blade. It was a crisp piece of work; you may judge for yourself if you visit Altamira.

"Nice job for a rainy day. You know, it's a wonder those fellows didn't stamp us all out with their sharp little hoofs. I mean, before we could hunt them. The One showed us how to save ourselves."

The painter nodded, and continued wiping. "The One must be strong," he commented. "To be the strongest is most of all."

"Eh? How do you make that out? The bison is stronger than you. There are some perfectly enormous bones . . . you're crazy. If strongness won, we should be the bones."

"The One gives us of his strongness."

"But it is not of the arm. I have been dwelling with this. It is something I wanted to give you. The One is with us. When we fight, He takes a side. You are weak, He takes your side. Your arm is no better—"

"Yes, it is!"

"But you bleed just as much. And you die. But there is something . . . you die, but your side wins. Those who killed you feel the One against them."

"I know what you mean."

"We must tell the others."

"Yes."

As they came out of the cave on poised footfalls they saw that the rain had stopped. A chill wind came, the breath of the Ice Lands. They looked up. How much more than blue was the sky!

II

Man knew he was weak. But also he knew he persisted. His persistence, he saw, was in a form the animals seemed not to share. His collective consciousness, his portion from Deity, had a seed by which it kept alive and grew. The sense of Right was distinct even where the application confused itself. His first fictions, or myths, were to settle this application, and called in his god or gods for the decision. The most perfectly preserved of these fictions are in that portion of the Bible which we call the Old Law or the Old Testament. From one literary standpoint this ancient Jewish literature is merely a marvelous collection of fictional arrangements. All these stories are eminently affairs with a plot—a plot being an arrangement of scenes and incidents creating uncertainty as to the outcome. And the outcome was highly uncertain until Deity spoke. It can never escape our notice how the Jewish Jahveh comes in at the crisis to solve the plot, and a plot so often otherwise unsolvable. Now he speaks with Moses on Mount Sinai, now he intervenes from a burning bush. What, in the way of plot, could transcend that first story of all, the most fascinating fiction in the world, the tale of Eden? It stands, after these thousands of years, as the supreme story, the most perfect instance of what man can do with the truths of his world by way of adapting them to his physical and emotional needs with the means of art, and an art flawless and serene.

> Always the generations pass
> Like sand through Heaven's blue hour-glass

and presently the Greeks are writing plays—that is, fictions to be acted and spoken—finer than any that have been written since. But the rôle of Deity remains for some time unchanged. At a certain point in the drama the heavens theoretically open and an Olympian is heard speaking, straightening out the helpless snarl into which these mortals have tangled themselves, solving the plot, decreeing the end of the story. This intervention is the *deus ex machina*, or god from the machine, a phrase we sometimes still use to denote a solving device. But we have to remember that it was not a device in those days.

At least, not at first. The divine epiphany—that is, the appearance or other unmistakable manifestation of the god—was apparently habitually used by Æschylus, who kept it for the last of three grouped plays. Uncontented with a god or goddess, he often brought in half Olympus; and in most instances his deities walked the ground with the other actors. Sophocles generally dispensed with the epiphany. Was Deity "going out"? Had man's habit of mind, fixed for tens of centuries, undergone a change as though it were some mere fashion of dress? Yes. Perhaps the man of his time who was most conscious of the change, and most nearly cognizant of what it was, is the dramatist, Euripides.[1]

III

Euripides used the *deus ex machina* rather more than was the new fashion. As he grew older, he increased his use of it. "There are some plays," says Gilbert Murray, "like the 'Iphigenia in Tauris,' in which, so far from the

[1] The best short study is *Euripides and His Age*, by Gilbert Murray, his translator and interpreter. (New York: Henry Holt & Company; London: Williams & Norgate. 1913.) Murray's incomparable translations of the plays are published by the Oxford University Press (American branch in New York).

god coming to clear up a tangled plot, the plot has to be diverted at the last moment so as to provide an excuse for the god's arrival. Euripides evidently liked a supernatural ending, and when he had to do without a real god —as in the 'Medea' and the 'Hecuba'—he was apt to end with winged chariots and prophecies."

Euripides was hostile to the gods of his race and time. Why, then, did he go out of his way to bring them into his plays? Murray suggests two things. The first is that "the poet can use his gods for delivering his essential moral judgment on the story; the condemnation of revenge, the pity for mankind, the opening-up of a larger atmosphere in which the horror through which we have just passed falls into its due resting-place." The second is the effect of beauty and "the antique, peaceful close" which a divine epiphany confers. But Euripides's main purpose lies deeper.

He was hostile to the Olympians because, as gods, they were no better than they should be—that is to say, less good than they should be. At the same time they were the gods of his people and nothing, with any immediacy, would take their place. Sophocles and others might ignore them and the awkward problem they presented to nerves and mind. For his part, Euripides would bring them constantly before the people in their unsatisfactory as well as their satisfactory aspects. The people would be disturbed, angry, upset; they would feel and remember. They might begin by execrating Euripides but some day they would more or less admit him right. But there was something else for vital consideration. Deity had once been stainless. If the gods were less than stainless now, it was because in representing them, man had not been able to avoid endowing Deity with some of his own human imperfections. A chance existed that man could be brought to see this. A chance existed to rehabilitate the gods. It must have been evident to Euripides that man and his Deity are inseparably conjoined; the elevation of one cannot proceed without the other. If now in his drama he showed Deity as jealous or vengeful, then he would show the god as sublime, passionless and just. "But the one failure," we can imagine him reflecting, "would be to leave the gods out entirely. . . . We seem to be headed that way."

We were. Something had happened to mankind that is still of such effect, twenty-three hundred years after Euripides, as to make Gilbert Murray discuss the appearance of Deity in Euripidean drama with an air wholly defensive and apologetic.

It was the rise of the rational faculty to an influential share in man's activity. Shall we examine this new development for a moment?

The filament of nerve to direct the muscle, nervous ganglia or centers, and finally a directive brain. Physical sensation; then a continuance or renewal of sensation, memory; emotion; in rare instances, imagination. The mind evolves the rational faculty as a further means of coördinating work that is increasingly heavy and complex. The Reason is to coördinate and act critically, to sort and sift, to select and reject, to modify and make smooth. But from the first it tends toward usurpation. Like the child of the populace it forgets its source and is conscious only of its power. It becomes dictatorial;

instead of a patient and modest critic of emotions and fitter and joiner of impulses we have a censor, an arbitrary tyrant, determined to rule or ruin.

Already in Euripides's day the Reason is touched with arrogance. Man has had gods and Reason has had nothing to say about them, not having come into its fullness of power; but henceforth all this is to be changed. The new censor can be heard in its plans:

"The emotions belong to me. And I am very doubtful about this old standby, Deity. All very well, no doubt, in the past; less necessary now that *I* am on the job. Perhaps not necessary at all? We shall see. Man seems to be profoundly attached to the Device (for It can't be anything more). In any case I am going to reform Deity considerably and make It into a Person or Persons of whom I can approve."

IV

Always we find it easier to go to the past from the present, from the known to the unknown; and perhaps we can best comprehend the Greek dramatist who wrote his plays so many centuries ago by contrasting him with a Greek dramatist of our own day, Thomas Hardy, whom we think of as a novelist. Hardy, too, reached a final conviction about the gods, namely, that it was impossible to leave them out of the story. We have only to recall the comment at the close of the eleventh chapter of *Tess of the D'Urbervilles:*

D'Urberville stooped, and heard a gentle regular breathing. . . . But where was Tess's guardian angel? where was the Providence of her simple faith? Perhaps, like that other god of whom the ironical Tishbite spoke, he was talking, or he was pursuing, or he was on a journey, or peradventure he was sleeping and was not to be awaked.

Or the sentence that concludes Tess's tragic story:

> "Justice" was done, and the President of the Immortals (in Æschylean phrase) had ended his sport with Tess.

When this sentence was criticized, Hardy cited Gloucester's lines in *King Lear:*

> As flies to wanton boys are we to the gods;
> They kill us for their sport.

And since the world had changed so that a divine epiphany was not possible in his novels, after he had ceased to write novels, in his character as poet, Hardy created a massive play, *The Dynasts,* of nineteen acts and one hundred and thirty scenes. Here Deity, as Hardy conceives of it, is the whole show; Napoleon and other mortals are "flesh-hinged manikins." Was this the attitude of Euripides?

By no means. The ancient Greek's spirit was also one of moral revolt and of much denial. But where Hardy has no hope, "Euripides at times 'hath deep in his hope a belief in some Understanding.'" He remembers all the glory that his gods have raised up in man—the courage, the love, the sacrifice, the submission. These were deeds that the rational faculty had no share in; they were irrational, unreasonable, beautiful, and they made men like gods. Where Hardy has surrendered unconditionally to the logical apparatus in his brain, Euripides was able to keep Reason in its place as a coördinator and critic. And in the end we find him expressing, in his profoundest play, the *Bacchae,* "a rather different attitude toward the pieties of the common man."

> The simple nameless herd of humanity
> Have deeds and faith that are truth enough for me.

Man was coming more and more to accept as knowledge only what Reason would ratify, and Euripides declares:

> As for Knowledge, I bear her no grudge; I take joy in the pursuit of her. But the other things are great and shining. Oh, for Life to flow towards that which is beautiful, till man through both light and darkness should be at peace and reverent, and, casting from him Laws that are outside Justice, give glory to the gods!

V

For a while Christianity was able to restore ficticn to its great rôle.

There was a splendid flowering of miracles and miracle plays in which Deity, most often in the Person of Jesus, or archangels, angels, Mary, Apostles, and saints, made the epiphanies and solved with simplicity the human crises. People recognized a God in their daily lives and welcomed Him with delight in their stories. But the rational faculty, against which the emotions so frequently and vigorously rebelled, kept reasserting itself. We must seek a convenient landmark of the change in some plot familiar to almost all readers. We find it in Shakespeare's *Merchant of Venice.*

Every reader of this book can be assumed to know the tale of the pound of flesh. Here Shakespeare has exactly the kind of plot that Æschylus or Sophocles or Euripides was accustomed to handle. But he was handling it in an altered world—a world to whom the real presence of Deity was lost. Shakespeare could not use a divine epiphany to solve his plot. He could not rise to a majestic climax in which he opened the heavens and allowed a Voice to be heard; he could only open a lawbook, pointing to the letter of a law therein, with its crossed *t*'s and dotted *i*'s. And the voice? Portia's, a little shrill.

See how, in this instance, the rational preoccupation has cheapened man's fiction. Was there ever a more silly or preposterous collapse of plot, a more banal defeat of drama, than in *The Merchant of Venice?* All the elements of drama are present, the matched struggle proceeds bravely up to a knotty crisis—and then the whole business goes into moral and emotional bankruptcy. There is no divine justice here, only a cheap flood of base emotions let loose over the discovery that one trick can thwart another. Every one knows that the interpretation of the law given by Portia and upheld by the court is the merest quibble such as would be overruled instantly in any present-day tribunal of standing. One would not have to carry the matter, in our time, nor, we may suspect in any time, to the Lord Chief Justice of England or to the Supreme Court of the United States to find out that a contract for a pound of flesh implied the right to inflict whatever inevitable loss of blood was entailed. Shylock would be instructed to go ahead, using "all due care." And this is the stuff that, on a vast scale in America, is required reading for boys and girls in high schools!

Shakespeare, who had to provide plays and who knew what would be theatrically effective, is no more to be judged by this piece of contrivance than a climate by one week's weather. Characteristically, he embellished *The Merchant of Venice* with such beauties of mood as his genius could fit into it. But we have to notice further, in the instances of his great plays, how handicapped he was by inability to use the *deus ex machina*—not as a solving device, which was merely occasional in Greek times, but as a way of attaining final emotional meaning and spiritual reconciliation. There is not one of them—*Hamlet, King Lear, The Tempest, Othello,* or any other—which does not beseech the rôle of Deity and leave a definite impression of spiritual frustration because an epiphany is not forthcoming. And *Macbeth* . . . if the *Electra* of Euripides is lifted to the heights by the appearance of the gods, as even the most rationalistically-minded allow, what could not Shakespeare have achieved with the same "device," had he been free to employ it!

The enduring wonder, to be sure, is the grandeur he did achieve, the breadth of his moral gesture in the great plays, where Hamlet and Lear and Lady Macbeth and the rest move fatefully through lives in which Deity may be invoked but on which the Eternal never sheds its timeless light. Euripides, Shakespeare, Hardy; a deepening twilight of the gods, a darkness fallen on man. . . .

VI

Such is the history of the oldest element in man's fiction. "*The Trojan Women* of Euripides," said Gilbert Murray, "is only the crying of one of the great wrongs of the world wrought into music"; and all literature of recent centuries is haunted by the loss mankind has sustained, though it be self-inflicted. Often the crying of that loss has wrought music no less than great; and there are in existence mutilations so beautiful that, like the armless Aphrodite, we cannot imagine how they could exceed had they come down to us in their perfection. So-called "realism" is, after all, only a brave and often ingeniously successful attempt to make the best of what is left to us; just as so-called "romanticism" is a less successful attempt to provide us with a substitute for the exaltation that was our heritage. We may glance back to a time in the beginnings of the novel, when Defoe practiced a realism so minute as to deceive his readers, who thought nobody could possibly report *Robinson Crusoe* with such exactitude unless he had worn goatskins and found the footprint in the sand. But with what did Crusoe's lonely thoughts consort most often—or rather, with Whom? Nothing in literature is more pathetic than the pleasure the poor fellow took in the sentience of the creature, Friday. To Friday, alone, in his master's position, his gods might have appeared easily, with boundless comfort to his spirit and with actual assistance; to Crusoe there appeared—Friday. For the rest the man from civilization dealt, in Hardy's phrase, chiefly with "certain impersonated abstractions." He was, after all, too highly civilized to dwell with his God.

We must resume the melancholy task of following plot in its modern degradation, restraining our sense of the ridiculous and voiding ourselves of inclination toward a morbid curiosity. Our attitude should be compassionate and uncondemning: This was a beautiful and, as we once conceived, a semi-divine, creature who has been soiled; but traces of her beauty remain and we can never forget what loveliness she had.

We all know that the eighteenth century was the Age of Reason. The rational faculty had a chance to show what it could do for mankind. The French Revolution was followed, in art as in political action, by fifty years of romantic tendency, best crystallized in the music of Robert Schumann and the poetry of Percy Shelley. In 1823 music witnessed an unparalleled epiphany in Beethoven's Ninth Symphony. An antique splendor had for a moment revisited the earth in the "Ode to a Nightingale" and the "Ode on a Grecian Urn." But prose fiction with a feeling for plot was in rather miserable case. The Gothic novel had indeed been accomplished, in which dungeons, ghosts, wailing noises and haunted people simulated tragedy.[1] It is difficult to find anything else even faintly reminiscent of the *deus ex machina* until Edgar Allan Poe had the keenness to see that a first-rate detective was the best available substitute for the god from the machine.

Poe's early prose had been much on the order of the Gothic novel, but more highly conceived. He dealt with

[1] A favorite example is Horace Walpole's *The Castle of Otranto*.

the horror of the brain, though generally, as in "The Fall of the House of Usher" and "The Assignation," he found it expedient to employ all the Gothic trappings. A marked overemphasis and unrestraint, of which words italicized and hectic punctuation are merely symbols, have reduced these tales of Poe's in the estimation of all except the generation immediately following him. Behind these pathetic imaginative creations it is easy to see a nature made for the molds of Euripidean tragedy. What is all this conjuration of mysterious violence but the despairing cry for *katharsis,* for spiritual purging, for the old, the immemorial plot that invoked the gods? What is the fascinating cleverness of "The Gold Bug" and "The Murders in the Rue Morgue"? It is the ruse, outwardly successful, of a man denied by the world he inhabits the descent of Deity and the ascension of man.

The transformation of plot was complete. A *homo ex machina* had been substituted for the *deus ex machina,* with all the difference generally subsisting between a god and a man. A god may sometimes step in before things have gone irrevocably far; it is all luck if a man happens along. A god could solve a plot; a detective could only come along afterward and mouse about with clues. For a while the element of drama, or struggle, seemed to have been fatally weakened. All that plot any longer consisted in was a situation in which people stood around, speculating how something had been wreaked. The interest in the solution of a crime or mystery was the merely curious interest of missing blocks in a puzzle picture or missing letters in a crossword puzzle. The rational faculty, although it had developed the great type of the modern novel, as we shall presently witness, was very uneasy at its failure to retain the satisfactions of the oldest fiction; and it set to work to see what could be done to restore them. The Lady Plot was now the most ordinary jade; what course could she adopt to give herself a semblance of charm, an atmosphere of allurement?

Obviously the detective story was little more than a tedious post mortem. An effort must be made to come in on the real drama and have the detective, or other inexpensive substitute for God, match wits and strength with the antagonist, human or circumstantial. There must be a race to do and to prevent. The interest would be almost wholly finite and the emotions would be of the most everyday character and the morality would consist chiefly in a feeling of greater social security. But a simulacrum of vitality would be presented.

One of the better examples of what could be accomplished with this improved technique is the story called *The Circular Staircase,* by Mary Roberts Rinehart. A courageous woman, Rachel Innes, with a practical sense of humor takes a house for summer residence and immediately finds herself in the path of an unknown and desperate enterprise. Very early in the narrative a man is murdered; but it quickly becomes clear that this crime is only an incident to some end unattained by the murderer. The real crime is in process of commission; and the murder will be solved only when the continuing threat is comprehended and defeated. But what is the real objective? Gradually it becomes clear that some one is trying to enter the house, and to gain access to a particular spot in the house. The story develops as a race to do and to prevent, with discovery of purpose as the only means toward the enemy's frustration and capture.

Here is a tale which cheerfully accepts its place on the lower levels of art and makes the most of its opportunities as a piece of fiction. The reader may inquire why the much more intricate stories of Wilkie Collins are not adduced for illustration. The answer is that their very complexity makes them unduly difficult to adduce. One would have to digress at too great length. There is another point about Collins: He was, to no inconsiderable extent, a novelist of character, and notably in his greatest tales, *The Moonstone* and *The Woman in White*. Character in *The Circular Staircase* is sufficient and deft, but is wholly subsidiary to plot.

It must not be supposed that writers since Poe with a natural bent for plot development have not ever striven to recapture the elevation of mood, the emotional purge, lost to them by the world's apostasy. Among the isolated and special instances none makes a deeper impression than a short story by Melville Davisson Post, "The Doomdorf Mystery." [2] Here the reader will find a true epiphany —the finger of God on the trigger of a gun—which the merely rational mind may construe, if it likes, as nothing but focused sunlight heating and exploding a charge of gunpowder. In his several books of detective stories with Father Brown as the detective, G. K. Chesterton has restored some of the elder feeling to fiction. The number of writers who have essayed the gesture toward Deity in at least one tale is large, and includes such an unlikely

[2] The opening tale in his book, *Uncle Abner: Master of Mysteries.*

talent as Michael Arlen's.[3] For the most part they have found themselves too greatly handicapped by their audience.

If we seek, outside the work of Thomas Hardy, a modern novel that uses plot in the service of ennobling emotion, we find a singularly perfect example in W. B. Maxwell's *The Devil's Garden.*

William Dale, an English rural postmaster, self-educated, honest, enthusiastic, has by his overzeal as a public servant got himself complained against; by his dangerous pride and lack of tact, run close to dismissal. He is, in fact, saved from dismissal only through the intervention of a rich neighbor and ex-Cabinet Minister, Mr. Barradine. Dale's wife appeals to Barradine who has long been a friend of her aunt and who has known her since childhood. The joy of his reinstatement has not worn off when Dale discovers that his wife has had to give herself to Barradine in order to enlist his aid. By degrees he forces the truth out of her: She was one of not a few girls with whom Barradine amused himself. When she married, that relation ended—it had always been hateful to her—and she has lived cleanly in the eleven years of their marriage until this crisis arose. She loves her husband; and the realization that his pride and spirit were at stake was decisive with her.

Dale, in rage and humiliation, allows her to return alone to the country. A fortnight's vacation has been ordered before he is to resume official duty and he disappears in London. He reappears a little earlier than he must, for Barradine has been found dead in his grounds, his

3 "The Ancient Sin" in his collection, *These Charming People.*

horse having bolted, and Mrs. Dale is one of a number remembered by legacies in the dead man's will. Barradine's death, Dale tells his wife, makes it possible for him to return to her. He does not like the legacy but to refuse it would call for some explanation. It is used to buy a farm, for all the heart has gone out of Dale as a postmaster.

Their life on the farm is placid and marked by kindnesses to people less well off than themselves. They have no children and adopt a homeless young girl. We follow the manifestations of Dale's strongly-assertive temperament. Religious experiences lift him out of fits of moroseness and despondency, and a paternal love for the adopted child grows up in him. But as the girl grows into young womanhood he makes the hideous discovery that he covets her even as Barradine once coveted a woman.

> He struggles, he is horribly torn; and at the supreme point of his moral agony it is divulged to the reader, through Dale's own self-torturing memories, that long ago, at the time of his disappearance, he had killed the man to whom his wife had sold herself. . . . He is about to commit the same wrong for which he has murdered a man. The revelation is so placed as to re-interpret his whole previous life and character.[4]

Conscience is the *deus ex machina*. The unhappy man's thoughts are directed toward suicide. He makes a humiliating failure of a half-attempt. It is part of his punishment that no glimpse of his agony comes to those about him. The end follows swiftly. The larger part of Bar-

[4] *Some Modern Novelists,* by Helen Thomas Follett and Wilson Follett, pp. 348-350.

radine's money had gone to found an orphanage for girls. This structure catches fire and Dale dies in the work of rescue.

"An example of technical adroitness as nearly sufficient in itself as it could well be, yet rigidly subordinated to a purpose which is other than technical."[5] What purpose? What really constitutes, in this arresting novel, as in the fiction of an older day, the rôle of plot? What must be the justification of an arbitrary presentation of scenes, of the withholding of the most relevant fact, of the invention of necessary incident, of an artificed arrangement, of a certain use of coincidence, accident and design?

Recall the origin of plot. It was used to show the working of a mysterious—and at first, a divine—justice in human lives. It inspired faith and strengthened hope; it stirred to the condemnation of evil and to pity of the evildoer. And chiefly it cleansed the soul of littleness and meanness and everydayness; to this end it was not afraid of miracles and it made them mean something.

Is it not as true to-day as in all the past that plot can be used to accomplish these things? Yes, that is the rôle of plot. Whenever it is employed as a device not without dignity, appealing to the emotions aroused by the mysterious, the just, the beautiful and the divine—when it is used as of old to raise up hope, to invoke and sustain faith, to repudiate evil and to make men more brave; to give a greater spaciousness to the soul—then nothing can surpass its appeal to consciousness and memory, now as in the beginning, hereafter as now.

This is the function of the plot that we have latterly

[5] *Ibid.*, p. 349.

come so to despise. The truth is, we see so little of plot except for plot's sake that we cannot grasp its proper function—and we have forgotten its genesis. It seems to us no more than a kind of vermiform appendix producing complications more often painful than interesting.

Literary values aside, then, the tests of a writer's use of plot are rather simple. If he has constructed plot for plot's sake, his work is at best a thing to divert the mind for a few moments or hours. Close on the heels of this main issue comes the further test of meaning. Granted that in the particular instance plot affords the best vehicle for what the writer wishes to communicate, we must judge the communication itself. The ignoble and the base are ruled out but otherwise there is no restriction upon the variety of meaning, only a condition as to its form. It must both be clear in itself and clarify its material; some bit of life must be held up to the reader in a fashion that will make all life seem clearer. The chief consideration in art being always an economical use of means and material, plot must avoid any unnecessary artificiality. Thus, in *The Devil's Garden,* the author omits a single scene in the chronological order of his story, withholding it for its appropriate, and terribly effective, disclosure at a later point. It is a single liberty with the reader, taken where a ton of contrivance could accomplish nothing, and where a failure to contrive at all would rob the communication of meaning of all its intensity.

But when we have stated the artistic requirement that unnecessary artificiality be shunned, we have said all. The subject cannot be specified. Rash generalizations against the use of coincidence, for example, are silly. A plot may need to employ coincidence, or more than one coincidence, if thus the story's meaning can best be expressed or enforced. We must bear in mind that coincidence is only the rational faculty's term for something it has observed but cannot explain; and that what one part of us terms coincidence, an older and stronger part of us recognizes as miracle. Coincidence, if used, is a hinge of plot, and comes under the strict injunction against plot for plot's sake. Every detail of plot must continuously subserve the end of conveying meaning; every artifice must surround us with significance; and plot must still come to us as a revelation if no longer as an intimation of immortality vouchsafed to humble men.

VII

Before we have done with plot, in the history of fiction, we must notice the romantic novel, so-called.

As we shall observe later, romanticism is the appetite of the emotions; and since they respond only to living, it is a zest for life. More common in youth, romantic feeling may exist at any age, as in the work of William De Morgan or Arnold Bennett, where it is constantly combined with realism of the most exact description. But this, the real romance, is not what we mean, characteristically, when we speak of romantic novels: We mean Sir Walter Scott and the kind of books he brought into existence. They need not be historical but they must be adventurous and glowing and they are generally full of plot.

These tales represent, of course, the old instinct with which fiction began. After the rational faculty had expurgated Deity, the thoroughly finite novel (as one form of fiction) came into existence. We have seen how the original structure of plot crumbled to pieces. The Walter Scott–Robert Louis Stevenson tale is one of the pieces. How bravely, like ants with a heavy morsel of surpassing richness, men have toiled to make this fragment securely theirs! Again to take the familiar example, Scott's *Ivanhoe,* we can scarcely too much admire the painstaking. To be sure, Scott is helped by writing of a time when Deity was still largely real to mankind; he has but to reproduce the mood of the spectators to make it almost seem as if Heaven smote Bois-Guilbert with Ivanhoe's weapon.

The rational faculty, having destroyed what it could not replace, set up its own standards for emotional responses, and the first of these, in its primitive form, was the Fact. Richard the Lion-Hearted actually lived; therefore he is interesting in a novel. Thus the rational faculty, laboring hard, and quite unconscious for some time that it wins on false pretenses. For a hundred thousand men have lived, and a thousand kings, but only a few, like this Richard, have interest. Actuality really means nothing, as plenty of historical novelists and even historians were to find to their cost. There are a great many Napoleon Bonapartes, utterly unlike, all based solidly on Fact, and this after the man has been barely a century dead. It is probable that the Bonaparte of Tolstoy's great novel, *War and Peace,* is one who never existed; but to-day he does exist and he will exist for years to come. Why? The rational faculty boggles in its answer.

The romantic novel is the *pot-au-feu,* but not every cook is a Frenchman, not every dish is the veritable soup. It tries to blend—a little—the novel of character, which we shall soon be discussing, and the fiction of accident and design, which is, in finite terms, all that is left us of the fiction of plot. It grasps, this romantic novel, at the historical background, hoping that the presence of an actual person or two will command our respect if emotion be little. It grasps at every clutchable straw; we are prayed to read the book because it pictures some bygone age and is thus "instructive." But the soup is often flavorless and not seldom a mere reheating more than half cold. The true romance may be present, the zest for life; but that is another matter.

Scott remains the finest figure in this compromised fiction. We may take him at his best, with either *The Heart of Midlothian* or *Ivanhoe* or what you will. Beside this best of Scott may be ranged any five other "romantic" novels to make a select six, champions of them all. Here is a suggestion for the other five:

Alexandre Dumas: *The Three Musketeers,*
Victor Hugo: *Les Miserables,*
James Fenimore Cooper: *The Last of the Mohicans,*
Robert Louis Stevenson: *Treasure Island,*
Joseph Conrad: *Victory,*

but other fives are equally possible, though perhaps it would be difficult to name a five superior. Well, then, these six. The first thing to notice is that none, unless it be our choice from Scott, relies on historical characters, though *Treasure Island* invokes an actual pirate or two.

In every one, though most weakly in Cooper, the true spirit of romance is felt, the eager appetite for life—but this has nothing to do with form or plot. The Dumas, Hugo, and Conrad are rich in their creation of character. We remember Porthos, Aramis, and D'Artagnan when we have forgotten all their adventures. It is, indeed, character that rules all these roosts: Jean Valjean, Uncas, Long John Silver, Heyst and Lena, and plain Mr. Jones materialize instantly before us while we still only half remember their fortunes. The augustness of older fiction, the investiture of accident and design that were in themselves miracle and meaning almost regardless of the actors, does indeed hang broodingly over the people of *Les Miserables* and over the principals of *Victory.* Why? Because neither Hugo nor Conrad was one to submit tamely to finitude. For that matter, Dumas rebelled a little and makes us feel the touch of destiny, of divine retribution, in *Monte Cristo;* Stevenson escaped from his bondage in *Dr. Jekyll and Mr. Hyde.*

No such thing as the romantic novel of our easy allusion has ever existed, but this does not mean that we shall discontinue our talk of such. It is a convenient term for tales with a definite amount of plot, mostly of a mechanical nature; some amount of character; an occasional infusion of historical matter—the whole usually kept firmly on the ground. There may or may not be romantic feeling, just as in novels that eschew plot almost entirely and center the interest wholly on character. But are there such novels? A-plenty. Arnold Bennett's *Clayhanger* is wildly romantic. The scene is an ugly English provincial manufacturing town. Edwin Clayhanger's father has managed to build a house in a little better street, a new part of Bursley.

> . . . The hot-water system of the new house, simple and primitive as it was, affected and inspired Edwin like a poem. There was a cistern room, actually a room devoted to nothing but cisterns, and the main cistern was so big that the builders had had to install it before the roof was put on, for it would never have gone through a door. This cistern, by means of a ball-tap, filled itself from the main nearly as quickly as it was emptied. Out of it grew pipes, creeping in secret downwards between inner walls of the house, penetrating everywhere. One went down to a boiler behind the kitchen range and filled it, and as the fire that was roasting the joint heated the boiler, the water mounted again magically to the cistern-room and filled another cistern, spherical and sealed, and thence descended, on a third journeying, to the bath and to the lavatory basin in the bathroom. . . . A room solely for baths! And a huge painted zinc bath! And a vast porcelain basin, with tiles all around it, in which you could splash! An endless supply of water on the first floor!
>
> At the shop-house . . . to take a warm hip-bath was an immense enterprise of heating, fetching, decanting, and general derangement of the entire house; and at best the bath was not hot; it always lost its virtue on the stairs and landing. And to splash—one of the most voluptuous pleasures in life—was forbidden by the code. Mrs. Nixon would actually weep at a splashing. Splashing was immoral. It was as wicked as amorous dalliance in a monastery.[6]

The true romance, the vigorous, unspoiled emotional appetite, the zest for life. Yet *Clayhanger* has no plot; is

---

[6] *Clayhanger,* by Arnold Bennett, Book Two, Chap. IV, section iii.

wholly finite; deals entirely with the commonplace, and concentrates on character.

VIII

The proper study of mankind is Man, as Pope put it so pithily. Centuries before, the rational faculty had reached that conclusion in considering the perplexing problem of fiction.

Whatever may be unknown, criticized Reason, had better be left for the present out of reckoning. Let us first ask ourselves, "What do I know?"—and the answer will be sufficiently disconcerting. Said Reason: "We can, at least, strive to know ourselves. We can endeavor to know ourselves better. Insofar as we accomplish that, we do something to make ourselves better."

Fiction had always assumed this and on the unspoken assumption had proceeded with instinctive art. However, the oldest fiction recognized nothing that we should call "character" to-day. Its *personæ* were the embodiments and expressions of traits general to mankind. Thus, in the story of Adam and Eve, Adam is Everyman and Eve, Everywoman. Adam is not a particular man nor is Eve a certain woman. The story is therefore of universal validity. No modern story can possibly have so wide an application, such force. Ruth, in *The Book of Ruth,* is simply the self-sacrifice and devotion of a woman in love. The story is timeless. The heroes and heroines of Greek legend were molded in the same way, to show by possibly extreme instances the effects of emotions and passions common to all mankind. The first touches of what we should call characterization are noticeable in

Greek drama, chiefly in Euripides. For example, in an early play, the *Alcestis:*

Admetus, a king in Thessaly, was fated to die on a certain day, but, in return for his piety of old, was allowed to find a substitute to die for him. His old father and mother refused; his young wife, Alcestis, gladly consented. Amid exquisite songs of mourning she is carried to her grave, when the wild hero, Heracles, comes to the house seeking hospitality. Admetus, with primitive courtesy, conceals what has happened and orders him to be given entertainment. The burial is finished when Heracles, already revelling and drunken and crowned with flowers, learns the truth. Sobered at the touch he goes out into the night to wrestle with Death amid the tombs and crush his ribs for him till he yields up his prey. . . . But amid all the romance Euripides cannot keep his hand from unveiling the weak spot in the sacred legend. Alcestis, no doubt, is beautiful, and it was beautiful of her to die. But what was it of Admetus to let her die? An ordinary playwright would elude the awkward question. Admetus would refuse his wife's sacrifice and she would perform it against his will or without his knowledge. We should somehow save our hero's character. Not so Euripides. His Admetus weeps tenderly over his wife, but he thinks it entirely suitable that she should die for him. The veil is not removed from his eyes till his old father, Pheres, who has bluntly refused to die for anybody, comes to bring offerings to Alcestis's funeral. A quarrel breaks out between the two selfish men, brilliantly written, subtle and merciless, in which Admetus's weakness is laid bare.[7]

Admetus, weeping tenderly over Alcestis, but thinking it entirely suitable that she should die for him, is genuine

[7] *Euripides and His Age,* by Gilbert Murray, Chap. III.

characterization, not just a personification of male selfis ness in general—old Pheres, declining to die for anybod is that. The quarrel between the two men, insofar as i bares his egotism to Admetus, is false characterization; the eyes of such egotism can never be opened to its own excesses. But the quarrel hammers the lesson home to the audience as, perhaps, it would not otherwise be driven home. The fundamental axiom of all characterization sticks out in this early example: Behavior. A writer ought to characterize only through the behavior—the words, acts, and thoughts—of his subject. Character can never, properly, be told about; can never be hearsay. If in fiction the author characterizes through his own mouth, or that of another person, we may tolerate the device to save time or for other expediency; but we may also reject outright.

And immediately we seem to collide with one of the most tenaciously held prerogatives of the novelist, his author's omniscience.

> The specialty of the novel is that the writer can talk about his characters as well as through them or can arrange for us to listen when they talk to themselves. He has access to self-communings, and from that level he can descend even deeper and peer into the subconscious. A man does not talk to himself quite truly—not even to himself; the happiness or misery that he secretly feels proceed from causes that he cannot quite explain, because as soon as he raises them to the level of the explicable they lose their native quality. The novelist has a real pull here. He can show the subconscious short-circuiting straight into action (the dramatist can do this too); he can also show it in its relation to soliloquy. He commands all the

secret life, and he must not be robbed of this privilege. "How did the writer know that?" it is sometimes said. "What's his standpoint? He is not being consistent, he's shifting his point of view from the limited to the omniscent, and now he's edging back again." Questions like these have too much the atmosphere of the law courts about them. All that matters to the reader is whether the shifting of attitude and the secret life are convincing.[8]

Is there a real conflict here? No, the fundamental axiom of *all* characterization is: behavior. "The writer can talk about his characters"—yes. He may do it to save time or to induct the reader into a mood. But he runs all the risks of such license. "He commands all the secret life"—yes. But by its fruits in the behavior of his character shall we know whether he commands it truly. The soliloquy offers no difficulty, for speech, whether in company or alone, is a species of behavior. All proper characterization—proper in method—is indirect, that is, the character thinking, saying, doing. All direct characterization—the author or another character telling about somebody—is hearsay. The author is making a bargain with his readers and the warning is always in plain sight: *Caveat auctor.*

The discussion on which we have entered does not properly belong here and should be reserved for later on, when we study method. But it must be pushed to a certain point, now that we have lapsed into it, and partly because it will guide us in our glance at the history of modern fiction. Let us take a very recent example of the

[8] *Aspects of the Novel,* by E. M. Forster (Harcourt, Brace: 1927), pp. 127-128.

novel, widely read in its year both in England and America, and note the author's method in a vital piece of characterization.

The novel is A. S. M. Hutchinson's *If Winter Comes*. The particular characterization is Mabel Sabre. Enough of the story may here be recalled to refresh our recollection.

Mark Sabre, the hero, is a wistful and highly idealistic man, shy, unsocial, quixotically humane in all his impulses, of deep emotional attachments. He has a dream of writing a history of England. The idea of his country provokes in him a tremendous emotional response. He is not much interested in people unless, perhaps, they seem to him to embody an ideal. He is wholly kind.

Mabel Sabre is his wife. A quite ordinary, average woman, concrete and practical, interested in her home and her neighbors, and childless, she has lived all these years of her married life without in the least comprehending her husband. She should, of course, long before this have grasped that he is a little boy sailing his white dreamboats in the blue of heaven. But it is from the first apparent to the reader that her incomprehension is at least as much Mark's fault as hers. He has never tried to interest himself in *her* ideals and objectives—which might have been a patient means toward gaining at least her tolerance for his own.

The problem of the novelist, Mr. Hutchinson, is at the outset to show the gulf that separates this pair. He has a further problem: He wishes to enlist our sympathies for Mark. This should be simple enough. We all like Mark Sabres unless we have to live with them;

sometimes, even then, we succumb to their charm. But Mr. Hutchinson is singularly uneasy, over-anxious, strained. Afraid, it would seem, to rest Mark's case on its very real merits, he opens his novel with the words: "One Hapgood, a solicitor, a useful person. . . ."

Useful is right! From the very first page Hapgood is resorted to for direct characterization of Mark and Mabel—especially Mabel. And such direct characterization! As a friend of Mark, Hapgood hates his wife with a hate explosive and vehement. Poor Mabel Sabre hasn't the ghost of a chance; and it becomes shockingly evident that Hapgood, after all, is only Mr. Hutchinson's device for hymning hate. As we read on we realize that it is the author who is damning Mabel Sabre, from start to finish—only he was afraid that if he said these things about her, in his omniscient author's rôle, we should exercise our reader's right to challenge his omniscience and reject his conclusions. He cannot show us—he does not show us—his warrant for these spiteful findings in Mabel's behavior; and has resorted to this trick of Hapgood. We may all read his novel, for passion and prejudice interest us and give us the dear delight of controversy; but our final feeling is one of oblivious contempt.

This is an extreme example of the betrayal which direct characterization can effect. Mr. Hutchinson's failure in omniscience was vast. He was not only without a humane knowledge of Mabel Sabre, he grasped Mark in only one aspect. Any woman could have told him that Mark, from the feminine standpoint, is impossible material for a husband. Any married man could have told him that no wife on earth tolerates well the presence of another woman under her roof. (It should perhaps be explained, for the benefit of any who may not have read *If Winter Comes,* that as the novel develops Mark befriends a young unmarried woman who is pregnant; insists on bringing her into his home; and remains injured and inarticulate when Mabel misunderstands this action and tends to suppose that Mark is father of the child.)

One sure method of eliminating hearsay, at least so far as the principal character is concerned, is to have him tell the story. This is our complacent and instant deduction; but it is not true. "A man does not talk to himself quite truly—not even to himself"; most certainly he does not talk quite truly to the world in general. He does not describe his actions quite truly; and of necessity he becomes the unavoidable means of directly characterizing every other actor, no matter how honest he may be; they even more than himself are coated with hearsay. So much further we progress into method at this time, but only so much; and only because our next example is of this type; for now we have to resume the history of the novel of character, of which the first great master was Daniel Defoe.

IX

Historically speaking, Defoe was the first only in English; Cervantes in Spain, a century earlier, had produced *Don Quixote,* in which the Knight and his squire, Sancho Panza, are beautifully and consistently put before us. Yet do they belong, in what has come to be their universal and enduring aspect, with the fiction of old—embodiments, the Knight of pathetic human make-believe, the squire of a literal-mindedness just as pathetic if less liable to broken bones. But Defoe is another matter. In him "the proper study of mankind" attained to such intensity of perception and skill of relation that in over two hundred years, we have developed only one superior and none who is his equal.

E. M. Forster, the novelist, in his engaging book, *Aspects of the Novel,* reviews Defoe's *Moll Flanders* more aptly than any one else has done; and what follows is a faulty paraphrase of his analysis.

Moll is all the story. Defoe's book has only such form as his heroine gives it. "She stands in an open space like a tree." Early in life she is seduced by a younger brother and then she is married to an elder. "She takes to husbands in the earlier and brighter part of her career," not to prostitution, "which she detests with all the force of a decent and affectionate heart." Mr. Forster is of the opinion that some great experience befell Defoe himself, while he was in Newgate Prison. "We do not know what it was, probably he himself did not know afterwards . . . but . . . out of its vague, powerful emotion Moll and Roxana [9] are born." Moll had, more or less simultaneously, three or four husbands, one turning out to be a brother. "She was happy with all of them, they were nice to her, she nice to them." There was a draper husband whom she never cared for a great deal but with whom she could fall in agreeably over the idea of a trip to Oxford. They went out and back in a coach-and-six, were bowed down to as a lord and his lady, "saw all the rarities at Oxford" and "talked with two or three Fellows

[9] *Roxana* is another of Defoe's novels.

of Colleges about putting out a young nephew, that was left to his lordship's care, to the University, and of their being his tutors . . . and thus having lived like quality, indeed, as to expense, we went away for Northampton, and, in a word, in about twelve days' ramble came home again, to the tune of about £93 expense." "Contrast with this," Mr. Forster invites us, "the scene with her Lancashire husband, whom she deeply loved. He is a highwayman, and each by pretending to wealth has trapped the other into marriage. After the ceremony, they are mutually unmasked, and if Defoe were writing mechanically he would set them to upbraid one another, like Mr. and Mrs. Lammle in *Our Mutual Friend*. But he has given himself over to the humor and good sense of his heroine. She guides him through." The scene is as follows:

"Truly," said I to him, "I found you would soon have conquered me; and it is my affliction now that I am not in a condition to let you see how easily I should have been reconciled to you, and have passed by all the tricks you had put upon me, in recompense of so much good-humor. But, my dear," said I, "what can we do now? We are both undone, and what better are we for our being reconciled together, seeing we have nothing to live on?"

We proposed a great many things, but nothing could offer where there was nothing to begin with. He begged me at last to talk no more of it, for, he said, I would break his heart; so we talked of other things a little, till at last he took a husband's leave of me, and so we went to sleep.

Well, then, as time goes on she "turns from husbands to thieving; she thinks this a change for the worse and a natural darkness spreads over the scene. But she is as firm and amusing as ever." When she robs a little girl returning from the dancing class of a gold necklace she is chiefly stirred by the dangers to the child, by anger at the parents for "leaving the poor little lamb to come home by itself, and it would teach them to take more care of it another time." Mr. Forster well observes: "How heavily and pretentiously a modern psychologist would labor to express this! It just runs off Defoe's pen, and so in another passage, where Moll cheats a man, and then tells him pleasantly afterwards that she has done so, with the result that she slides still further into his good graces, and cannot bear to cheat him any more. Whatever she does gives us a slight shock—not the jolt of disillusionment, but the thrill that proceeds from a living being."

At last she is caught in a shop, arrested, sentenced to death and then transported to Virginia as a mitigation. Her Lancashire husband is being transported also, and after a few further incidents the end is reached with a resolution to lead better lives. And now, as illustrating the true nature of the finite fiction by the witness of another mind, and a mind of great keenness, note Mr. Forster's comment:

> Her penitence is sincere, and only a superficial judge will condemn her as a hypocrite. A nature such as hers cannot for long distinguish between doing wrong and getting caught—for a sentence or two she disentangles them but they insist on blending, and that is why her outlook is so cockneyfied and natural, with "sich is life" for a philosophy and Newgate in the place of Hell. If we were to press her or her creator Defoe

and say, "Come, be serious. Do you believe in Infinity?" they would say (in the parlance of their modern descendants), "Of course I believe in Infinity—what do you take me for?"—a confession of faith that slams the door on Infinity more completely than could any denial.

X

When we turn to Samuel Richardson and his *Clarissa* we note the first rank growth—and still the commonest—of fiction reduced to finitude. The elder fiction had offered, with its God or crevasse through which the glimpse of Infinity was gained, an adequate channel for human emotion. The finite novel could not in many an instance carry off the flood, either of author or reader. Hence the advent in fiction of what we call Sentimentality: Obstructed emotion makes a swampy edge at points along the river of life, in which grow weeds. Or to abandon the figure—not a particularly good one—the something in man which went out to meet the sky, and now found the sky empty, searched across the plain, among finite objects and fellow-humans, for a lesser satisfaction. Not Defoe, perhaps, and not all men felt this ancient need very strongly or often; many of those who felt it most remained, and now remain, unconscious of it to the end of their lives; unconscious, that is, of its real nature. The woman who, from selfishness and vanity, had denied herself a child, would be indignant if you told her the true source of that sickening sentimentality lavished on her little and feeble pet lapdog. Man, having denied himself Deity, may never suspect that natural channel for the emotions heaped up within him.

Richardson's *Clarissa* is sufficiently summarized by Austin Dobson:

> Entangled henceforth in an inextricable network of lies, intrigue and deception, the poor girl, alienated from her friends, and unsuspecting in her own goodness and purity, is decoyed into the company of some of the most worthless of her sex and finally betrayed while under the influence of opiates. After various experiences in a spunging-house, and different hiding-places, she finally settles down, broken-hearted, to die. Her relations reject her; and though Lovelace, in his intermittent moments of remorse, is willing to marry her, her pride and inherent nobility of character make such a solution out of the question. Serene in the consciousness of her innocence, "unviolated"—as she says—"in her will," but mortally wounded, Clarissa gradually fades away, and finally dies, leaving her suddenly awakened relatives distracted by remorse for her fate, while Lovelace, who has richly deserved the gallows, is compassionately killed in a duel by her cousin and guardian, Colonel William Morden.

That is a dispassionate outline of the course of the novel—one that aroused extravagant praises in the eighteenth century, which you will remember as the Age of Reason, but which remained very unsatisfied underneath. In France the Abbé Prevost, himself the author of *Manon Lescaut,* translated the work of Richardson for the emotional benefit of his countrymen. And as *Manon Lescaut,* a strictly contemporary tale, shows that what was happening in English fiction was happening elsewhere—was, indeed, a development of finite fiction as a whole—we may just glance at the French masterpiece.

For masterpiece it is. We have the word of Anatole

France and de Maupassant for it. We may feel that it has excessively sentimental passages and that, in the words of Mr. Burton Rascoe, "all this anguished pity for a capricious—though beautiful—wanton is a trifle more than is necessary." [10] But that is not all the tale offers.

The story is told by the Chevalier des Grieux, a young man of excellent family, destined for the Church. An accidental meeting is followed by an infatuation for Manon the hopeless nature of which none realizes at first. They are married; she remains physically faithful to des Grieux just eight days. A concerted effort is made by the Chevalier, his family, his best friend and the Church to break off the attachment; it fails. Neither imprisonment nor religion nor separation has the slightest effect upon the Chevalier's malady; and although he knows the truth about Manon, whose rascally brother (if he is her "brother") has much hand in the affair, des Grieux cannot help himself in the slightest. They are both deported to New Orleans, a miserable collection of huts in a savage wilderness; Manon dies; des Grieux is found lying insensible on her grave.

The immeasurable superiority to *Clarissa* is largely inherent in the story itself. If we take the chiefly "sympathetic" figures in the two books, des Grieux, in spite of all our impatience with him, is a nobler creature than Richardson's heroine. His physical love of Manon is so plainly the mere fleshly hinge of some really transcendent and ennobling emotion; whereas Clarissa's mentality is never able to rise above the fact that Lovelace has got

[10] In his preface to the edition of *Manon Lescaut* published in 1919 (second edition, 1924) by Alfred A. Knopf, New York.

into bed with her. It is, of course, outrageous that Lovelace should; but to make it the whole of her life, as she does, is sentimentality that could hardly be exceeded. The Freudians would offer a more cynical explanation, but we can let it pass with saying that it is a denial of the spirit.

But if Clarissa denied the spirit, Manon took the limit of license in the other direction. The book appears less sentimental to Prevost's countrymen for a reason that Mr. Rascoe states very well: [11]

Properly to appreciate "Manon Lescaut" is to get an inkling of the workings of the French mind in dealing with problems of the heart. Essentially the attitude of the intelligent Frenchman is that the sentiment of love and the physiological act of love are separate and distinct things: they may be found inseparable and indissoluble, and frequently they really are, but if they are not the dereliction is not so appalling as we of Puritan tradition fancy it. A philosophical treatment of the subject may be found in M. Camille Mauclair's two recent volumes, *De l'Amour physique* and *La Magie de l'Amour*. . . . There is a love, M. Mauclair points out, based upon physical requirements, and there is a love based upon intangible qualities of attachment and affection. Physical unfaithfulness is quite compatible with a steadfast heart and is even to be commended when the facts warrant.

Manon, you see, understood that philosophy perfectly. The Chevalier, to tell the truth, understood it only imperfectly. . . . Manon considered her beauty a vendible commodity, affecting in no way the disposition of her love. With the one she could assure the luxuries which would render the other

[11] *Ibid.*

more delightful. Her plaint might well have been, "I have been faithful to thee, Chevalier, in my fashion."

But although where the focus of *Clarissa* is trivial, that of *Manon Lescaut* is of great and serious moment, the French work can no more avoid sentimental excesses (however less they offend us) than does the Englishman's. In truth, unless one were Defoe-minded, the practice of fiction was now beset with great difficulty, the difficulty of controlling emotion, or rather, of finding purely human and finite subjects worthy for deep emotional exercise. As it happened the next of the English novelists was of Defoe's stamp, though painting with broader strokes. Henry Fielding produced in *Tom Jones* a very perfect and robust specimen of the novel of character, one that rouses all the ordinary passions of daily living and that is as unsentimental as may be.

If sentimentality was the first and most dangerous "escape" captured by emotion from the hard bondage of finitude, there was not long to wait for another. Fantasy—to adopt E. M. Forster's term—arose with Laurence Sterne and is the real vitality of Sterne's *Tristram Shandy*. Forster distinguishes carefully between the element he calls fantasy and another, which he calls prophecy. We shall be able to understand the difference more clearly if we defer study of it until later, when Dostoevsky and Tolstoy and Herman Melville break upon us. For the present we have to note that Sterne's classic has the sense of human impotence strongly upon its story, of human helplessness and restiveness under an unknown constraint; and this uneasy, half-humorous, one-third despairing, one-sixth hopeful feeling is so marked that no reader misses it in the midst of the general humor or the delight in characters; no, not even he who reads Sterne to snigger over what seem to him sly indecencies misses the fantasy in which the story is floated.

But it is the year 1775 and Jane Austen has been born.

XI

An inconspicuous young woman, daughter of a clergyman and not even a resident of London, was to do more for the novel of character than any one before her or since.

Emma, composed between 1811 and 1816, first published in 1816, will answer our purpose. It is not quite the last of the half-dozen novels by which we know Miss Austen, for *Persuasion* appeared two years later.

And first we shall notice the touches of modernity in it. They deserve attention because the style of conversation is outmoded, and so are the fine lines of social distinction on which Jane Austen's novels flourish, as carefully trained as a vine on a trellis.

> Mrs. Goddard was the mistress of a school—not of a seminary, or an establishment, or anything which professed, in long sentences of refined nonsense, to combine liberal acquirements with elegant morality, upon new principles and new systems—and where young ladies for enormous pay might be screwed out of health and into vanity—but a real, honest, old-fashioned boarding-school, where a reasonable quantity of accomplishments were sold at a reasonable price. . . .

"Seminaries" were to thrive for fifty or more years after

this was written; but what is really modern—that is, of our time rather than the author's—is the attitude. And not so much the attitude on education as the attitude toward affectation. The modernity hits us in one phrase, "long sentences of refined nonsense"; in the one word "nonsense" coming after that particular adjective, if you will.

After being long fed with hopes of a speedy visit from Mr. and Mrs. Suckling, the Highbury world were obliged to endure the mortification of hearing that they could not possibly come till the autumn. No such importation of novelties could enrich their intellectual stores at present.

"No such importation of novelties!"—but that whole sentence might as easily come from Arnold Bennett, writing a century later. We must not convey a false impression. There is plenty of the "fair mistress of the mansion" kind of thing in Jane Austen. The point is that no one else, writing in her time, presents us with aught but the fair-mistress-of-the-mansion manner. These flashes of dry, delicate but downright humor, of unsentimental common sense, are what make it a pleasure to read Miss Austen to-day, along with other qualities which we shall examine. There is, moreover, a very good suspicion that some of Miss Austen's conventionally elaborate expressions are ironically intended.

Another thing and a more vital: There is no thought of plot in Jane Austen's stories. It would be inaccurate to say that she discarded fiction's hereditary structure; to try to use it seems not to have occurred to her. She knew its existence, of course; there it was, in plain sight, mangled and twisted for the purposes of the Gothic novel, so-called, that literary chamber of horrors which she satirized in her own *Northanger Abbey.* But there is no evidence that it entered her brain to employ it in the old sense; with the possible exception of Defoe, she was the first to grasp its entire inutility for what the novel had come to be. For although we have dealt with the history of plot without any more accurate definition than that it is "an arrangement of scenes and incidents creating uncertainty as to the outcome," we cannot continue with so loose a description; the time has come for a tightening of terms and a re-definition. We now see that what we meant by plot, in older fiction, could not be simply that. Even Jane Austen offers "an arrangement of scenes and incidents creating uncertainty as to the outcome." We shall call any such arrangement—using the name general in our day—an "action." Every story has one. What, then, is—or was—a plot?

We know perfectly well what we mean; definition is not so easy. Most writers lay the emphasis upon causality; if one thing follows another, they say, you have narrative or mere "story," in the sequence of time, but if one thing begets another, or there is a series of begettings, it is a plot.[12] But we can scarcely allow the matter to rest so simply; few fictions on earth avoid all trace of causality; causality is no plot where the issue is inescapable or foreseen. Is plot the touch of deliberate artifice introduced into structure, like W. B. Maxwell's with-

[12] This would make out those long genealogies in the Old Testament to be plots, wouldn't it? The reader is assured that no reference to *them* was intended, in speaking, a while back, of the plot-stories of the Old Testament.

holding of the key scene in *The Devil's Garden?* Probably not, since many or most of the older fictions show no such practice, and since the particular artifice may vary so widely. No, plot is not in the arrangement. If we analyze what we feel when we hear the word we shall find it to be a form of high anticipation as distinguished from the gradual, steady growth of our interest. The high anticipation that is expressed in the proverb about it being the unexpected that happens. A form of speculation as opposed to a cautious six per cent. In one word, a risk; we may add, a sound risk, or one that turns out to have been sound. The real hallmark of plot is an action which proceeds visibly toward some risky and considerable crisis in which all that is crucial to the action, and to one or more of the principal characters, is put to the touch. We note that there is also an implied action which proceeds *invisibly* until the crisis supervenes, when it comes to the surface, visible for the first time, and having usually the appearance of an unexpected side thrust, an unforeseen flanking movement, an intervention, an envelopment. Thus in so many of the Greek dramas the implied action was the life of the Olympians and their constant concern with mortals, leading to intervention in the crisis of the action. In *The Devil's Garden* the implied and non-visible action is the working of conscience and moral ideas in William Dale. Quite obviously, plot in this true sense is but little adapted to the novel of character, because the implications of character are not withheld from the reader except the author cheat or the reader be stupid. When the crisis is reached, the author may not safely acquaint us with a new and hitherto unrevealed trait of the hero or heroine, display of which shall turn the action. There is an example of this flaw in a recent novel, *The Green Hat,* by Michael Arlen. The author brings off his book with a flourish by the simple—too simple—expedient of making his heroine, in the last chapter, a totally different character from the representation of her up to that point. There is a scene of great passion, after which she goes out and kills herself by hurling her motor car against a giant tree. The passionate scene, the sudden drench of emotion, the swift and final action, sweep us off our feet. It is only afterward that we realize, with a degree of wrath or amusement, the trick played on us, an impersonation of a high order to make a solution and an ending otherwise unattainable.

Such dashing counterfeits, a ruse on that order, had no place in Jane Austen. She cultivated to perfection a native garden with neither forcing beds nor hothouses. We return to her, after a century and longer, because we sense her clear conception of the finite novel's natural growth and structure—because we realize anew every year the exquisiteness of bloom her garden yields. She no more thought of plot than she thought of geometrical flower beds; it was foreign to her purpose and would have been fatal to her aims. "The proper study of mankind is Man." In her the rational faculty spoke up, all at once, in decided tones and with indisputable utterance. "Look here," it said, "whatever may be Unknown, there is much that we do know, can know, ought to know and must know if we are to live our lives to their fullest. An important part, and likely the most important, of the fullness of life and wisdom of living is our knowledge of each other and ourselves. It can do us no harm to be largely practical, to observe closely, to weigh the customs of the society we live in and consider our social relationships, to balance masculine attitudes against feminine attitudes and to be endlessly inquisitive, patiently inquisitive, about men and women. If we can never know each other completely, no pains are lost that we take to know each other better. Here is A, with these traits, and B, with this disposition, and here is what happens when they come together. It may not be a plot but it *is* a clash, a struggle, a drama, however unobtrusive. And it's the sort of drama you live with and look upon every day. Watch it: you may learn something."

And so Miss Austen, under this mandate, set to work. She had a special equipment for the work: She was a woman. Somewhat later we shall have occasion to consider the profound differences between men and women as these differences invade fiction, and largely transform it from the woman's point of view. Just now convenience and, possibly, an instinct for plot, dictate that we limit ourselves to a single point. That is the point of Jane Austen's undeviating femininity. It is both subtle and constant. It shall be illustrated without any present comment. If the illustrations do not convey the point, pass it; both the illustrations and their significance may become luminous later. All are from *Emma*.

It was a melancholy change; and Emma could not but sigh over it, and wish for impossible things, till her father awoke, and made it necessary to be cheerful.

From his habits of gentle selfishness, and of never being

able to suppose that other people could feel differently from himself, he was very much disposed to think Miss Taylor had done as sad a thing for herself as for them. [Miss Taylor has married.]

It was now some time since Miss Taylor had begun to influence his schemes; but as it was not the tyrannic influence of youth on youth, it had not shaken his determination of never settling till he could purchase Randalls.

Emma allowed her father to talk—but supplied her visitors in a much more satisfactory style. [A meal.]

She particularly led Harriet to talk more of Mr. Martin, and there was evidently no dislike to it. Harriet was very ready to speak of the share he had had in their moonlight walks and merry evening games. . . . "He had gone three miles round one day in order to bring her some walnuts, because she had said how fond she was of them, and in everything else he was so very obliging. . . . His mother and sisters were very fond of him. Mrs. Martin had told her one day (and there was a blush as she said it) that it was impossible for anybody to be a better son, and therefore she was sure, whenever he married, he would make a good husband. Not that she *wanted* him to marry. She was in no hurry at all."

"Well done, Mrs. Martin!" thought Emma. "You know what you are about."

Here are only a few short examples from the first four chapters of a book of fifty-five chapters. And only one is an episode, or an approach to it. For the more adequate illustration of Miss Austen's talent, the reader must go direct to *Emma*. There he will find the point of femininity in the action itself, from beginning to end:—in Emma's ambitious plan to make a match for Harriet and her steps toward it; her conflicts with Knightley; her rapid conclusion, on learning that Frank Churchill is to revisit Highbury, that any apprehension or embarrassment she feels is not for herself but for him, "who had undoubtedly been always so much the most in love of the two"; etc., etc.

Miss Austen's frequent modernity, on which we touched first, is perhaps no more than a happy accident; her quality of femininity is enough to insure her of literary immortality by its timelessness. It is a *way* of observing, rather than of recording. Its instant and enduring success depends only upon the continued existence of her sex, which now seems probable. We may look after her and see many men among the novelists, some of them our greatest, learning her manner of perception and copying it with varying skill despite the serious handicap of being males. But we shall find no one who can surpass her; and hardly any who kept as strictly and wisely in the finite novel's finitude, cultivating with intensive and fruitful art the earth about them. For the most part they cannot refrain from stealing glances at the sky—and neglecting the corner by the stone wall. For the most part these later ones have toyed with the idea of plot, putting their flowers of character into beds of unconvincing patterns. But, we may ask, without Jane Austen, would they have produced flowers at all? Would Thackeray have been able to make Becky Sharpe unfold her petals on a prickly stem? Would Dickens have triumphed? or Wilkie Collins have tickled us? Would George Meredith have even seen his rôle, much less have galloped, however ridiculously, to champion that sex? Henry James could not have written and Arnold Bennett would have had to design pottery. We may well exaggerate a little in recognizing a debt so vast owed to a lady.

XII

A note on Jane Austen, before we relinquish her: Is not her method false in a most vital respect? For she always characterizes directly—tells right off in her plain and practical manner what the newcomer is like. Of course, if she gave us nothing else, her fault would be severe. But her direct characterization is invariably followed, and at once, by a scene in which she truly characterizes, a scene in which the new person lives, moves, breathes and has his whole being in an embodiment, as a rule exquisitely fine, of everything that has been premised about him. For Miss Austen is the most Euclidean of novelists, immediately "demonstrating" and irrefutably proving everybody she gives us. Her direct characterizations represent a certain economy of our attention, for which, in our reader-laziness, we are seldom anything but grateful. They are of about the value of a dramatist's stage-directions. That they are sometimes a little tiresome, and nearly always superfluous, is only just; we should have small use for a writer in whom we found nothing to grumble at.

But now we are down to the last hundred years in our abbreviated history of fiction—abbreviated and unduly narrowed, for the drama and poetry are fiction, too. But so, we remember, are other arts—sculpture and music and painting. They are all fictions, that is, adaptations of truth to meet man's physical and emotional needs. We shall appeal to them for frequent illustration; for this parallel and that divergence; but it is evident that we shall need to follow the furrow in which we find ourselves—prose fiction, and that generally of the so-called novel length. Shall we make much sacrifice of wisdom in so doing?

We shall sacrifice a great deal. No one of man's forms of fiction is inherently better than another. The full philosophy of fiction, as we have it to-day, is contained in not less than all the forms, and will extend itself as new forms come into gradual being. But to one or more, and usually to several of the existing forms, any given man or woman is nearly always insensible. To a philosophy of all fictions every reader must find himself a little cold. Nor can a printed work properly present the subject, except by makeshift. We should have to see sculptures with our eyes, as the discourse proceeded, not merely view them flattened in the reproduction of photographs. The Boston Symphony or some equivalent would have to play, reaching our ears by more perfect acoustics than the radio as yet compasses. Velasquez, in something better than the best of four-color process plates, would be indispensable; and television is not ready for the enterprise. But the printed forms of fiction are more immediate and certain. We have only to choose our examples from the best-known or more easily procurable novels to deal as equitably as possible with all who read these pages.

We sacrifice much, but we make certain gains. One is the triumph of the single form we have chosen. Prose fiction—and from the term printed plays are properly excluded, a play not being a play unless and until it is acted—surpasses all other fictional forms in its scope for the inclusions of those troublesome truths that must somehow be adapted to man's physical and emotional needs. Sculpture is limited to relatively few figures, to a relatively simple design, and is frozen or fixed; music is a peculiar language; painting shares the disabilities of sculpture except that it adds color and loses one dimension (sculpture used to employ color, too; does still, somewhat too narrowly); poetry uses its appeal to physical sensation and memory merely as a springboard for the imaginative leap that too few are capable of. But the drama? Surely words and actors can be as far-ranging as words alone? No, for a number of reasons. Our attention is concentrated on the stage for a few hours, and the strain cannot be prolonged. We receive the fiction with a certain self-consciousness, be it ever so slight, as one of a company, to whose reception we are sensitively aware. And we cannot make our intelligence and emotion the sole and proper test in our reception—for there is the actor, whose intelligence and emotion conditions the author's and conditions ours. With the fewest exceptions, also, a play must succeed commercially; the playwright in most instances therefore sharply constricts the truths he will work with. On prose fiction, and especially on the novel, this necessity to make money has exercised infinitely less pressure.

On the whole, then, if we strive to extract the philosophy of fiction from the novel almost exclusively, we shall not be doing so badly in aim or intention. We shall cut ourselves off from the full wisdom; we may hope to master more perfectly wisdom in our single field, which is also the most embracing.

XIII

With the finite novel firmly established, we need do not much more than just glance at its individual manifestations, mainly the effects of temperament in its practitioners. For the purposes of our short history of fiction, that is enough; such other review as we need is only apposite when we enter into Method. Charles Dickens, whose opportunities for observing far exceeded Miss Austen's, was a victim of finitude as she never was. But if he could not invoke the gods, at least he could show men some of the ways in which they were sunk, and did. It is a noble thing to have bettered English prisons and English schools; but something less than to give a wisdom of living for every generation. Poor Dickens was often sentimental; and the degree of his sentimentality is just the measure of his impotence in finitude. His boundless and exuberant creation of character is a persisting joy. It will be well to stop and ask ourselves why. For most of his characters were simply reiterated expressions of a single trait or attitude—what E. M. Forster so happily calls "flat" characters. And many of them were caricatures, though often amiable and delightful ones. But they have a curious vitality, as G. K. Chesterton points out. As we read Dickens some of this vitality passes into us; we take it with us when we look at people for a little after. But what we chiefly get from Dickens is the convenient and dangerous method of simplification.

If we observe with more vitality, we also tend to focus on one outstanding characteristic; we begin making flat characters from the life around us and it is the greatest fun—generally harmless, if we press it not too far.

Balzac rejoiced in finitude; was perhaps the first who wished to show that it is really infinite in its light and shade. We think of him as founding, with his Human Comedy, modern realism. It can be true only in the sense that others, misunderstanding his method, used it feebly. For Balzac himself was a substantial creator of living men and veritable women. When he wrote, men and women had not become so tedious as they have since, nor so hopeless as Zola was to make them. How to overcome this encroaching tedium was the secret problem that gave Flaubert many dreadful days. He spent them, usually, holding his head in his hands while he groped for a word. Just one word! *The* one, inexorably. But Flaubert's quest of days for the word, weeks for the paragraph, resulted in a new species of tedium, that of a style which seriously distracts attention from the subject, as if an interesting woman should make the mistake of appearing before us in a costume that competed with her own charms.

Since Flaubert, it has dawned on us slowly that literary style—prose which in any degree obtrudes itself as prose—is something less than the most enviable condition in a novel.

With Deity erased, the sweep of emotion, as we have seen, became often a stagnated flood of sentimentality; the rational faculty's efforts to take the place of Deity's *action* have never progressed beyond the purely passive declarations of morality. Another standstill; and one much more fatal for mankind. For when man believed that Deity would do something about wrong and injustice—and equally something about virtue—his fictions had an efficacy impossible in codes of behavior dependent on a social consensus. Contrast the older fictions with such modern ones as the novels of George Eliot and the difference will be clear. If man wreaked a cruelty of old, the god could and did punish him. But if a character sins in George Eliot, Hetty in *Adam Bede* for an instance, only the faraway tradition of the god can be invoked. In the famous scene of that novel of George Eliot's, Hetty is in prison for having abandoned and so having killed her baby. Dinah comes to see her. How hard Dinah labors to make Heaven seem present and real! How strangely and pitifully inactive are the effects of the scene! Hetty, after all, is without any clear vision or any clear emotion. Perhaps the chief element in her mixed and stifled feeling is disappointment that her hope was not fulfilled—that some one did not happen along and rescue her baby. And the effects on the reader are as lamentably weak. "She ought not to have done it. Of course it will be necessary to hang her; or at least, she must be transported abroad. Dear, dear! Perhaps she needs a mixture of tenderness and severity. But there isn't much we can do about her, poor thing, except view her as an Example." The finite stands helpless before the infinite—helpless and acutely uncomfortable. The God whom Dinah invokes has no reality for the reader, who hopes, however, that He may become real and somehow active for Hetty. . . . It is all rather futile.

The mistake of such fiction, we see, lies in its refusal to recognize an impotence, its endeavor to postulate potency where none any longer is viable. But in *The Scarlet Letter* Hawthorne found the right way. Impotence descends upon the story of Hester Prynne and Dimmesdale from the outset, as it does upon the characters in a Russian novel. We know there is no God, except as a half-forgotten legend; there is no One to intercede, no One to intervene. Such effects as we shall get will be perfectly finite—the stir of conscience, which is haunted by the old Legend and gives forth faint ancestral echoes of the God who once was manifest; the collision with morality, society's poor instrument to take the place of divine action. And that is why we can read *The Scarlet Letter* and receive an enduring impression that *Adam Bede* and its like never give us. Hawthorne is honest as George Eliot knew not how to be. Herman Melville is honest; Dostoevsky and Tolstoy are honest —those novelists whose work Forster rightly denominates by the word "prophecy." What is meant by "prophecy"? It is not merely a singing, a tone of voice; it is not H. G. Wells voicing a hope of a future better than the present. Mr. Forster puts it luminously when he observes: "In Dostoevsky the characters and situations always stand for more than themselves; infinity attends them; though they remain individuals they expand to embrace it and summon it to embrace them; one can apply to them the saying of St. Catherine of Siena that God is in the soul and the soul is in God as the sea is in the fish and the fish is in the sea."

Prophecy in this sense is perhaps the only respect in

which fiction, since the coming of finitude, has successfully recaptured some portion of its loss. It is as if an active man were crippled by slow disease and pinned to his chair; after a while imagination, a gift he had never had occasion to exercise and did not know he possessed, comes to his partial rescue. To remain not too inconsistently finite but always to imply the infinite, the extension beyond, was to conquer some good out of what otherwise had been a scarcely mitigated evil. Herman Melville's *Moby Dick;* Dostoevsky in either *The Brothers Karamazov* or *Crime and Punishment;* Emily Brontë's *Wuthering Heights;* some of D. H. Lawrence; and E. M. Forster himself, at least in his finely-executed *A Passage to India,* are all specimens of prophecy, of what we may call the overreach. We can now distinguish the main developments of fiction, philosophically speaking, from the coming of the finite limitation to our own day. It will be more vivid to imagine a few novelists as speaking, each trying to express his creed abstractly.

Defoe: Of course I believe in infinity and Deity. But really, my time is all taken up with Crusoe's quite marvelous ingenuity on his island and Moll's good humor with her husbands. The world is so full of a number of things! Human nature, principally.

Jane Austen: I believe I shall give myself the pleasure and satisfaction of writing about a heroine whom no one will much like except myself. Emma is certainly capable of serious folly but there is stuff in her. I am not much concerned with Deity, for I know my place, and take a pride, as well as comfort, in keeping it.

The Abbé Prevost: People are what they are. Readers will see in the conduct of M. des Grieux a terrible example of the strength of the passions. The story will really be a moral treatise reduced agreeably to practice. A little sentimentality in a good cause can do no harm.

Herman Melville: I suspect we are all damned but I don't see it, as Hawthorne does, in terms of the problem of personal salvation. I see it as the chance to dream of Paradise.

Dostoevski: I am all humility, gentlemen. I recognize that there is something lost or misplaced. I conceive we spend our whole lives looking for it. If you don't mind, if you will pardon me, I shall try to show that hunt going on in every person I draw. We carry on the business of life, stupid and ecstatic and terrible, and all the while we are listening for something, expecting Somebody. . . .

George Eliot: God ought not to be so difficult when we have the Ten Commandments and social morality. It is our duty, with these incontestable and written evidences—Moses personally received the Commandments from God in an interview—it is our duty, assuredly, in all the circumstances, to posit God.

XIV

Does such verbalization seem unfair? For those who may be shocked by it, let us sum up the philosophy of fiction in another way:

First was fiction a means of integrating man's life with Deity, and Deity's with man's, in the fullness of this life and toward a life everlasting.

As man's physical mechanism developed, his dependence upon it increased, his preoccupation with it and from it absorbed him more and more; finitude was his world and the rational faculty his toy in its exploration. All his fictions changed.

Finite fiction perfected itself in the novel of character. Its maladies were two: sentimentality, resulting from emotional excess with insufficient outlets; morality offered as moralizing, a weak, passive substitute for the old action by Deity.

As offsets finite fiction achieved fantasy, with its brief escapes for emotion, and prophecy, with its extension beyond finity into the void, its overreach. But the prerequisite of both these achievements was and is humility, the confession of impotence and an irrecoverable loss.

There may, of course, be future gains for finite fiction. We hope for them but we do not know. The clues, if any are, must lie as seeds in fiction relatively contemporary.

It is useless to mourn the reduction of fiction to the finite basis unless we are prepared to mourn the history of mankind for the last two thousand years. That history may now be changing; and as the mind of the race changes, so will fiction change with it. Our generation and many generations to come must accept cheerfully for fiction only the finity that is all mankind receives as the aspects of daily life. The heavens have closed; we must make the blue vault ring hollow from the spaces beyond if we can.

CHAPTER III

THE MATERIAL OF FICTION; OR, THE MIND OF THE READER

LIFE, for the purpose of the novelist, consists essentially of human relationships. This abrupt and inaccurate definition will usually serve; and most of the apparent exceptions, on a closer scrutiny, seem at least partly to fall within its wide circle. If a story deals with a man and his God, the man's half is within the circle; if a story deal with a man and his dog the case is the same. This is to ignore the fact that in such stories both dog and God are likely to be assimilated to humanity. We may suppose a story to be concerned only with one man or woman, excluding surrounding objects as far as possible and carefully not humanizing them in their appearances. Something like Thoreau's *Walden*, but with greater inattention to all but Thoreau. That story, in all probability, will still be the story of a human relationship—the subject's with himself, or more precisely, of one part of his self with some other part. Mr. E. M. Forster has pointed out that life as we live it consists of a good deal besides human relationships. We are born and die; we spend a third of our lives in sleep, and an important total in eating. Dickens began a novel with a chapter entitled "I Am Born," but the text somewhat disappointed the expectations not unreasonably aroused.

We have no memory of birth; giving birth is another matter. The business of dying can be represented, but it is interesting to notice that the representation is hardly convincing unless it is made in terms of the severing of human relationships. Our memory of sleep is short-lived with respect to most dreams, non-existent in respect of the time we do not dream. Eating is sharp in sensation and not negligible as a memory. Fiction takes it into variable account.

What is the explanation? Why does fiction deal almost exclusively with one major aspect of life, ignoring or minimizing the others. For it is perfectly true, as Forster observes, that we do not spend most of our time in loving or hating, nor in the intermediate phases of personal adjustments. The answer is found in another curious condition to which must be applied the term Dimension.

We breathe, eat and sleep in the familiar and necessary three dimensions and the fourth dimension of time. Time as a dimension hardly belongs to man in his more savage states; civilized man has developed it to a degree that sometimes appears excessive. As D. H. Lawrence amusingly puts it in his *Mornings in Mexico:*

> The white monkey has curious tricks. He knows, for example, the time. Now to a Mexican, and an Indian, time is a vague, foggy reality. There are only three times: *en la manaña, en la tarde, en la noche:* in the morning, in the afternoon, in the night. There is even no midday, and no evening.
>
> But to the white monkey, horrible to relate, there are exact spots of time, such as five o'clock, half-past nine. The day is a horrible puzzle of exact spots of time.

But although these are the dimensions of physical existence, they are not the dimensions of living in any sense that human beings will agree to, from childhood to oldest age. Living is a matter of intensity, or interior dimension—what Forster calls the "life by values."[1] Since man discovered the thing he calls emotion, physical sensation and memory have been kept busy supplying the raw material for emotion to feed upon. And emotion, feeling, impresses us solely by its intensity or strength, like an electric light or other source of illumination. True, emotion lasts a certain time, but when it is upon us we are scarcely conscious of time. It has, no doubt, some range that corresponds to length, breadth, and height or depth in spatial objects. But of this range *at the time* we are hardly cognizant. Only its incandescence truly matters.

And the incandescence is indifferent to our concepts of space and time. Either it is single in its temporal and spatial dimension or else it includes those we know and an infinite further dimensional series. It is its own interior dimension—measures itself and is measured by us purely from its intensity. It gets this singularity, no doubt, directly from physical sensation, which has the same pronounced trait; and memory is obedient to both.

How is intensity attained? Mere abundance of physical sensation will not supply it; like every other form of energy it derives only from proper fuel. Quantity wears out the mechanism, like unlimited coal of inferior quality dumped into a furnace. Very limited physical sensation

---

[1] These references are to *Aspects of the Novel*, by E. M. Forster, this and the one immediately preceding, to his discussion in Chapter III.

and a scantly supplied memory will achieve far more, if the quality is rich, if the kind is right. And the kind that promotes intensity has been found to be active rather than passive. The ascidian, reaching out with its feeler, got rather more sensation from expanding and contracting its own muscle than from what it touched. Its physical sensation was hardly less when it touched nothing. Man, developing emotion, has strengthened immeasurably this faculty of auto-sensation, so that it is almost impossible for him to feel fervently where his own activity is not involved.

His activity is most doubtful of success—and therefore most rewarding in a happy result—where it is exercised upon his fellows. He can move rocks and stones, tame or kill the animals. But he has no such certainty among his equals. His hate will probably not kill, his love will not infallibly bless or protect. Actually the sole dimension that he receives constantly as physical sensation and experiences constantly as emotion is the distance between him and some other human soul. He is part of a circumference in which are included all other humans of whom he has knowledge. Those he hates and loves stand closest to him; those to whom he is most indifferent are the full diameter away. And the circle is always changing, but for him, the changes are his changes. Sometimes, receiving love from one toward whom he feels nothing, he is annoyed or upset. What does this person mean by shoving around, by trying to short-cut along an arc? Stand back there, you! But, oh, come hither, *thou!*

He wishes to exercise a mysterious force like the force

of gravity, a power to attract, and he cannot find out how to do it. All his life long he is preoccupied with this problem. He does things with his body—runs errands with his feet, bestows caresses with his hands—but the pull he desires to exert is not in these activities. To eat is no longer the keen pleasure it was, unless he is fed by the one who stands on his right. Sometimes he feels he would rather withhold food from that one on his left than eat; more often he takes exquisite pleasure in putting his choicest food before the one whom he wishes to draw most closely to him.

To be active, active, in this unknown dimension of intensity is all his life, really. Space and time are most often irrelevances. When they are the foes of intensity, delight is to him in overcoming them.

II

Since this is life for the purpose of the novelist, the truths of life that a novelist uses are the verities of feeling. Others scarcely count. If a novel be painstakingly exact in every respect and yet be insincere we have small use for it, though an intentional insincerity can sometimes give us moments of great fun. A terrible sincerity excuses all sorts of faults.

In other words, emotion may be more powerful than art. The fictioner seizes upon his special truths of life, the facts of feeling so to speak, and struggles to adapt them to human physical and emotional needs. Art is his most powerful ally in the process; but it is important to reflect that the art cannot be purely literary. It must be an art of the mind, of the emotions, of human nature.

There is a sharp limit upon what can be accomplished by verbal dexterity and the suavities of prose style. The writer's position differs little from that of the public speaker in a serious cause. He *may* be fluent, polished, skillful toward a climax, and this may induct the listener fully into his view; but he may only stammer forth his argument, without logic or arrangement or felicitous expression and conquer about as completely. After all, how one handles it is a little less essential than what one has hold of.

An axiom of art—one of very few—requires that the nature of a material be respected. A worker in steel has no business pretending that it is wicker. The body of a motor car cannot properly resemble a perambulator, for steel is not basket-work and does poorly to pretend it is. Fiction is not psychology, in spite of the delusion so recently current but now somewhat receding. It is not photography, either, a reminder still frequently necessary. Novels that depend for their proper appreciation by the reader upon knowledge of some special kind fail in art to just the extent of that dependence. We shall have occasion in a later chapter to consider at some length Arnold Bennett's novel, *The Old Wives' Tale*, but there is a passage in the preface to that work which must be cited here. It illustrates the right approach of the artist whose art is fiction.

With regard to the French portion of the story, it was not until I had written the first part that I saw from a study of my chronological basis that the Siege of Paris might be brought into the tale. The idea was seductive; but I hated, and still hate, the awful business of research; and I only knew the Paris of the Twentieth Century. Now I was aware that my railway servant and his wife had been living in Paris at the time of the war. I said to the old man, "By the way, you went through the Siege of Paris, didn't you?" He turned to his old wife and said, uncertainly, "The Siege of Paris? Yes, we did, didn't we?" The Siege of Paris had been only one incident among many in their lives. Of course, they remembered it well, though not vividly, and I gained much information from them. But the most useful thing which I gained from them was the perception, startling at first, that ordinary people went on living very ordinary lives in Paris during the siege, and that to the vast mass of the population the siege was not the dramatic, spectacular, thrilling, ecstatic affair that is described in history. Encouraged by this perception, I decided to include the siege in my scheme. I read Sarcey's diary of the siege aloud to my wife, and I looked at the pictures in Jules Claretie's popular work on the siege and the commune, and I glanced at the printed collection of official documents, and there my research ended.

Mr. Bennett's material was fiction, that is, human relationships between certain not at all extraordinary people. It was not a military operation, nor a political crisis, nor national history, nor public drama. Joseph Hergesheimer's *Java Head,* a tale of Salem, Massachusetts, in the days of clipper ships, and of a seaman who came home with a Chinese bride, is a beautiful and satisfying novel; if it has a fault, it is the reader's consciousness of the ninety-odd histories, diaries and works on Chinese philosophy, etc., which Mr. Hergesheimer read as a preparation for his story. The bones of this research come through at the corners of his story. But because the verities of feeling are there, too, we make only minor complaint.

The artistic canon requiring respect for the material's nature is most conspicuously violated, perhaps, in program music. Pure music—instrumental and orchestral works—is accompanied by a detailed description in words of what it is supposed to represent. This vice has not penetrated as yet into fiction and we are not called upon to listen to a symphonic interpretation while we read a modern novel—though it is not at all impossible that we will be, and the hint here given may prove most indiscreet. These hermaphroditisms come about from a worry about intelligibility. Meaning is often unintelligible, or only partly intelligible; feeling is always intelligible. It is feeling, emotion, that is deficient in these anxiously documented works—and as music allows emotion to flow most freely, the deficiency occurs oftenest in that form of art. Let us select a person who cannot read as being least subject to the obsession of meaning. We will take any extended passage of that most incoherent work, James Joyce's *Ulysses,* and read it aloud to him. If he shows anxiety, we will warn him that it doesn't *mean* anything particular. In reading we shall be careful to give no more than natural emphasis to the words and expressions—profanity shall have merely its proper expletive force and obscenity its proper accent of lewdness, that is all. And when we have finished our auditor will be perfectly clear as to the feeling of Joyce in that passage.

Ours is an exploration and a quest; we must be bold

to press on to the point toward which all these thoughts about the material of fiction are leading us. That material, we have said, consists of human relationships, but on the most important of these we have not touched—the relationship with the reader.

It is worth repeating for clearness and emphasis: The material of fiction necessarily includes the mind of the reader. Of the human relationships with which a work of fiction may deal, that with the reader is the most important and the controlling relationship. Any attempt to construe material apart from the reader, as if fiction were produced in a vacuum and uttered in a void, must result in failure.

The objection may be raised that, of course, every fictioner considers that his work will have an audience, if only of a few; that he cannot fail to make this audience a part of his undertaking. And this may even be true; the trouble is rather in the nature of that consideration than in an absolute lack of it. Too many novelists take the reader for granted, just as too many have been overconscious of his existence. If it is base and futile to "write down" to an imaginary audience, it is the height of ineptitude to assume that the audience can meet every demand the writer may choose to impose upon it. A writer who would not think for an instant of twisting the verities of a character in his story, of requiring that character to do something alien to his nature or beyond his capacity, will often completely disregard the whole race of men and women outside his book. But a book, in itself, is nothing but a production of the printing press and bindery; it becomes a book when somebody reads it. If, as has been plausibly argued, a critic to some extent re-creates a novel, or makes a new creation by the interaction of his mind with the author's, then the same thing is true of the book and any reader, in degree however different.

A moment devoted to this theme will not be wasted. We have just said that a book becomes a book when some one reads it. We may go farther and say that the book is what the reader makes of what the author has written. It is not what the author intended the reader should make, necessarily; it is probably almost never quite that. The author, writing his book, has entered into a human relationship—one of those enterprises in which simplicity, skill, courage and seductiveness must be at their utmost, but one in which no commandment can be enforced, no compulsion exerted. If the author does not place himself in the reader's situation, so far as he can; if he does not undertake the sympathetic comprehension of the reader at least as thoroughly as he does that of his hero or heroine, what chance is there that he will succeed?

He need not concern with a particular reader, and he errs gravely if he thinks of some body of readers, except, it may be, from a consideration frankly commercial. (As this is a discussion of the philosophy of fiction, and not the business of fiction, we need not pursue the exception.) Nor is the author to suppose readers as a whole to have special characteristics. Though they are only a part of humanity, they are drawn from it by no process which insures their peculiarity in any respect, unless it be a mental vitality a little greater than that of their fellow-humans. The things which will be accurate about readers will be just as applicable to humanity in general; and it should not add perceptibly to the author's problem, who must understand his characters, to understand his readers as well.

With this qualification: He can re-value one of his characters by showing him through the mind of another, by illuminating him through his, the author's, mind. With the reader he cannot do this; he is dealing with an equal and must take his chance. But he has only to know as much as he should know about men and women to make his chance more than reasonably good.

Unfortunately, he often knows far too little. Let us go over some of the requisites. The very first, by ancient agreement, is the effect of reality by which a story imposes itself on him who reads. Reality has many aspects; it ramifies into endless detail—goes into the turn of a sentence and depends sometimes on a choice between virtual synonyms. Modern advertising copy-writers and poets share an acute appreciation of reality's refinements; they know it is a goal very far off. Here is an instance of its delicacy. Arnold Bennett's reputation was made by *The Old Wives' Tale.* Fifteen years later he produced a novel called *Riceyman Steps.* There was no question in his mind or his publishers' that this book was his best since *The Old Wives' Tale.* Moreover, it had to a peculiar degree the same sense of life's richness in mean surroundings. How proclaim the fact so as to confer reality in the mind of prospective readers? If one said, "by the author of *The Old Wives' Tale,*" there was no reality. A direct comparison might only challenge skeptical unbelief. But if one said: *"Riceyman Steps.* By the hand that wrote *The Old Wives' Tale*" —so much, no more—one said it all, in a phrase that was vivid, real and true. So much for the breath of reality in the merest phrase, a substitution of three words for two. Reality in this sense is like a pulse beating at every moment of a sustained piece of work—a pulse of which the reader is always conscious, for which he continually listens. And where this kind of reality is unfailingly present, the slightest cutting makes the work bleed.

But it is with reality in the larger sense that we must deal in this chapter.

The first general consideration is an old one usually stated as Plausibility versus Probability. It points out that in life anything may happen, but that no such license applies in fiction. A newspaper headline might proclaim the collapse of Brooklyn Bridge, or another of the great bridges spanning the East River in New York City, with a loss of life in the hundreds or thousands, and we would all believe it; but at the writer who should introduce such an occurrence in his fiction we would all scoff heartily. His only chances to make us accept the disaster would lie in (1) such demands upon our sense of reality from the outset as would make the bridge disaster seem plausible, or (2) the *fait accompli,* showing the thing as having happened. The second method is the more interesting; he might open his story with the confused thoughts of a man or woman struggling in the water, dimly and very gradually realizing what had occurred between the seat in the crowded car, the opened magazine, the fascinating article and its unfinished sentence, and the icy, suffocating present. . . .

At any time life can bring down a bludgeon on our heads and compel our credence. The fictioner must always persuade us to believe. Where his purpose is too far from the paths of easy persuasion, his best, and nearly his sole, chance is to imitate the coercions of surrounding life. Those coercions, by making a complete change of the life external, usually (but not always) compel a quick adjustment of interior to exterior reality. In the imitation of life, the older fiction had an immense advantage; on occasion it could and did disregard probability as completely as life disregards it. It was under no such compulsion as we are to-day to make Event either strictly probable or wholly plausible, and this was a great enfranchisement, for, of course, Event is unconcerned with probability or plausibility. These two demands of the rational faculty, legitimately exercised in regard to human action in works of fiction, are simply bedevilments of the fictioner in the spheres where human action may influence but cannot control.

As things are, the writer is compelled to keep to events inherently probable or else made plausible. Divine accident must be sugar-coated so that the reason may swallow it down, very much in the manner in which some fiction sugar-coats a moral pill. Where the improbable is admitted, the chief means of achieving plausibility is by reference to human action; thus in the example just before us most writers would feel it expedient to explain the bridge's collapse by some fault of the engineers.

Most criticism of fiction is conducted from the treacherous premises of a rational faculty which came into vitality long after fiction was born. It has, a little, the air of the precocious infant judging the action of an adult. It makes four possible classifications:

Plausible and probable.
Plausible but improbable.
Implausible but probable.
Implausible and improbable.

The application of such tests to a work of fiction resembles an effort to make arithmetic do the work of analytical geometry. Presumably a story that was both implausible and improbable would be subject to unrelieved condemnation; yet, to cite only one instance, G. K. Chesterton's *The Man Who Was Thursday,* already a semi-classic, comes within the definition.

We shall find—we shall always find—the exploration of fictional reality impossible except we light ourselves by the mind of the reader. This, it may be thought, is not the brightest of illuminations; and it is not. Neither is it the dimmest. What, precisely, the mind of the reader accomplishes for the writer is a steady lambency in which there is scarcely any wavering. Some things remain in shadow, outside the circle of that mind; others are plain as pikestaffs. If the light never much intensifies, neither does it wane; though fixed and not portable, one can know where to find it. The task of the writer is to bring things outside its periphery, within, as one fetches an object under the rays of a street lamp. And that, by the way, is exactly what the mind of the reader is, a lamp lighting the streets along which the vast majority of lives come and go—so far as we are concerned, must come and go perpetually.

The mind of the reader, that is, the mind of the race, is not developed to the point of imagination. It is not the mind of the poet, we have to remember, nor the higher mathematician. It can do no more with the things beyond its ken than the street lamp. All its mature pleasures, and all its pleasurable emotions, are derived from the process we call recognition.

Recognition depends solely on physical sensation and memory. It consists of the exercise of memory always, of both sometimes. Music, sculpture, painting, since they always involve physical sensation, can with more safety lessen the appeal to memory than can writing, which must give physical sensation too but cannot do it directly. It follows that the writer must involve rather deeply the memory of his reader, whether by appeal to his memory as an individual or to the memory of the race, so-called. The constant resort to one human faculty must be free from tiresomeness, avoiding any effect of iteration; probably this would be impossible of achievement were not the memory the most easily stimulated and most unwearying faculty of the mind. The writer will naturally almost never appeal to memory directly, and his indirect action toward it will, at its best, resemble the most complete and sustained evocation of which we have knowledge. We often speak of a book casting a spell over the reader, but there is only one spell that can be woven, though the way of its weaving is of thousandfold variation.

Recognition, the reader's re-knowing through memory

and revived physical sensation, is not only the single most important thing in writing but a staggering percentage of the whole affair. We must not narrow it down in any reckoning, or in any definition. It includes the memory of traditional knowledge. The writer, perhaps, wishes to tell a story of Monte Carlo. The reader has never seen Monte Carlo. Nevertheless he knows Monte Carlo perfectly well out of a tradition of the place. The writer, let us suppose him E. Phillips Oppenheim, is on absolutely safe ground in presenting a Monte Carlo of the Casino, adventurers male and female, hushed-up suicides and a sapphire sea. Recognition will be entire; plausibility and probability, that Tweedledum and Tweedledee duo, will grace the scene. It is only when Mr. Oppenheim undertakes to present an unfamiliar and unrecognizable Monte Carlo that difficulty arises. It arises instantly and it is terrible as the face of an unscalable Alpine cliff. For this reason Mr. Oppenheim will be at the utmost pains in dealing with it. His people will be extraordinarily recognizable; and he will begin as far as possible with the recognized Monte Carlo and present nothing else for quite a while. At length, very circumspectly, some strange facet of the place will be brought into view. Mr. Oppenheim will not dwell upon this aspect, no matter how great its final importance in his story. To this method of ingratiation the fictioner is constantly compelled to resort wherever recognition by the mind of the reader cannot be predicated.

No recognition of a particular place can be assumed for that mind; it knows everywhere and nowhere. Paris,

London, New York, San Francisco; interior Africa, the Arctic igloo, the Xanadu of Kubla Khan; St. Peter's in Rome, the Taj Mahal, the Acropolis, Sancta Sophia; Lake Como and Lake Louise, Mount Everest and Mont St. Michel—these have their traditional aspects, which is to say their fictional reality, the shapes men have given them, more incontestable than their forms in nature and being. We are all acquainted with that extreme instance of the disappointed traveler at the Mediterranean's gateway, a tale which suggests that it may yet be necessary to letter the rock with words to the effect that the Prudential has the strength of Gibraltar.

Certain primary recognitions can, however, be assumed for the mind of the reader in regard to people. Even villages of only a few hundred souls are microcosms of humanity. All the ordinary human motives and traits are observable in such small communities. The writer is advantaged by human friction. One may live at the foot of a mountain all his days and remain incurious and ignorant of it; a human neighbor rubs against one. And the reader himself is human.

A confounding of realism with reality has caused no little trouble in modern fiction, and we shall have to examine the mind of the reader to find just where the trouble lies. A large hint of it is contained in what we considered a moment ago—traditional knowledge, fictional reality. There is a traditional Monte Carlo, fictionally real—apart from any other reality it may have. What does this mean? Writers, since this present Monte Carlo began, have with remarkable consistency chosen certain aspects of its look and life for report. Each writer had his series of human relationships to present, his verities of human feeling to convey, his interior dimension of intensification to control him, and in the case of the first writers using this background, Monte Carlo, insofar as it differed from most scenes, was only an obstacle of blank non-recognition to overcome in the mind of the reader. Now the method of realism, so-called, is a scrupulous attention to physical detail, to begin with, in the confidence that such detail, cumulatively presented, will arouse physical sensation in the reader. Realism is an attempt to leave memory out of the equation, to form an equation directly with the reader, and chiefly and at first by means of the eye. It is an attempt at word-visualization; it cannot cut out memory since a word is itself the formulation of a memory, but it minimizes memory all it can, it sacrifices the incessant and indirect appeal habitual to fiction for a direct appeal. Leaving the outside scene and coming to interior action, realism still tries to be as literal and visual as it possibly can, emphasizing minutiæ and deeming nothing tangible or physical, nothing that visualizes, irrelevant for its purpose. Or, if it cannot be made visual, then audible, tasteable, smellable. It is really an attempt to bring back into language the sharply sensuous quality with which languages were saturated before the Greek mind invented abstract terms. The realist cannot go back to ancient Hebrew, for example, and substitute for such a word as "virtue," "sweet-smellingness" or "good-tastingness," but he can do much to revive the sensuous simplicities in which fiction, and even emotion, began. His obvious danger lies in over-attention to surfaces; his less obvious danger is in fatiguing the reader and in distorting the image of what the reader would naturally see. There is a vase on a table in a room, but one entering that room frequently may never see it; it may even not be seen, and thus not be part of the room, in the case of a first entrance. Realism was not long in developing beyond the region of externals causing physical sensation into the more personal region of perceptions themselves. It is realism—that is, the reach toward vividness and immediacy—when the author represents objects and events wholly in terms of some person's sensation of them.

He wasn't going to open his eyes just yet and let in Emmy's pink hair that tufted the ruffled pillow of her twin bed. Had switched out its flame the last thing at night. Without looking, he knew well how her pink puff absorbed the henna—went into the roses painted on the footboards.

"I love pink," she said frequently.

The color leaked through the lace lamp shade by his bed, the sofa massed it in the corner.

"Don't put your feet on the velvet," she'd warned. "It's been done over for Agatha's début. . . . And your scarfpin, John. . . ." His scarfpin had left a hole in the pin cushion. Brutal of him to jab such a delicate thing!

A man felt coarse in a woman's room, a hedgehog in a handkerchief box; got ruffled over, smothered in pink schemes of Emmy. So it was hard to breathe. If he died, would she cover him with a pink marble tombstone?—Dr. John Farraday garlanded—doves somewhere and an urn?

Drowsy, head on the pillow, no need to move for a while. Eyes closed, he could dial New York; had the feel of it.

Just the way the air edged his cheek told the time—seven-thirty precisely.[2]

This is the "stream of consciousness" method, a more advanced form of realism, carried to its furthest point—so far—by James Joyce in *Ulysses,* and refined most intricately—so far—by Marcel Proust in *Remembrance of Things Past.*[3]

Realism's big gain is its intensification. Where human relationships are concerned, its externals help little and its interior method is one-sided and disadvantageous; the writer must hop from inside one mind to the inside of another, and then another, and back again, if the relationships are to be fairly presented; no single mind, however fine, is sufficient (though Henry James was always looking for one), unity, except in method, goes all to pieces and the reader's agility may tire. More than the reader's agility may tire: the gain of intensity is so great that the reader almost lives the life of each character; the over-stimulation and the demand on versatility make for rapid and total exhaustion. So much realism may defeat reality; it is all the reader can do to live one character in life, his own, intermitted with startling moments in which he lives the life of his neighbor. But in a highly developed realistic novel of the present he may be called upon to live six people at once.

---

[2] Opening paragraphs of *Black Stream,* a novel by Nathalie Sedgwick Colby.

[3] Title of C. K. Scott Moncrieff's English translation of the continuous novel, *A la Recherche du Temps Perdu.* One cannot ask for it, however, at least in America, under that title. One must assemble through a bookshop, from various publishers, *Swann's Way* (two volumes), *Within a Budding Grove,* etc.

We have been drawn away from our Monte Carlo example, which must now seem of such simplicity as to resemble crudity. A realistic Monte Carlo, in the first fictions about the place, was certainly the aim. The most striking aspects were realistically presented. But then memory, a digestive-reproductive process, a cow's cud, stepped in. Its intervention is the constant foe of realism, with writer and reader alike. Soon it became impossible to write about Monte Carlo without the memorable identifications—the Casino, the adventurers, the whisked-away suicides, the sapphire ocean. As impossible as for Homer to omit "wine-dark" or "many-sounding" when he mentioned great waters; as impossible as it used to be for an American newspaper to speak of a "brewer" merely—he was always a "wealthy brewer." [4]

We should now be in a position to make a few tentative determinations of reality. This problem of the ages for the philosophers will give us the least possible bother at this stage of our survey, since we have not to worry about objective reality at all. All that worries us is what may be real to the reader whose path is lit by a street lamp, not by the moon.

We may say at once that what he has experienced through his senses and re-knows through memory is real. What he knows for the first time, if received through some sense directly, is real. (From this category writing is by its nature excluded, unless it employs actors.) What he re-knows racially, in the form of in-

[4] Samuel Rewey, of the staff of *The Sun,* New York, editing reporters' copy, used to grumble: "'Wealthy brewer' should be one word. If English had half the facility in compound words of German, it would be!"

stinct or "inherited memory" is real, though in any given instance his re-knowledge is less safely assumed. What he re-knows individually, as a tradition past his critical challenge, "his" Monte Carlo, "his" Abraham Lincoln, is real. All these are quite incontestable forms of fictional reality.

What is there, in the way of reality, outside these four classes, which the novel or story may in even slight degree hope to achieve? We may fear there is not much; we shall do well to adopt that attitude. The aspects of reality on which fiction founds itself are existent—human relationships, the verities of feeling, the intensification by which we transcend the life in time. A writer depicting an unrecognized human relationship or an unacceptable verity of feeling may count, of course, on the reader's knowledge that some form of relationship always *is*, that some kind of feeling always flows; he may count on this but he cannot count much. And now where does realism come in and how far will it carry the writer with the reader? We have seen that it is the strongest appeal to the intensification faculty, to the interior dimension of living, but easily goes too far. But it is, after all, only a method; where it achieves reality it does so through the three classes accessible to writing, plus the intensity it emphasizes.

On what the reader re-knows from memory of personal experience the fictioner can count little; on what he re-knows racially, the dependence is heavy. The appeal to his re-knowledge as an individual can be endlessly subdivided—to what he knows as a Frenchman or German or American, as a Catholic, as a war veteran;

to what she knows as a widow or a woman of society or a factory worker. But the first and most natural division is to what the reader knows as a man or a woman, regardless of nationality or condition in the world. Note that this appeal is double, to what the reader can reknow racially as well as individually and traditionally. There is always the chance, of course, that the appeal will be threefold, including reader memory of personal experiences.

It would seem, then, that sexual recognitions—the man re-knowing as a man, the woman as a woman—would be one of the very greatest forms of fictional reality. It is; but there is perhaps no reality in which most writers are so greatly deficient. To put it succinctly, most men are entirely ignorant of all women, of the feminine perceptions and recognitions, that is. We are upon the threshold of the most fascinating subject in all fiction—in all life governed by the interior dimension. We cannot develop it fully, but let us not be afraid to be disproportionate in our attention.

III

The biological background is well known: and men have studied women closely enough. Schopenhauer and Weininger out of bitterness, the ash of death in their mouths, explored for the truth, and found it in one version; we cannot receive the findings because of the depth of their dye in personal experience. But equally (or even more) is it impossible to receive the findings of a fantastic chivalry like George Meredith's. To go about it impersonally and with more coolness, woman still rests securely on her nervous system; as a sex she has so far been able—happily able—to resist the masculine tendency toward over-ratiocination. Very roughly, the difference is that woman still thinks with her nerves, man with his brain. While in theoretical biology this may make woman less developed than man, in actual practice it makes her vastly his superior in the business of living and the wisdom of living.

Here is the commonest occurrence, as the best example: A young man has asked a girl to marry him. We will suppose her unconstrained by circumstances; she has only to settle whether she loves him. That, in fact, has long been settled, but she knows enough about men to know how to act appropriately. She tells him that she must think over his proposal. She tells him that because she knows it is a formula which he will understand and accept; but it must not for an instant be supposed that she means any such thing as he assumes her to mean. He, being a man, supposes she is going to go through the exercises of the rational faculty, search for reasons for and against, reflect, ratiocinate. In point of actuality she is going to do nothing of the kind—being woman, she could scarcely operate that way even if she so desired, which would be most unlikely. No, she will not think it over in any sense comprehended by the man. What she will actually do will be to verify her sensations.

Her nervous system has been recording with instantaneous precision all the physical sensations this young man has caused her. Now memory will repeat these sensations and the nervous system will re-test and relate them. His face, his hair, his eyelashes, eyes and mouth;

the feeling of his lips pressed against hers and the penumbra of that instant; his clothes and manner of wearing them; his hips and carriage; the color of his neckties; the texture of his skin; the shapeliness of his hands and the contact of his palm; his manner with other people in particular instances and on both special and ordinary occasions; the cross-current of what people say of him; his ability to order a meal for them both in a restaurant, his poise, energy, initiative, and assurance. All these sensations and a hundred others will be gone over again and again by memory and nerves. It is not a thought-process at all, as men understand thinking, but caution, correlation, *verification.* All these things were definitely known in the moments of their first experience, but they must be checked, especially as the fine mesh of recent memory sifts them. They, and nothing else, are to be the reasons for accepting or rejecting this suitor. Abstract considerations have no place in the reckoning.

It has happened many times, and will happen frequently until the race expires, that a man has learned some portion of this procedure, completely misunderstanding it. We will suppose our young woman's verification to have resulted in a "No" to the suitor. Her family is disappointed, her brother of about her own age or maybe a bit older is flabbergasted. He upbraids, demanding her reasons, and in the irritation of their quarrel his sister flashes out that, well, for one thing Nicholas wears such horrid neckties, he is so awkward at ordering a meal with the waiter hovering behind, and then his skin, so rosy with that *bursting* look, like a pink-and-white sausage. And Brother is horrified. Good Lord! Women are silly! Nance knows that Nick is the salt of the earth, a square-shooter, kind, generous, not a mean impulse in him—damned able, too, with a big career ahead of him, a fellow of the most absolute integrity. . . . But Brother is wrong, and his sister is right. She is going to have to look at that too exuberant complexion every morning across the breakfast table; all her life she would see those neckties and feel, at intervals, the angry humiliation of his timidity with the waiter. She is not, in any sense real to her, going to live with Nicholas's business integrity, nor will his career be in the twin bed. She has obeyed a sound and infallible instinct. She has made her decision for no reason at all —and for the best of reasons.

We do not mean that the rational faculty does not struggle to have its share in the business; that Sister does not waver and fluctuate as the considerations it urges upon her straggle into the procession of her "thoughts." We do mean that with womanly wisdom she settles the question from quite another basis, an older, a sounder, a more practical. Practicality, the intense practicality of the fully-developed nervous system, is the trait which most distinguishes women from men. If their reach is not seldom less high, it usually results in a securer grasp. That grasp, indeed, that extraordinary tenaciousness of purpose, has sometimes dire and tragic results. A wife will drive her husband beyond his strength, or in a path alien to his capacity, until he breaks; a mother will insist, with fondness and fierceness, on realizing some ideal of her own in her child, an ideal that is not the child's, and disaster is the issue.

But let us consider another example, this time directly related to writing—a fictional application of what we have under view. A young man of exceptional education and a writer produced his first novel and a publisher had it under consideration. But not long; rejection was inevitable and Mr. B. inherited the task of explaining to the author the reasons for the rejection. As so often happens, Mr. B. could not really explain; too much was wrong all through the manuscript. But in an effort to deal fairly he wrote a long letter to the author in which he stated this and continued:

The best I can do is to cite a representative instance. It occurs early in your book. Two young people are in love. Deserting an evening party, they stroll out together under the trees of a garden. You devote a paragraph to what was going on in the young man's mind, and you do him very well. You show him with his head in the clouds, his feet only partly on the ground. He is filled with a vague but overwhelming emotion—a generous outpouring of something that wells up within him. He imagines this emotion to be personalized, to be centered upon the girl whose arm is in his, who walks by his side. The truth is perhaps more nearly in the saying that he is "in love with love." The reader divines that, under the conditions, almost any other equally attractive young woman would do as well.

But now you proceed to the young woman, and in a paragraph about her, indicate that she is in much the same mental state. This, if you will allow me to say so, is completely wrong. The chances are that she is dwelling intently on one concrete question: "I wonder what it will be like when he kisses me." She is dealing with all aspects of this moment to come, intimately, pursuingly. But there is more: she is formulating in her mind the means by which the moment shall be brought to pass. There is a bend in the path, a little ways ahead, where by a slight pause, a half-turn, brushing against him . . .

The defect I have endeavored to illustrate is one that runs all through your story. The women are unreal.

Unreal, that is to say, to other women. The woman reader of fiction is not, in most cases, able to analyze the defect in so many novels and stories. She is only able to say: "Well, the woman in that story didn't seem real to me." One cannot expect her to tell why; it is the business of the fictioner to know why. It is, indeed, much more his business than that even of the critic, because in this matter the failure is usually a lack of creative detail, and to tell what is wrong requires the creative gift possession of which should have made the story right. Yet sometimes a woman can put her finger on the something-missing and it is often the subtlest sort of failure. There was an excellent novel published a few years ago, one of those stories dominated throughout by a fascinating woman. Women who read the book through respected it as an achievement, but their reading was attended by an almost continuous murmur of complaint. And one of these complaints showed the masculine author's lack of finesse. He had just described an entrance of his heroine. His reader looked up, she exclaimed, with a touch of exasperation:

"I don't want to know that Sophy came in wearing black. I want to know what she looked like, in black!"

That was typical of the difficulty women found while reading this novel, an undue struggle to invest the heroine with feminine reality, a continual absence of those little recognitions which women make. Here is another example:

A certain publishing house had brought out a third novel by a highly promising young man. His first two books had attracted more than usual attention, but this new story seemed to the publisher by far the best, and the best chance of the three. It dealt with the amusing adventures of a man of forty or thereabouts, still rather youthful and still unmarried. Various young women made up their minds to capture him, with or without the aid of their mothers. The episodes were varied; one or two were extremely pathetic; one or two were bold but free from offensiveness and very laughable. In the end the hero's wariness did not save him.

The publisher highly recommended this book for its entertainment to his stenographer, a girl with no more than a high school education, but intelligent, with no cheapness about her. A few days later he asked her how she had enjoyed it.

"Why, I didn't think it was so good."

The publisher pricked up his ears. He was going to hear something of the first importance.

"Oh! Why not? I thought it was the best fun."

"Well," she answered. "You see the author never once shows what it was all those girls saw in Dash that made them so crazy about him."

The book had a lamentably poor sale.

Reality for women is the novelist's constant affair. It

is an accomplishment of the greatest inherent difficulty for men, and only a few have excelled at it. George Meredith championed women but apparently understood them only superficially. Arnold Bennett and Robert Hichens are both highly remarkable in their understanding and the reality of their portrayal. Joseph Conrad walked among his women humbly, realizing his ignorance of all but a few. Booth Tarkington has been praised for his heroine in *Alice Adams,* and quite deservedly, but it is a question whether she is as good as Cora Madison in *The Flirt.* Practically all that men have learned about the art of reality for the women in their fictions is derived from Jane Austen, whose sense of feminine values was and is unerring. For though customs and social relationships vary, the values that women put upon certain things vary hardly at all. There is, of course, considerable personal variation; but so there is among men.

We will consider an instance of the sex difference and then illustrate feminine reality by a few excerpts from various novelists.

Our instance is a husband and wife who attend a party together.

They may remain together during most of the evening but a week later, asked to recall the event, they relate details very far apart. The discrepancy is not merely that of two pairs of eyes, it is a sexual difference. The woman has really observed, and now remembers, those things that concerned her as a woman—the fit of a dress, the look Mrs. Bard gave her husband when he told about his mother's cooking, John Croyden's prowl to keep beside Cora Mallock and the strained look about his wife's eyes, the food, the service, the snub administered in a way only women perceive or understand. . . . Our lady, and most of her sex, are busy on such occasions and others that are no occasions at all, assembling from the materials at hand the elements of one or more human dramas.[5]

And the husband? It is hardly necessary to indicate the gulf which divides his recollections from his wife's. In all likelihood he observed not one single thing that she did. His chief reminiscence is as to the kind of a time he had, good or bad. He remembers a story some one told. He recalls vaguely that he thought Mrs. Neilson a remarkably pretty woman. Poor old Blanville looked seedy; his son's bankruptcy must have got into him for a lot of money. His memory of the food is confined to some item he particularly liked or disliked.

But obviously, if a man is going to write fiction and make it convincing to the mind of the feminine reader, especially where his women are concerned, he must cultivate very thoroughly the technique of feminine perception, he must know the woman's scale of values, he must achieve a reality with which mere realism has nothing whatever to do, except as an incidental and occasional means toward his much greater end.

Now for some illustrations of feminine reality from the work of writers who have mastered this technique, or to whom it comes as something innate. The authors shall not be named until after all the excerpts have been quoted; you are invited to assign each bit to the proper author as you read it.

---

[5] From the chapter on Kathleen Norris in *The Women Who Make Our Novels,* by Grant Overton. (Revised edition, Dodd Mead, 1928).

Marsellus, silenced during the soup, came in with a warm smile and a slight shrug of the shoulders. "Building is the word with us, Sir Edgar, my—oh, isn't it! My wife and I are in the throes of it. We are building a country house, rather an ambitious affair, out on the wooded shores of Lake Michigan. Perhaps you would like to run out in my car and see it? What are your engagements for to-morrow? I can take you out in half an hour, and we can lunch at the Country Club. . . ."

The engagement made, Louis turned to Mrs. St. Peter. "And won't you come, too, dearest? You haven't been out since we got our wonderful wrought-iron door fittings from Chicago. We found just the right sort of hinge and latch, Sir Edgar, and had all the others copied from it. None of your Colonial glass knobs for us!"

Mrs. St. Peter sighed. Scott and Kathleen had just glass-knobbed their new bungalow throughout, yet she knew Louis didn't mean to hurt their feelings—it was his heedless enthusiasm made him say untactful things.

Now she saw him on a height, and that seemed as it should be. She knew that physically she was going to mount up to him, and to join him on his height, and to stand beside him on it, looking over the prospect he saw. But she had a longing to be able to join him on another height too, and to see what he looked out on from it. She had that longing, but with it came another longing, intimate, searching, and horribly full of sex—the longing to draw him down from his isolation to her, to lure him from his contemplation of the infinite to a narrower contemplation—of her, to force him to concentrate on her. He had taken possession of her because of his difference from all other men. Now she had a terrible longing to force him to become like all other men.

A very little quiet reflection was enough to satisfy Emma as to the nature of her agitation on hearing this news of Frank Churchill. She was soon convinced that it was not for herself she was feeling at all apprehensive or embarrassed—it was for him. Her own attachment had really subsided into a mere nothing—it was not worth thinking of; but if he, who had undoubtedly been always so much the most in love of the two, were to be returning with the same warmth of sentiment which he had taken away, it would be very distressing. If a separation of two months should not have cooled him, there were dangers and evils before her: caution for him and for herself would be necessary. She did not mean to have her own affections entangled again, and it would be incumbent on her to avoid any encouragement of his.

She wished that she might be able to keep him from an absolute declaration.

His arms were folded across his knees, and thus lifting his face towards Emma, close by her, he looked fixedly at her. She noticed in his eyes small golden lines radiating from black pupils; she even smelt the perfume of the pomade that made his hair glossy. Then a faintness came over her; she recalled the Viscount, who had waltzed with her at Vaubyessard, and his beard exhaled like this hair an odor of vanilla and citron, and mechanically she half-closed her eyes the better to breathe it in. But in making this movement, as she leaned back in her chair, she saw in the distance, right on the line of the horizon, the old diligence the "Hirondelle," that was slowly descending the hill of Leux, dragging after it a long trail of dust. It was in this yellow carriage that Leon had so often come back to her, and by this route down there that he had gone forever. She fancied she saw him opposite at his window; then all grew confused; clouds gathered; it seemed to her that she was again turning in the waltz under the light of the lustres on the arm of the Viscount, and that Leon was not far away, that he was coming; and yet all the time she was conscious of the scent of Rodolphe's head by her side. This sweetness of sensation pierced through her old desires, and these, like grains of sand under a gust of wind, eddied to and fro in the subtle breath of the perfume which suffused her soul. She opened wide her nostrils several times to drink in the freshness of the ivy round the capitals. She took off her gloves, she wiped her hands, then fanned her face with her handkerchief, while athwart the throbbing of her temples she heard the murmur of the crowd and the voice of the councillor intoning his phrases.

Without saying anything Elsie went downstairs into the shadowy shop. A dozen or so letters lay on the floor. "I'll give him two or three to quiet him," she thought, counting him now as a baby. She picked up three envelopes at random. "He'd better not have them all," she thought. The others she left lying. She had no concern whatever as to the possible business importance of any of the correspondence. Her sole concern, apart from the sickroom, was the condition of the shop. Ought she to clean it, or ought she to "let it go"? She wanted to clean it because it was obviously fast returning to its original state of filth. On the other hand, while cleaning it she might be neglecting her master. None but herself had the power to decide which course should be taken. She perceived that she was mistress. Naïvely she enjoyed the strange sensation of authority, but the responsibility of authority dismayed her.

"Are these all?" Mr. Earlforward asked indifferently, as she put the three letters into his limp, shiny hand.

"Yes, sir," she said, without compunction.

Franklin again paused, his eyes on hers. With a little effort he now pursued. "You know of my romance, Miss Buchanan, and you know that it's over, except as a beautiful and sacred memory. You know that I don't intend to let a memory warp my life. It may seem sudden to you, and I ask your pardon if it's too sudden; but I want to marry; I want a home, and children, and the companionship of some one I care for and respect, very deeply. Therefore, Miss Buchanan," he spoke on, turning a little paler, but with the same deliberate steadiness, "I ask you if you will marry me."

While Franklin spoke, it had crossed Helen's mind that perhaps he had determined to follow her suggestion—buy a castle and find a princess to put in it; it had crossed her mind that he might be going to ask her advice on this momentous step—she was used to giving advice on such momentous steps; but when he brought out his final sentence she was so astonished that she rose from her chair and stood before him. She became very white, and, with the strained look that then came to them, her eyes opened widely. And she gazed down at Franklin Winslow Kane while, in three flashes, searing and swift, like running leaps of lightning, three thoughts traversed her mind: Gerald—All that money—A child. It was in this last thought that she seemed, then, to fall crumblingly, like a burnt-out thing reduced to powder. A child. What would it look like, a child of hers and Franklin Kane's? How spare and poor and insignificant were his face and form. Could she love a child who had a nose like that—a neat, flat, sallow little nose? A spasm, half of laughter, half of sobbing caught her breath.

"I've startled you," said Franklin, who still sat in his chair looking up at her. "Please forgive me."

A further thought came to her now, one that she could

utter, was able to utter. "I couldn't live in America. Yes, you did startle me. But I am much honored."

The examples given are from the following authors and books, in order: Willa Cather, *The Professor's House;* Robert Hichens, *The Unearthly;* Jane Austen, *Emma;* Gustave Flaubert, *Madame Bovary;* Arnold Bennett, *Riceyman Steps;* Anne Douglas Sedgwick, *Franklin Winslow Kane.* Were space unlimited it would be pleasant to quote other and longer passages, from men and women alike, from so-called "popular" authors and from authors of an enshrined literary tradition. It is hard, for instance, not to draw upon the portrait of Barry du Spain, as seen through the eyes of his adoring but bewildered and hurt young bride, in Kathleen Norris's *Barberry Bush.* It is equally difficult not to quote a page or more of Frank Swinnerton's perfect study of four people, *Nocturne.*

It is not likely that any one who reads the examples given above will be in much doubt as to the feminine point of recognition, and thus of reality, in each. But we may as well be explicit. In Miss Cather's passage, it is Mrs. St. Peter's sigh, the little hurt she feels for her other son-in-law and her daughter, Kathleen, when Son-in-law Louis speaks with scorn of glass doorknobs. Mr. Hichens deals with the dualism of the feminine soul; Jane Austen with the feminine capacity for inverting the situation. "She was soon convinced that it was not for herself she was feeling at all apprehensive or embarrassed—it was for him"; and with this quickly and comfortably established, Emma has no trouble deciding on a course when she and Frank Churchill shall meet again.

Flaubert is presenting the side of physical sensation, so tremendously more important in woman's life than in man's. Emma's confusion of her lovers in her day-dream is entirely typical of her sort of woman. Arnold Bennett's power to comprehend feminine mental processes was never more beautifully illustrated than in Elsie's behavior with the dozen letters; it is an attitude known to all women—still the child, feed the brute, lie to him for a larger good. Folded in with this state of mind, in Elsie's case, is her intense preoccupation with the problem of cleaning the shop; any woman will realize how great that preoccupation was, how beside it all else sank to insignificance.

In the last example, from Anne Douglas Sedgwick's fine novel, the point is Helen Buchanan's instant visualization of a child with the unsatisfactory nose of the man who is proposing marriage to her. It is spontaneous and it is wholly her own. Franklin Kane has included a generality about children in his elaborate statement, but this is not the cause of the flash in Helen's mind, for at that moment she merely thinks he is about to ask her advice on whom to marry, or where to look for some one in marriage. No, it is the woman, the woman whose eyes and nerves translate the words of the man into a physical reality based on the physical reality confronting her. It is, indeed, Everywoman who lives in Helen Buchanan under that moment's crucial pressure.

Enough, perhaps, has been said to suggest the rôle which reality for women plays in fiction, a rôle not less vital than woman herself plays in the human drama. The subject is endless, and as a subject must by us be abandoned here. There are other problems, chiefly of fictional structure, and the mind of the reader bends us to necessary determinations regarding these.

And first, sequence.

IV

By sequence, we mean the time dimension of fiction.

There is no use in making a bugaboo of time. It may be a handicap; but, as even E. M. Forster, deploring its existence, points out, it is absolutely necessary to intelligibility.[6] Somewhere and somehow the fictioner must indicate the order of events. He may do it openly and methodically, like Scott, or may disguise or blur it, like Marcel Proust; and just what he does will be determined by the effects he desires to produce. He cannot ignore it unless he is willing to join the great minority of Gertrude Stein.

In fiction intended for a large number of readers, sequence must in the main, and with only slight and passing exceptions, be chronological. This is absolutely true in respect of fiction that is published serially, or in instalments—or, one should perhaps say, that is to be read with intervals between. *There* any lapse into the past, glance into the future, or transposition of sequence must be wholly contained within a single instalment, or even the sharpest and most attentive reader will become confused. It does not matter that this strict requirement

[6] For an amusing discussion of the time element, see Chapter II, "The Story," in Mr. Forster's *Aspects of the Novel.*

has sometimes been disregarded, or rather, it matters only as convincing evidence of its force. Those who, in 1912 or thereabouts, attempted to read as a serial in a New York Sunday newspaper, Joseph Conrad's intricate novel, *Chance,* will understand the impossibility of attempting to follow serially anything but a straightforward narrative. A more recent example is found in the magazine publication of Edna Ferber's *Show Boat.* This story opens with the birth of Kim Ravenal in a storm on the Mississippi River, but immediately drops back to the childhood of Kim Ravenal's mother. It deals very fully with that mother's life as a child and with her growth to womanhood. The result was that, although the magazine used a generously long first instalment, the first chunk of the story ended and the second began many years before the scene with which the reader started.

Such technique has its frequent justifications in a book, and we shall duly consider what they are in our next chapter; in serial fiction such a form of construction is fatal. This cannot be said of skips of time, although, if they are long skips, matters of years, the magazine editor will use every effort to bring them in the middle of an instalment. Coming at the end of one instalment and the beginning of the next, they bewilder the reader with a sense of having missed something, either an instalment in between or a portion that the editor has cut from the story.

No excuse is necessary for continuing some distance further a discussion of the requisites in fiction intended to be published serially. A vast deal of fiction is first published and read in this fashion, a considerable percentage of it being the best contemporary work. The mind of the reader is more often busy with a magazine than with a book, we may suspect. It is not a snobbish mind; and while we may long for it to attain a better power of discrimination, we shall do nothing to bring that about by ignoring it as it is. Our philosophy of fiction derives quite as much from that mind as from the creativeness of the fictioner, whose transcendentalism is usually influenced no little by the desire to be read.

Now it may be truc that the story, as story, appeals to the gaping caveman in us; that it is the lowest form of fictional exercise. Possibly, in its simplest forms, it appeals only to our ignorant curiosity, with its "What next?" But of what use to groan over the fact?—less a fact than a specimen of academic analysis. The appeal of "What next?" is scarcely found in what science would call the pure state. One might as well concentrate a gloomy vision on the indubitable circumstance that human existence is insured by animal heat, blind to the exquisiteness of children or the felicities of adult companionship. In any fiction, the interest of "What then?" must inhere; and obviously, in any fiction that involves long waits for the reader, this interest must be specially intensified at certain moments—the moments when the reader is compelled to halt.

Serial suspense is a trick, no doubt; those who have essayed it vainly often so call it. But that it can also be an art should be patent to minds less jealous. It is not in the least inconsistent with the profoundest characterization or the loftiest emotion—with any of the richness with which fiction can be endowed. Simply it requires something peculiar to itself, a combination of reasonably rapid movement with the development of periodic crises. That it need have nothing else much—no literary values, only the cheapest human values—is unfortunately true. It is also true that the crises or hold-over points may be highly artificial and wholly misleading; the suspense is a fake but the reader does not know it and at the beginning of the next instalment a decoy scene leads him away from the discovery that he has been imposed upon. But this does not mean that the mind of the reader prefers a bogus article to a genuine, only that he will have the article, bogus or not.

Sequence, the dimension in time, which, we must remind ourselves, does not insist upon a chronological order in a work of fiction, but only insists that time be sufficiently indicated, may be the hampering difficulty that some writers proclaim it—for them. It cannot be said that most writers are expert enough to offer such a complaint. Only when one is the master of sequence may he properly wish to pass beyond it. But most writers fumble with it all their lives.

Why? Sequence, in a work of fiction, is the warp, the life by intensities is the woof of story. Here is a continuous procession of events, but only a few of those events have emotional intensity, and thus importance, or even relevance, in fiction. The majority of fictioners have all they can do in a lifetime to acquire sufficient skill in judging intensities. Does this particular occurrence qualify by intensity for inclusion in the story? And how much of it must be included—which is another way of saying, how long shall it run? The "how much," of course, matters principally in relation to what else has to be told. There is the further difficulty that with each new story these problems of judgment must be faced anew, from start to finish. No, most fictioners have their hands more than full with the proportioning and patterning of intensity's colored threads in designs ever varying and with results ever anxiously uncertain; they are not hampered by the Time Warp, rather are they grateful for it.

In this, their first and fundamental problem of structure, Sequence is their ally oftener than their passive enemy. It is far less friendly when the fashion of telling a story confronts them. Since fiction can appeal directly to none of the senses, unless acted or at very least recited, read aloud, the writer is bound to simulate a direct appeal as often as he can. This appeal is naturally and most often and easily toward the eye, as being the most active and amenable sense. The writer wishes to make the reader *see* the story in the literal fashion of having it form retinal images. He therefore usually endeavors to write his story in a succession of what are called scenes.

A scene is a piece of writing in which one or more characters act before the reader in a given setting. Any change in actors or setting, or lapse of time, initiates a new scene.

The setting may be fully described or merely indicated. The actors may be holding a conversation or one may be murdering the other. If only one actor is present, his thoughts will constitute the scene. They may project a scene within the scene.

The essence of the scenic method is that the writer *shows* the reader—so far as his skill permits, puts the occurrence before the reader's eye.

The other fashion is narrative. Strictly, narrative is a telling-about, instead of a putting-before—a device for covering necessary ground or imparting requisite information with rapidity and clearness, a concession squeezed out to Sequence by a reluctant and grudging Intensity. Pure narrative in this sense is no longer very common, and where writers are compelled to resort to it they break it up with constant scenes. In the modern short story pure narrative is often reduced to a sentence, a phrase—just the connective tissue essential to indicate the lapse of time and to lead adroitly from one scene into the next. The structure of such stories is much more analogous to that of plays than to the structure of the novel. Realism of the "stream of consciousness" type automatically excludes narration, is all a scene or scenes in somebody's head. Pure narrative is so infrequent that it is customary to speak of narrative in a looser way. So loosely taken, all of Book II of Willa Cather's novel, *The Professor's House*—the part called "Tom Outland's Story"—can be called narrative. It goes incessantly into scene, but by comparison with the first part is, as a whole, "told about."

Just as the old descriptions of writing have been relegated to obscurity, being analytical but not useful—Description, Conversation, Action, etc.—so will probably pass our modern and briefer division of Narration and Scene, if pressed too closely. The two frequently fuse; and to parse a given passage for the narrative and scenic elements is an exercise of not much value. The business of the writer is incessantly to ask himself: "Am I putting before the reader, or am I telling him about?" And where space and proportion permit, he will transpose narration into scene for the sake of the greater vividness generally resulting.

But not always. For the choice between the two methods is not exclusively the issue of vividness or the conveniences and necessities of primary form—by which we may sum up Intensity's tricks with Sequence. An unbroken succession of scenes may deprive a story of all repose, the people of all dignity, the reader of enough time to savor emotions properly; a narrative passage may be essential to some mood into which the reader should be inducted or in which he should be sustained. We may be reminded of what John Galsworthy says in his preface to that very fine fiction, R. H. Mottram's *The Spanish Farm:*

"The Spanish Farm" is not precisely a novel, and it is not altogether a chronicle; and here the interest comes in—quite clearly the author did not mean it to be a novel, and fail; nor did he mean it to be a chronicle, and fail. In other words, he was guided by mood and subject-matter . . . I do not think the serious critic can miss the peculiar unforced feeling of novelty its form has given me. You do not put it down saying: "I see perfectly what form the fellow was trying for, but he didn't bring it off." You put it down thinking: "The fellow didn't seem to be trying for any form, but he did bring it off."

We know the self-conscious chronicle in fiction, and its—as a rule—artificial effect. "The Spanish Farm" is as far from that as it is from the dramatic novel. It just goes its own way, and quietly defeats the search for parallels.

It should be unnecessary to say that Narrative, as we have here used it, is never precisely identical with speech by a character. Such a speech, if of any length, generally moves into the scenic method, dramatizes moments of the narration. The device of having a character tell about an event or series of events may be economical purely, but is more often resorted to for some inflection which cannot be conveyed with vividness otherwise. An excellent example is Turgenev's *The District Doctor*.[7] The peculiar poignancy of this love story lies in the fact that the lover himself tells it to a friend. A shabby, middle-aged man, dulled by routine work, acquiescent in a stupid marriage, he brings to the telling a kind of anguish which articulates what words cannot. The inflection which Turgenev wishes to place is of fresh hurt, of a wound still bleeding internally despite all the lapse of years. No other narrative device would serve half so well.

But at this juncture some one is sure to raise the question, once so weightily argued, as to the point of view. The serious argument for it, that there should be *a* point of view, may be found in Percy Lubbock's *The Craft of Fiction;* a spirited rejoinder is offered by E. M. Forster in his *Aspects of the Novel*.[8] Mr. Forster thinks it necessary that the author should "bounce the reader," and

---

[7] In his book, *A Sportsman's Sketches*. This particular story is available for American readers in the Modern Library volume, *Best Russian Short Stories,* edited by Thomas Seltzer, as well as in other collections.

[8] Closing pages of Chapter IV.

concludes that if he is able to do so he may shift the point of view at will. He is practical rather than logical in this attitude. Not only may his attitude be commended in this matter, but we may urge it upon ourselves in every fictional inquiry. For fiction is pragmatism, too; what works is valid, and what doesn't work, no matter how theoretically perfect, is a waste of everybody's time. The author must in every instance determine the point of view from which, predominantly, his fiction will take its departures. He may then stick to this throughout, or lapse from it when he pleases, provided he has considered well what he is doing and does it with reasonable effect. The mind of the reader is not exigent in the matter, and there is no reason why the critic should find heavy fault on technical grounds.

What works is good. In the chapters immediately following we are to study the workings. We shall study them analytically, by considering representative novels of several sorts, and synthetically, by some progress toward the construction of novels of our own. Then some of the observations on method in this chapter which may have seemed too generalized or abstract will possibly take on clearer meaning; any error into which we have fallen, find, perhaps, at least partial correction.

CHAPTER IV

FIRST STUDY IN METHOD. NOVEL OF CHARACTER

THE novel of character is dominant in our day —so far it dominates the fiction of our century as it did the fiction of the nineteenth century. We shall therefore proceed to study it first, and if possible with more amplitude than any other species. We shall scrutinize, one by one, the following examples:

Jane Austen: *Persuasion*
Arnold Bennett: *The Old Wives' Tale*
Joseph Conrad: *Nostromo*
Willa Cather: *A Lost Lady*

Finally we shall try our hand at the beginnings of a novel of our own. Thus to the subjects of this chapter, enumerated above, let us add one more:

Laboratory: *The Strain Runs Out*

A few words explaining the selections made for study are in order.

Probably no one will criticize the choice of a work by Jane Austen. If the novel of character does not owe its existence to her, it owes her its consummated perfection. As a presentation of character solely, it has advanced not at all since her day, a century behind us.

Mr. Bennett's greatest book has been selected for a

variety of reasons, aside from its intrinsic greatness. It is the first great landmark of modern realism—realism as a literary method, not simply as a camera pointed at surrounding objects. It also signalized the end of a period of twenty years in which romanticism, or something that passed for romance, made fashionable by Robert Louis Stevenson, and imitated by a hundred inferior writers, carried all before it. But there is another reason: *The Old Wives' Tale* is quite as much a novel of outside forces as of human agency, in particular the compulsion of Time; and we shall have to consider this special effect, this quality usually called "epic" but more nearly prophetic.

Nostromo is prophetic, too, and of such scope, both in relation to Space and Time, as to obscure in most minds the fact that character is the main subject. It shows, better, perhaps, than any novel of our day, how much can be brought into the novel founded on Jane Austen without impairing its structure. Especially does *Nostromo* show how far the character novel, grounded on a realistic method, can reach toward infinity. But Conrad's work is full of these gestures toward the supreme attribute of ancient fiction.

Willa Cather's smaller masterpiece is worth our study for its extreme narrative simplicity, its absolute realism achieved without any resort to the heightened realistic methods.[1]

[1] The reader of this book is earnestly requested to read each novel himself before so much as glancing at the study of it in the ensuing pages.

THE PHILOSOPHY OF FICTION

I. JANE AUSTEN

Persuasion

Persuasion is the last of Jane Austen's six novels. We know that it was written between 1811 and 1816; it was first published in 1818. So much may be admitted to our knowledge; but it will perhaps be a useful exercise if we consider the book purely as a book, assuming that we know nothing of the author beyond her name.

The date of composition may be allowed because the general style of the book at once reveals it, more or less approximately. Suppose, then, that this novel saw light for the first time in our day, the author being totally obscure, what should we say of it?

We should find in it plenty of faults; it is not so certain that we should detect its merits. The faults are very open ones; conspicuous; the book's real distinctions lie deeper. They lie so deep that the better part of a century has been necessary to bring them to a proper estimation.

The story is simple, in spite of fairly numerous characters and the plenitude of incident. Anne Elliot, second daughter of a baronet, has been persuaded from a marriage of the heart with Captain Frederick Wentworth, a young naval officer, eight years before the book opens. Accident brings him back into her life after he has gained his rank in the navy and acquired a very decent fortune in his share of the prize money from captured vessels. The problem is whether these two will find their way to each other again—or rather, whether Captain Wentworth will come to love Anne after such a lapse of busy and changeful years and fortune; for Anne's love, once given, has never been retracted.

It seems a slender subject for what we should nowadays call a full-length novel. Possibly most contemporary reviewers would be a little scornful of this single thread spun out to so great a length, not recognizing that in its very simplicity the story is peculiarly hard to tell. A modern short-story writer, to be sure, would polish off the whole business in seven or eight thousand words, using as few characters as possible and a highly selective and scenic method. And yet, on due consideration, it is impossible to term Miss Austen's work padded. If we lay her novel alongside the contemporary short story we find that an intricate, necessary and sound design finds no more room than it needs.

How does this come about? The answer is that the short story's whole endeavor is slightly but sufficiently to individualize its pair of lovers; Miss Austen's final effort must be to assimilate them into the race. The two writers will start from opposite assumptions and proceed toward contrary (but not contradictory) conclusions. The short story writer, in effect, says to the reader: "There are men and women. They fall in love. But you will be particularly interested in *this* couple." The novelist may be imagined as saying: "Anne Elliot and Frederick Wentworth fell in love. Of course, I think their case interesting or I should not be telling you about it. But, really, they are interesting quite as much for their connections and the rules of their society, their civilization, under which they had to act, as for themselves, or nearly so. It is not for me to be free with large generalizations; but if you care to follow out the instance I think it may deepen your impressions of human nature."

Accordingly, *Persuasion* does not open with its subject at all. Miss Austen's first care is for Anne's family and general surroundings. Sir Walter Elliot, of Kellynch Hall, her father, is presented in all his ineffable vanity of rank, and Elizabeth, Anne's older sister, who is equally as vain and selfish as the father. Throughout the book we are to see everybody and everything either through Anne's eyes or from a point just back of her shoulder, as it were, and with a sympathy for her even when our comprehension is superior. But Miss Austen begins with straightforward, succinct narrative. Sir Walter, Elizabeth, Anne and the family friend, Lady Russell, are stated for our information in a business-like manner. Mrs. Clay, Elizabeth's intimate, a widow not held free from designs on Sir Walter, is brought in. A scene or two preliminary to the rental of Kellynch Hall serves the double purpose of confirming by their behavior what Miss Austen has so flatly asserted about these persons and of setting in train the events necessary to bring Captain Wentworth back into Anne's life. These events must not appear the contrivance of the novelist, and Miss Austen is a good deal too skillful to let them seem so. It has been settled that Mr. Shepherd may lease Kellynch Hall to one Admiral Croft. There has, so far, been no mention, even, of Frederick Wentworth. We have been looking on idly while Miss Austen expeditiously sets forth the change in the Elliot fortunes. And we are come to the final paragraph of Chapter III.

> Mr. Shepherd was completely empowered to act; and no sooner had such an end been reached, than Anne, who had been a most attentive listener to the whole, left the room, to seek the comfort of cool air for her flushed cheeks; and as she walked along a favorite grove, said, with a gentle sigh, "A few months more, and *he*, perhaps, may be walking here."

With admirable dramatic skill, fixing our attention upon her once and for all, Miss Austen conducts us in one sentence into Anne's innermost secret of the heart. "*He* was not Mr. Wentworth, the former curate of Monkford . . . but a Captain Frederick Wentworth, his brother," commences Chapter IV, and we follow on through the necessary summary of facts, assenting—for the moment pleasantly unconscious that there is anything of contrivance, with the sense of one of life's accidents strong upon us. Yet stronger than anything is the spell of Anne's murmur as she walked alone; a whole new world, a world of delicious reality that has nothing to do with Kellynch Hall, is opening before us.

It is from the security of this world that we view the expansion of the story in incident, characterizations, motivations and gestures. Let us digress to a consideration of what appear, at first reading, to be the novelist's shortcomings. Making all allowance for the period, her conversations seem impossibly stilted. Was this because she could not write as people speak? No, she does the hearty manner of that bluff old sailorman, Admiral Croft, entirely well. Mrs. Charles Musgrove, Sir Walter Elliot and the rest are made to reveal themselves in every utterance. The reportorial manner of dialogue is a twentieth century innovation in fiction, along with the photography of scenes; Miss Austen evidently attempted something different. If we seek one word for the effect she was after we shall probably say that she wanted to make her people's talk contrapuntal, not merely expressive. She wished to combine several effects of equal importance, the obvious meaning of the thing said, the characteristics of the speaker, and various implications for the reader to catch on to, of which the dominant one was frequently a contemptuous satire of an artificial society. But there is another purpose in view quite as serious as the satirical one. Wherever the character of the speaker permits, the moral sense must assert itself, not as a proof of the character but as an improvement to the reader. The speaker—an Anne Elliot, a Frederick Wentworth, a Lady Russell—must, to take a phrase from Miss Austen's "Mansfield Park," think justly on all important points and embody this reflection in his remarks. It is not conversation, perhaps, so much as a series of observations; but equally it is not mere talk, a waste of the speaker's breath and the reader's time. If not seldom somebody's answer to a question takes on the aspect of a little homily, we may ask ourselves whether Jane Austen's dialogue or that general in twentieth century novels wears the better. In Jane Austen, though speeches are rarely realistic, they are never vapid; in spite of elaboration of words and phrases, there is exquisite sensibility as well as the sense.

But what shall we make of such a passage as the following? Captain Benwick, a forlorn widower, has been discussing literature with Anne. Only a summary of their talk has been given, including Anne's fine comment that "it was the misfortune of poetry to be seldom safely enjoyed by those who enjoyed it completely; the strong feelings which alone could estimate it truly were the very feelings which ought to taste it but sparingly." Miss Austen continues:

> His looks showing him not pained, but pleased with this allusion to his situation, she was emboldened to go on; and feeling in herself the right of seniority of mind, she ventured to recommend a larger allowance of prose in his daily study; and on being requested to particularize, mentioned such works of our best moralists, such collections of the finest letters, such memoirs of characters of worth and suffering, as occurred to her at the moment as calculated to rouse and fortify the mind by the highest precepts and the strongest examples of moral and religious endurances.

Is this a case like Mrs. Humphry Ward's, of whom it was complained that she told about the witty talk of her people at dinner but gave no specimens of their brilliance? Surely, Miss Austen is writing a sleazy passage such as any beginner nowadays would be ashamed of. No doubt she is at less than her best, but the paragraph must be considered in its context. Anne and Frederick Wentworth have now met several times, have exchanged civilities, have this night sat down at the same dinner table. Across the room, while she converses with Captain Benwick, Frederick and Captain Harville are entertaining the rest of the company. No word, no look for her! All that Captain Benwick is saying and all that she is saying is unimportant to her heart, except as a generosity of her nature toward an unhappy person. Hence Miss

Austen's offhand report of the conversation with Captain Benwick—and we may suspect that the satirical intonation is not absent from her description of the reading Anne prescribes for the lonely man. The suspicion is confirmed by the next sentences:

> Captain Benwick listened attentively, and seemed grateful for the interest implied; and though with a shake of the head, and sighs which declared his little faith in the efficacy of any books on grief like his, noted down the names of those she recommended, and promised to procure and read them.

This is in the best manner of the author's gently mocking tone—a tone that can become ruthless without raising its pitch by one adjective. And now the chapter closes, rightly, by a return to Anne, to proper perspective, to the exercise of the sense of humor:

> When the evening was over, Anne could not but be amused at the idea of her coming to Lyme to preach patience and resignation to a young man whom she had never seen before; nor could she help fearing, on more serious reflection, that, like many other great moralists and preachers, she had been eloquent on a point in which her own conduct would ill bear examination.

No appeal for sympathy! Yet the pathos of the scene and its coda is perfect, and not less than its humorous fatuity. The latter proceeds from the disproportion between Benwick's malady and Anne's medicine, the former comes out of the lamentable gulf between Anne's evening and the evening it ought to be. The humorous pointlessness can be expressed, as smaller effects always can be openly made in all fiction; the all-important effect cannot be stated anywhere at all, but must, as always, be achieved by a kind of envelopment of the reader. The reader may remain blandly unaware of what steals in upon him from all sides. But with the instant of awareness will come his unconditional surrender to the author. The effect has been made.

One more "fault" of Jane Austen's. So much has been said about her consideration for social lines that to rehearse the arguments would be tedious and empty. The alert reader will soon discover that this was a subject on which Miss Austen "thought justly," just as she required of her favored characters. If these just reflections are sought in epitome, perhaps they may be found in a passage near the end of Chapter XVI in *Persuasion,* in a conversation between William Elliot and Anne. Anne's father and sister have just broken their necks to make acquaintance with their "cousins," the Dowager Viscountess Dalrymple and her daughter.

Anne was ashamed. Had Lady Dalrymple and her daughter even been very agreeable, she would still have been ashamed of the agitation they created, but they were nothing. . . .

Lady Russell confessed that she had expected something better; but yet "it was an acquaintance worth having," and when Anne ventured to speak her opinion of them to Mr. Elliot, he agreed to their being nothing in themselves, but still maintained that, as a family connection, as good company, as those who would collect good company around them, they had their value. Anne smiled and said—

"My idea of good company, Mr. Elliot, is the company of

clever, well-informed people, who have a great deal of conversation; that is what I call good company."

"You are mistaken," said he, gently, "that is not good company; that is the best. . . ."

Where *Persuasion* is weakest is not in its arbitrary handling of narrative and scenic divisions, its conversational style, its restricted society, or any of the things usually complained of in Jane Austen, but in its action. Louisa Musgrove's fall in which she suffers concussion of the brain is not badly planned but is very poorly told; Miss Austen has no skill at such a scene and might better have given it to us at secondhand. Mrs. Smith, the school friend, who so conveniently possesses all the knowledge necessary to discredit William Elliot—and that directly to Anne—lacks a good deal in skill. But these are not vital defects; they are more than outshone by the felicity of our introduction to Anne's romance of the past, already discussed, and by the magnificent sweep of Chapter XXIII where Anne and Wentworth are brought together.

We must look at this chapter for a moment. It begins quietly with two older women gossiping half-audibly about a particular match, the ill of long engagements, etc. Wentworth is writing at a table some distance away; at something in the talk he sends "one quick, conscious look" in Anne's direction. While she is still excited by this, Captain Harville motions her to the window and shows her, not without feeling, the miniature that his brother-in-law, Captain Benwick, ordered of himself, to be a gift to his wife. Now she is dead and it must be set for presentation to the girl Benwick is about to marry. "Poor Fanny!" breathes Harville, "she would not have forgotten him so soon. "No," replies Anne, with feeling, "that I can easily believe."

And in a second we are deep in the animated discussion that arises between these two as to the degree of attachment in men and women respectively. It is a conversation full of overtones, so far as Anne's side is concerned. There is a slight noise; Wentworth has dropped his pen; Anne is startled to find him nearer than she had supposed; could he have been listening? "Have you finished your letter?" asks Harville, and Wentworth answers: "Not quite, a few lines more. I shall have done in five minutes." Harville and Anne continue their debate—a presentation which, interesting in itself, serves Miss Austen's final end of assimilating her lovers to the men and women of every age. At last Wentworth is ready to go, hastened by Mrs. Croft's move to depart. He leaves the room without a word or a look for Anne.

She has taken a few steps toward the desk when the door opens. It is Wentworth, with an excuse of forgetting his gloves. He crosses the room to the desk, his back toward Mrs. Musgrove, draws out a letter from under the scattered paper, places it before Anne with entreating eyes, and is out of the room while she is still collecting her senses.

It is the love letter.

Within the hour, the two are walking together and the explanation of Wentworth's whole behavior is before the reader and before Anne. It is convincing; and what more remains to be said of other people's fortunes is smoothly rounded off in a short final chapter. The book is complete, the subject is clear. It is persuasion, both of the mind and of the heart. It says that the cogence of the mind cannot be disregarded, but that the compulsion of the heart is supreme. The various considerations of safety and risk, of duty and conscience, are weighed to a scruple in the final conversations. Those who can bring themselves to think justly have no great trouble to speak with exactitude.

Old-fashioned. Finely conceived. As solid as the day it was written. You work through it slowly and are amply repaid, not only in substance but with a liberal measure of the exhilaration with which, despite all labor and fatigues, Jane Austen wrote.

II. ARNOLD BENNETT

The Old Wives' Tale

In his preface to *The Old Wives' Tale,* Arnold Bennett tells how he came to write the book. Dining one evening in a Paris restaurant his attention was attracted to a grotesque old woman at whose ridiculous mannerisms other diners, and even the waitresses, were laughing. It suddenly occurred to Bennett that the old woman had once been young, slim, perhaps beautiful. Her case was a tragedy, but no exceptional tragedy—simply the heart-rending trick life plays upon all of us. While he was considering the general subject he recalled Guy de Maupassant's "Une Vie." He determined to go de Maupassant one better and give two life-histories instead of one. The ambitious nature of the book made him hesitate, but at length he began writing it in the autumn of 1907. The first quarter, about fifty thousand words, was completed in six weeks. The work was interrupted by the execution of Bennett's fantasia, *Buried Alive;* was resumed in early spring, 1908, and pushed through to completion at the end of July. Published in the autumn of 1908, it was reviewed on the whole rather unfavorably and the sale was poor. It made its way in England gradually, but in America, where it was brought out a year or so later, critical acclaim and a large sale accrued to it from the first.

Arnold Bennett had come from pottery-making Staffordshire to London at about the age of twenty-one. After a good deal of journalism, his first novel appeared when he was thirty-one. A half dozen novels had been published when, at forty, he began to write *The Old Wives' Tale*. *Anna of the Five Towns* had been his second book, but most of the fiction preceding *The Old Wives' Tale* had been light in character.

On the personal side Bennett was, and is, unusual in a number of respects. In one aspect he has all his life remained the young man from the provinces who feels that he can conquer the great city, and who thrills to the intoxication of that ambition and to its material rewards and sensuous enjoyments. As a writer for the daily and weekly press he had acquired a habit of work very exceptional among writers of fiction. He possessed an extreme inquisitiveness springing from a breadth of interests very rare in one person; he is as keenly observant as possible. Frank Swinnerton says that if there is something in a room which you particularly do not wish Bennett to notice, you relegate it to an obscure corner before his entrance and endeavor to divert his observation when he has come in; Bennett then perceives it at once, says nothing for a while, and finally reveals his discovery by a unique remark!

No man, perhaps, has so nearly possessed Jane Austen's eyes, or had to so great a degree the "feminine malice" which is a friendly maliciousness—a blend of keen perception, intuition, slyness and a determination to tell. With all of Defoe's feeling for smoothness and plausibility, Bennett combines an audacity that Defoe was always covering up but that Bennett prefers to wear with a swagger. Sedulously busy with human affairs and the things of the earth, he is at the greatest pains to appear absolutely finite-minded. Continually finding a miracle in some humble and everyday occurrence, Bennett seems less to deny the existence of larger miracles than to affirm them superfluous. In many ways he gives the effect of a pose, or of a variety of poses; but if it is posing it is inseparable from the man's own nature. Bennett's knowledge of French literature was already wide when *The Old Wives' Tale* was written; and the work was begun and completed in France.

The first sentence of the book names the sisters who are its heroines and stamps them with the provincial character which is to be their characteristic throughout.

Those two girls, Constance and Sophia Baines, paid no heed to the manifold interest of their situation, of which, indeed, they had never been conscious.

Without pause, the novelist goes at once into an evocation of Staffordshire, first placed in relation to England as a whole, then pictured in a famous passage as if seen from above—a vision such as would to-day be possible from a low-flying airplane:

> On every side the fields and moors of Staffordshire, intersected by roads and lanes, railways, watercourses and telegraph lines, patterned by hedges, ornamented and made respectable by halls and genteel parks, enlivened by villages at the intersections, and warmly surveyed by the sun, spread out undulating. And trains were rushing round curves in deep cuttings, and carts and wagons trotting and jingling on the yellow roads, and long, narrow boats passing in a leisure majestic and infinite over the surface of the stolid canals. . . . One could imagine the messages concerning prices, sudden death, and horses, in their flight through the wires under the feet of birds. In the inns Utopians were shouting the universe into order over beer, and in the halls and parks the dignity of England was being preserved in a fitting manner. The villages were full of women who did nothing but fight against dirt and hunger, and repair the effects of friction on clothes. Thousands of laborers were in the fields, but the fields were so broad and numerous that this scattered multitude was totally lost therein. The cuckoo was much more perceptible than man, dominating whole square miles with his resounding call.

With gradual ease are we brought down to the draper's shop of John Baines, situated in St. Luke's Square, Bursley, one of the Five Towns in Staffordshire, and to the sisters. Mr. Bennett begins at once to distinguish the characters of his two girls. Constance is of a placid, contented type; Sophia is more imaginative and daring.

The difference is not made too immediately apparent. Their ages are sixteen and fifteen; and at that age they may seem strikingly alike, all *jeune fille,* and not much else.

For several chapters we move through incidents and episodes that appear perfectly spontaneous but are actually invented with great care—designed to induct us fully into the traits of Constance and Sophia, their father and mother; and to acquaint us completely with the assistant in the draper's shop, Mr. Povey. The time is underlined for us, the 1860's. In the fourth chapter, Gerald Scales is brought to our notice, the very personable salesman for a Manchester firm. We see him first through Sophia's eyes—see him invested with the glamour he has for her before she even knows his name.

Mr. Baines is ill, a last illness. Deftly, Mr. Bennett knots this thread with another, for Sophia deserts the sickroom briefly to see Gerald Scales in the shop, and in this interval her father dies. There follows a period of a year and a half in which Sophia sees nothing of Gerald, hears nothing from him. Contrasted with her secret and dire agony is the growing assurance of Mr. Povey, who has "ideas" about making the business more successful. Remarkable and amusing is the scene in which he addresses Mrs. Baines on the subject of her older daughter's affections, a gentle soul led by nervousness into a manner between rudeness and threat.

> "You know there's something between us!" he insisted.
>
> "How should I know there is something between you? Constance has never said a word to me. And have you?"

"Well," said he. "We've hidden nothing."

"What is there between you and Constance? If I may ask!"

"That depends on you," said he again.

"Have you asked her to be your wife?"

"No. I haven't exactly asked her to be my wife." He hesitated. "You see—"

Mrs. Baines collected her forces. "Have you kissed her?" This in a cold voice.

Mr. Povey now blushed. "I haven't exactly kissed her," he stammered, apparently shocked by the inquisition. "No, I should not say that I had kissed her."

It might have been that before committing himself he felt a desire for Mrs. Baines's definition of a kiss.

"You are very extraordinary," she said loftily. It was no less than the truth.

"All I want to know is—have you got anything against me?" he demanded roughly. "Because if so—"

"Anything against you, Mr. Povey? Why should I have anything against you?"

"Then why can't we be engaged?"

She considered that he was bullying her.

Very shortly comes the revelation that Sophia has run off with Gerald Scales. And Mr. Bennett, who can be as elaborate and discursive as a Dickens or a Thackeray, introduces an admirable piece of foreshortening into what is to be a lengthy perspective. There is a page or so embodying the disclosure about Sophia, something over a page to render the knells that begin tolling in the mother's thoughts; mention of a telegram from the runaway girl and a reassuring note a fortnight later; a paragraph for Mrs. Baines's surrender to destiny; a paragraph that telescopes weeks, perhaps months, and shows the mother leaving with trunks and parcels to spend the remainder of her life with her sister, in her childhood's home, this departure taking place "on the morning of the afternoon when Mr. and Mrs. Povey returned from their honeymoon."

Now the book has reached a parting of the ways. The author is not unwisely tempted, by Sophia's romantic flight, into an immediate pursuit of her and her adventure. He continues with the history of Constance. It is enough of a change that she is Mrs. Povey, that Samuel and she are master of the shop and mistress of the house respectively, that Samuel's revolutionary notions of selling draper's goods can now be effected without let or hindrance. The overshadowing change, of course, is in Constance's rôle. Mr. Bennett returns, fitly and incessantly to the state of mind succinctly celebrated by Emily Dickinson:

> I'm wife; I've finished that,
> That other state.

He is attentive to Constance's motherhood, which takes the form of an only child, Cyril. The birth of Cyril—Constance's experience of it—is given in a retrospection, four or five hundred words, no more; it is not easily matched among fiction's more normal accouchements. The penetration of the feminine point of view continues in such episodes as Constance giving Cyril her breast. In describing a children's party when Cyril is four and a half, Mr. Bennett's perfect touch is on the most recognizable detail of all:

Although the window was slightly open, the air was heavy with the natural human odor which young children transpire. More than one mother, pressing her nose into a lacy mass, to whisper, inhaled that pleasant perfume with a voluptuous thrill.

Everything, one is tempted to say, finds representation in these pages—everything fundamental in domesticity: the strangeness which a child makes between the parents, the mother's fatal incapacity for aught but tenderness, the child's amazing manifestations of an independent existence which, owing to its utter dependence, seldom appear other than heartless or depraved. Of great exterior events only a few are probable or necessary. Mr. Povey's cousin kills his bestial wife and Samuel exhausts himself in efforts to prevent Daniel Povey from going to the gallows. The efforts fail, Mr. Povey gets pneumonia and dies. Constance, a soft millstone around Cyril's neck, dies that familiar species of living death when his clay modeling wins him a London scholarship and takes him away from her, virtually forever.

For the history of Sophia we go back to a scene in London, following on her elopement with Gerald Scales in 1866. Gerald returns to the hotel with a vague excuse that there are difficulties in the way of their being married at once; it shall all be fixed up as soon as they reach Paris. Sophia falters at first, but soon uncovers the firmness that is in her. Not afraid of a scene, she forces Gerald to an unconditional surrender. When next we see them they are in Paris, duly married, and Gerald is beginning the extravagance which will waste away a legacy of twelve thousand pounds in less than four years.

The course is run in four chapters. Quite early in it, Sophia takes advantage of Gerald's besottedness to steal two hundred pounds from his pocket; and when he finally deserts her she still has this money. A little of it goes to pay back money that Chirac, Gerald's friend who has become her friend, had stolen to lend Gerald. More goes to pay for Sophia's care through a long illness with mucous fever in the house of two Frenchwomen, prostitutes and friends of Chirac's. With the last little remnants of fortune, Sophia sets up as keeper of a *pension*. She runs her boarding-house through all the tumult of the siege of Paris, and with true Five Towns thrift and persistence, makes and saves money. Her separate history concludes with the sentence:

> At the end of 1878, the Exhibition Year, her *pension* consisted of two floors instead of one, and she had turned the two hundred pounds stolen from Gerald into over two thousand.

We pass to the 1890's, when a young man, a friend of Cyril's, stopping at Sophia's boarding-house, guesses her identity. Saying nothing to her, he tells Cyril and Constance on his return to England. There is a letter from Constance to Sophia, magnificent in its simple affection, artlessness and native tact. Sophia, now beset by illness, returns to England; the two sisters are reunited, spend a little time together, and then pass on, Sophia dying first. When Constance dies, only Sophia's aged and feeble dog survives.

From one point of view, and the most obvious, Time seems the subject of *The Old Wives' Tale.* Constance and Sophia, it has been said, are "doomed to decay with a completeness rare in fiction." Very few novels, no doubt, have so well conveyed the sense of the ever-rolling flood that bears all its sons away. But if Time were Mr. Bennett's principal subject, is it not likely he would have been more concerned with it? He is not, as we can see on reflection, very considerate of the passing hour. He does not hesitate to telescope, foreshorten, abridge, omit. His treatment of Constance and Sophia, separately, is highly selective, underneath its admirable smoothness of effect. Cyril is a baby, Cyril is four and a half, Cyril is nine, Mr. Povey dies, Cyril is fifteen or thereabouts. The four years in which Sophia has to endure Gerald are as concisely dealt with. The sense of Time, indeed, comes upon these two women in Mr. Bennett's story with the uncertain incidence of its stroke in life. At odd intervals, they realize it—as when it comes over Constance that she has had nearly twenty-one years of married life. The completeness of that final decay no more makes Time Mr. Bennett's protagonist than Death. We feel Time's rôle in the drama, but only as the one unchanging pressure of all the circumstantial pressures.

Is his subject character? At once we feel ourselves much closer to the mark. Here are two girls of the Five Towns, sisters and singularly unlike—Constance, calm, rooted, of tenacious strength; Sophia, bold, relentless, hardy, but no less oak-like in her fiber. It is the same fiber in both, and it triumphs over every external agency with the sole exception of invincible Time. Mr. Bennett, we may tell ourselves, wished to show this toughness, this locust grain, in its splendid resistance, its power to defeat all but physical decay and its sturdy postponement of even that. Yes, this is a subject convincingly illustrated by his novel, first in the quiet life of Constance, then in the devastated life of Sophia. But a doubt or two arises. There is a good deal of the Five Towns in the story, but not quite as much as such a subject would imply. Sophia, indeed, is divorced with utter completeness from the Five Towns; from 1872 to 1896 she might be any hard-headed Frenchwoman; she takes on more than the color of her environment, and all its lessons of practical wisdom are assimilated into the stock of her character. Mr. Bennett is perhaps presenting the enduring traits of a family; but what family? The Baineses? The Symes of Axe, the family of the girls' mother? We see it is not so, and slip back to that point about Sophia, which gives us a better clue than any we have had before. Sophia, we reflected, might, for close on to quarter of a century, have been any capable and disillusioned Frenchwoman—with the possible difference of a sexual disillusion that the Frenchwoman would be less likely to have acquired. But Sophia, in other words, is a woman, in the peculiar sense in which Constance also is a woman; psychically and integrally. Paths far apart have brought out these sisters in the same place. Constance traveled the route of wifehood and motherhood and humdrum; Sophia's journey was steeper and lonelier. The physical reunion of the two girls gives a pleasing outward and tangible shape to a spiritual achievement we should like to see them consciously share.

Do we not feel that we have here come upon the true subject of the novel? It is not Time, it is not simply character, personal or familial or racial. It is sexual character, the Very Woman in Constance, the Eternal Feminine in resilient Sophia, that Bennett is writing about. It is not the *ewig Weibliches* universally celebrated in song and story, a species of allurement, but a strength that men have not, a strength that overcomes them in the long history of the race. It is physical, no doubt, but at all times it is psychical—an affair of the nervous system and not of the brain. And as we consider this, dozens of instances leap out of the story to confirm this last conjecture—Constance annexing Mr. Povey, besting him over Cyril, outliving him; Sophia defeating and outwitting Gerald Scales, holding Chirac off at arm's length, outliving her husband, too. But it is not so much in these issues of event that Bennett offers us his subject, it is in the constant choice of detail, the aspect he puts on all his detail, the incessant point of view. Everything through the woman's eyes! Only enough from the masculine standpoint to confer a sufficient reality on Mr. Povey and Gerald and Cyril! Sexual character, Woman's character as Woman—this is what he is concerned to give us, at every moment and on every page. No man ever did it better.

And this understanding throws, rightly considered, a sharp light on the style in which the book is written. Bennett, as all his readers know, has a highly individual prose. Over and above his fondness for particular words (such as "majestic") and his amicable irony of phrase there is something that has been reproached as a sly facetiousness. There are the places where he uses an exclamation point at the end of each of a string of sentences; and except where the serious nature of his scene makes it absolutely impossible he has been felt to move along with a spirit of levity a little unbecoming in the circumstances. But if we realize that this is his way of conveying the feminine intonation in crises great and small, the difficulty clears away without compelling us to assent to the method. What he is constantly striving for is plainly the eagerness and interestedness with which women receive all the occurrences in their finite worlds; their yearning over a trifle of gossip, their dramatization of every fleeting mood. His exclamation point seldom denotes surprise or astonishment; what it always does denote is nervous sensation, the excitement of event no matter how minor.

And realism? Nothing could be more marvelously realistic than this feminine perception, these sexual recognition-points of every experience. There is the realism of the "stream of consciousness" type, constantly gained by the view of what is passing in Constance's or Sophia's mind, but free from the over-intensity and incoherence into which the advanced "consciousness" writers have often precipitated us.

When we have found the subject of *The Old Wives' Tale* we have uncovered as well the source of that "epic" or prophetic quality that is so definite and so elusive of definition. Small wonder that a striking study of profoundly-rooted sexual character should feel epical—

ring with overtones of prophecy as convincing as those in the great chorus from Euripides's *Medea:*

> And Woman, yea, Woman shall be terrible in story.

The voice of Time, heard at the fateful moments of these sisters' lives, is prophetic, too.

Mr. Bennett, then, has succeeded in giving us, in the personal history of two women, something of all women. It is the measure of his accomplishment, we may feel, that no one who wishes to embody a woman in a work of fiction can afford to ignore *The Old Wives' Tale.*

III. JOSEPH CONRAD

Nostromo

The longest of Joseph Conrad's novels is also his most richly-peopled canvas. It has never been one of his popular books, but excellent opinion can be found to support the contention that it is his best. *Nostromo* is a comparatively early work, written in 1903-4—difficult and with rewards commensurate with the exactions it lays upon the reader. The difficulty is no greater, perhaps, than that encountered in *Chance,* but is more akin to the trouble one finds in reading *Under Western Eyes.* It will pay us to glance at Conrad's experiments with the novel.

They were made, principally, in three books, all subsequent to the one we are about to consider. In *Under Western Eyes,* Part IV begins where Part I leaves off, a disregard of chronology in the interests of drama and mood which we see in a less formal exercise in *Nostromo.* The extreme complexity of *Chance* has perhaps been best explained by Leland Hall: [2]

> His desire to give fiction as an art something of the plasticity of sculpture may account in a general way for another . . . characteristic . . . [a method] of telling a story by means of several observers and narrators. . . . In *Chance* he has achieved such results with it as to raise very pressingly the question whether or not he has broken quite away from tradition and created a new art of the novel. . . . He has employed at least four narrators: Marlow, Captain Powell, and Mr. and Mrs. Fyne, and there are others besides. Three of these characters play a part in the novel quite distinct from their parts as narrators; yet Conrad has handled all the complications which such a method must occasion so smoothly that the reader hardly realizes the difficulties that the author has surmounted. They are difficulties with which most authors would not choose to burden themselves. Indeed, Henry James wrote that *Chance* had proved Conrad the votary of the "way to do a thing that shall undergo most doing." But Conrad's success is beyond question, and the vindication of the method may be found in the intricate and perfect counterfeit of reality which *Chance* presents. It is a method which has given to the novel not a little of the plasticity of sculpture. . . . Flora de Barral and Captain Anthony are molded, as it were, by the subtle touches of many pairs of hands. . . . They move, not against a background, but in the midst of a circumfluent reality.

---

[2] In his chapter on Joseph Conrad embodied in John W. Cunliffe's *English Literature During the Last Half-Century* (revised edition, Macmillan, 1923). One of the most intelligent of the short accounts of Conrad's work.

In a much later novel, *The Rescue*—begun early, five-sixths completed, and then abandoned for about twenty years for lack of an ending—Conrad took a dramatic situation and suspended it longer and more successfully than anybody else has ever succeeded in doing.[3] It was not, of course, suspense for suspense's sake, but because these people in this situation were uniquely exposed to the study of them as individuals and to the vision of those secrets of the human heart which were Conrad's supreme subject.

Now all these experiments of Conrad's with the novel are made on a lesser scale in *Nostromo*—the inversion of chronology, the narrator device, the suspended situation—but here they appear as technical expedients, here they are subordinate to a general scheme and a controlling purpose.

The general facts of Conrad's life are well-known. He was a Pole by birth, the son of two scholarly people whose political ideas made them objects of suspicion to the Russian Government. When hardly more than a boy the young Korzeniowski (for that was Conrad's patronymic) went away to sea, at first on French boats. For a couple of years or so he was engaged in smuggling arms into Spain, arms for the Carlists, and in this dangerous activity, managed with a small Mediterranean vessel, came in contact with one Dominic, a Corsican sailor, an upstanding fellow who was later to have several incarnations in Conrad's fiction. Nostromo (Gian' Battista Fidanza) is the most considerable one.

[3] "Longer" refers not to the time of the action, but to its elaboration, at the greatest possible length.

Since *Nostromo* is laid in South America, readers may wonder if Conrad was much there. The answer is, No. On two or three voyages in 1875-6 he glimpsed the West Indies and the Gulf of Mexico; he may just have set foot ashore on the west coast of South America. It was while in the Gulf of Mexico that he heard the tale of the theft of a lighter loaded with silver, but forgot it until just over a quarter of a century later, when he came upon it again in an American seaman's memoirs. At that time Conrad was at a loss for a fictional subject, and at first he saw none here. "It was only when it dawned upon me that the purloiner of the treasure need not necessarily be a confirmed rogue, that he could be even a man of character, an actor and possibly a victim in the changing scenes of a revolution, it was only then that I had the first vision of a twilight country which was to become the province of Sulaco."[4]

Never was an imaginary country made as real as the Costaguana of "Nostromo," in spite of, or perhaps because of, a skillful blending of South American geography. We begin with the Placid Gulf, defined by a point (Punta Mala) and a peninsula (Azuera). At the head of the gulf lies the city of Sulaco, capital of the Occidental Province. Inland, but so close that from the gulf they appear to tower above the city, are stupendous mountains, the Cordillera, like the range of the Andes, with one particular vast snow-covered summit, Higuerota. Across the mountains lies the valley of Santa Marta, and on the eastern seaboard, the city of Santa Marta itself, capital of the Republic of Costaguana. Another seaport,

[4] In the Note printed as a Preface to *Nostromo*.

Cayta, lies on the western seaboard at some distance from Sulaco. A considerable campo, or table-land, separates Sulaco from the Cordillera, in the foothills of which, across a gorge, lies a mountain of silver, the San Tome mine.

In the Placid Gulf lies three small islands, one of which, the Great Isabel (as distinguished from the Little Isabel) is of the highest importance in our story. The Great Isabel is a mile long, with a spring of fresh water, two large trees, and a ravine extending its whole length and full of bushes.

The history of Costaguana is typical of all the countries of the South American continent. After the liberation from Spain, the republic was governed by a series of despots, in the brief intervals of frequent revolutions. The worst of these was Guzman Bento, whom Conrad has apparently modeled, for the extent of his reminiscent glimpses, on Francia of Paraguay. Coming down to more recent times, the Blanco (White) Party has succeeded in installing as Dictator with a five-year term one Ribiera. But eighteen months later Ribiera is a fugitive, crossing the mountains and barely escaping with his life on one of the boats of the Oceanic Steam Navigation Company, the O. S. N., for which Sulaco is a port of call. General Montero, head of the army, has revolted against him.

In the past there had been one or two efforts to secure the political separation of the Occidental Province from the rest of the Republic of Costaguana. The mountains had seemed a natural barrier. It had long been evident that if and when the San Tome silver mine was put into modern operation, this mine and its interests would be the controlling factor in the economic, and probably in the political, existence of the Occidental Province.

With this much of geography and history, we can perhaps safely proceed to *Nostromo* itself without more danger of losing our bearings than if we were perusing the novel. The danger, considerable there, hangs darkly over any one who must attempt the story in outline.

And first, the subject. It is the effect of avarice on strong and noble character. Gian' Battista Fidanza, a Genoese sailor who has found his way to Sulaco, is capataz de cargadores, or as we should say, boss of the longshoremen, for the O. S. N. Company. Captain Mitchell, the superintendent of the O. S. N., is very proud of him. The Europeans of Sulaco, accustomed to refer to Fidanza as "nostr' uomo," our man, have been the means of creating the nickname by which he is everywhere known. In truth, Nostromo, a commanding figure, a man of the people, is in many respects the most powerful person of the town.

Avarice is not natural to him; a certain vanity, the exaggeration of his self-respect and sense of power, is natural. A chance comes to him to steal a shipment of San Tome silver and he does it. In considering this subject Conrad developed several others of no less moment. One is the history of Latin America in terms of racial temperament; another, and a greater, is the bondage of material interests. These two fit into each other at a certain point, that point, in Latin American history, lying just beyond the time of the events related in *Nostromo*.

Part First, a quarter of the book, is almost solely devoted to setting the stage for the action to come, although Conrad's skill is far too great to convey the sense of standstill. An opening chapter describes Sulaco and its surroundings; tells—since this is to be a story of avarice—a legend of ghosts of gold-hunters on Azuera; and concludes with a sufficient description of the Great Isabel island.

The smoothness of transition from chapter to chapter is noticeable in *Nostromo*. From mention of the harbor of Sulaco, we pass to "the only sign of commercial activity within the harbor," the O. S. N. pier, and thus come upon Captain Mitchell, local superintendent for the steamship company. Directly he is telling us about the flight and escape of Ribiera; how the mob attacked the custom house; and how Nostromo at the head of his cargadores beat them back, at the same time protecting the property of the National Central Railway, which is building a line to go through the mountains and join Sulaco, at last, with the rest of Costaguana.

Captain Mitchell's narration is merely the means of getting us into a direct story of some events of that time. Having repulsed the mob, Nostromo rode past the hotel, halfway between the harbor and the town, kept by old Giorgio Viola, an Italian who had served under Garibaldi both in Sicily and in South America. To Viola, Nostromo is as his own son; but his wife, Teresa, mother of two young girls, Linda and Giselle, is more critical of the capataz. Her attitude is really an inverted affection for Gian' Battista; she probably aspires to him as a son-in-law. Viola's place is a resort of the Italians and is frequented also by the Signori Inglesi, the English engineers who are building the railway. We spend the day in this barricaded inn, where Teresa prays and moans out reproaches on Nostromo, and old Giorgio sits with a cocked gun across his knees. Nostromo, arriving finally, assures himself that the family is unmolested and rides off again to the pursuit of the looters he has put to flight.

In the fifth chapter we find ourselves back eighteen months to the time of Ribiera's accession to the dictatorship. He has just broken ground for the new railway and the O. S. N. is giving a dinner on one of its vessels in the harbor. At this feast various notables are assembled: the Dictator, Captain Mitchell, Charles Gould, administrator of the San Tome silver mine, and the chairman of the railway board (from London) who sits beside Mrs. Gould. The chairman, Sir John, has had an arduous journey, from London to Santa Marta by boat, in special cars on the Santa Marta coast line, the only railway so far existing, and then in a shaky old stage (diligencia) over the mountains. The stage has been upset twice in one day on the brink of deep ravines. Some uneasiness is felt by those at the dinner over the aspect of General Montero, head of the army. We desert the dinner table for a reminiscence of Sir John's trip over the Cordillera. Attention must be drawn to the beauty of Conrad's writing in this passage.

> He could not help being impressed by his surroundings during his halt at the surveying camp established at the highest point his railway was to reach. He spent the night there, arriving just too late to see the last dying glow of sunlight upon the snowy flank of Higuerota. Pillared masses of black

basalt framed like an open portal a portion of the white field lying aslant against the west. In the transparent air of the high altitudes everything seemed very near, steeped in a clear stillness as in an imponderable liquid; and with his ear ready to catch the first sound of the expected diligencia the engineer-in-chief, at the door of a hut of rough stones, had contemplated the changing hues on the enormous side of the mountain, thinking that in this sight, as in a piece of inspired music, there could be found together the utmost delicacy of shaded expression and a stupendous magnificence of effect.

Sir John arrived too late to hear the magnificent and inaudible strain sung by the sunset among the high peaks of the Sierra. . . .

Afterwards, late at night, pacing to and fro outside, he had a long talk with his chief engineer. . . . Of the young fellows at the table, to whom the survey of the track was like the tracing of the path of life, more than one would be called to meet death before the work was done. But the work would be done: the force would be almost as strong as a faith. Not quite, however. In the silence of the sleeping camp upon the moonlit plateau forming the top of the pass like the floor of a vast arena surrounded by the basalt walls of precipices, two strolling figures in thick ulsters stood still, and the voice of the engineer pronounced distinctly the words—

"We can't move mountains!"

Sir John, raising his head to follow the pointing gesture, felt the full force of the words. The white Higuerota soared out of the shadows of rock and earth like a frozen bubble under the moon. All was still, till near by, behind the wall of a corral for the camp animals, built roughly of loose stones in the form of a circle, a pack-mule stamped his forefoot and blew heavily twice.

In the sixth chapter we receive some account of Dr. Monygham, involving the first allusion to the days of Guzman Bento. The Doctor had undergone atrocious tortures at the hands of that tyrant, involving a betrayal of a conspiracy, and has ever since been marked by an immense distrust of mankind, reflecting the contempt in which he holds himself. Unpopular in Sulaco, Charles Gould has made him physician to the mine, and Monygham is devoted to Mrs. Gould. We move into the history of the Goulds, Englishmen domiciled in Costaguana for several generations. Charles Gould's grandfather had fought for liberation under Bolivar; an uncle had been executed by Guzman Bento; and Charles Gould's father, saddled with the perpetual concession of the San Tome mine and thus put at the mercy of the country's political scoundrels, had died from worry and despair. These events of the past are now directly narrated by Conrad, who tells of Charles Gould's education in England, his courtship of Emilia (Mrs. Gould) in Italy, his inheritance of the mine, and his steely determination to make it a magnificent success, redressing the terrible injustice that it did his father. Mr. Holroyd, an American capitalist, is interested by Charles and will remain a characteristic figure in the background, a person influenced by his favorable estimate of Charles Gould, his pleasure in a new hobby, and—results.

All this has moved us along to the end of the seventh chapter; the eighth, and last in Part First, shows the mine in prosperous operation, acquaints us with Don Pepe, Charles Gould's chief of police at San Tome, and brings in a characteristic figure of such countries, Hernandez, the bandit of the campo. Without jar, we find ourselves back at the dinner table where Sir John sits beside Mrs. Gould. Our General Montero offers an ambiguous toast that deepens the uneasiness of those present. A little later we are having another glimpse of Nostromo. He publicly repulses a girl who has claimed him as her lover, then, bending from the saddle, lifts her up on his foot, gives her his knife and lets her cut off all the silver buttons from his coat. Nostromo, indeed, is constantly appearing in passages in these chapters, always as a dependable and trusted kind of superior employee or as a species of popular leader and hero. It was he who escorted Sir John over the mountains. It is he on whom the Europeans instinctively call for special services, sure of his prestige and loyalty. The end of Part First comes with a brief renewal of Captain Mitchell's account of Ribiera's flight; it is to advance us again nearer to the hour of action.

Such, in brief outline, is the first quarter of the novel. Many incidents have been omitted, but only one considerable person—Don José Avellanos, an aged patriot and the author of a history, *Fifty Years of Misrule.* Of fine family, his life has included such extremes as Guzman Bento's abominable cruelties and the diplomatic representation of his country at the first courts of Europe. He is as typical of his country as Hernandez, the robber, and he is the father of Antonia Avellanos, whose European education has not destroyed her native grace, who is clear, courageous, and of great charm.

With Part Second we come to the forward movement of the novel, though not with perceptible haste. From an extended and reminiscent account of Don José Avellanos we emerge to meet his daughter. It is made clear that Holroyd and Charles Gould have financed the Ribiera dictatorship—the failure of which we already know. Now for the first time some account is given of General Montero's revolt, which precipitated the Blanco disaster. We move to a scene in which General Barrios, commanding the Blanco troops, is embarking with his army to go by water to Cayta. Barrios, a little world-weary, assures Mrs. Gould that soon he will return with Montero in a cage. All this has occupied two chapters; in the third we watch Antonia Avellanos and young Martin Decoud. Decoud, of an old Sulaco family, has been a Parisian dandy, and is now returned to edit a Ribiera newspaper in Sulaco, the *Porvenir*. He is completely cynical about his task, which, as he says, consists in calling Montero a "great animal" three times a week; he is cynical about everything on earth, apparently, except Antonia Avellanos. We enter the fourth chapter with a history of Barrios and proceed to a visit Mrs. Gould pays to old Giorgio Viola, who is her protégé. Viola's two girls are brought into more notice than they have received hitherto —Linda, the older, dark and intent, Giselle, the younger, blonde and acquiescent. There is a striking speech by Decoud analyzing, in his too cynical fashion, the defects of his countrymen:

"You are right, Don Jose. The natural treasures of Costaguana are of importance to progressive Europe . . . just as three hundred years ago the wealth of our Spanish fathers was a serious object to the rest of Europe. . . . There is a curse of futility upon our character: Don Quixote and Sancho Panza, chivalry and materialism, high-sounding sentiments and a supine morality, violent efforts for an idea and a sullen acquiescence in every form of corruption. We convulsed a continent for our independence only to become the passive prey of a democratic parody, the helpless victims of scoundrels and cutthroats, our institutions a mockery, our laws a farce—a Guzman Bento our master! And we have sunk so low that when a man like you has awakened our conscience, a stupid barbarian of a Montero—great Heavens! a Montero!—becomes a deadly danger, and an ignorant, boastful Indio, like Barrios, is our defender."

They are driving back to the Casa Gould, which is this afternoon a rendezvous for all adherents of the Blanco Party. Against the background of this noisy, semi-social, semi-political gathering we listen to Martin Decoud's further cynicisms, confided to Antonia and refuted by her to a certain extent. These refutations and rebukes bring the lover's protestations which Decoud is no less eager to utter. Hirsch, a hide-merchant from Esmeralda, a port down the coast, tries to get reassurances as to the political outlook from tight-lipped Charles Gould. At length Gould says calmly to Hirsch that there is a vast store of dynamite at the mine, enough to blow up half Sulaco and send his mountain crashing down into the valley. A little later Gould tells the railway engineer-in-chief the same thing. The explosive is his trump card against Montero or any other adventurer. As he says in answer to his wife's anxious questions, he is prepared to go to any length. . . . Passing on, in the sixth chapter, we have a long conversation after the gathering has dispersed between Decoud and Mrs. Gould. On pretext of finding Antonia's fan, the journalist has made his way back to communicate startling news—a dispatch which reports a victory for Montero, which seems to make clear that Montero's brother, Pedro Montero, has only to cross the mountains to possess Sulaco, since Barrios and his troops are out of reach on the water. Decoud's idea is that the Occidental Province must declare its independence, as the only ultimate way out. . . .

When the seventh chapter opens a sleepless and filthy Decoud is writing a letter to his sister in Paris to describe the events of the Three Days which have ensued upon the chapter just ended. News of Montero's victory has provoked rioting in the city, led by Gamacho and Fuentes, two Monterist deputies. A shipment of silver has been brought down from San Tome mountain and this, as well as general looting, has been the mob's objective. Decoud writes his letter from Viola's hotel in the dead of night. Soon Nostromo is to meet him and the two of them will take a lighter loaded with the silver out of the Placid Gulf to a small port just outside Costaguana where the next steamship, secretly instructed, may pick it up. The enterprise is attended with great danger. It is now certain that Pedro Montero is coming down the mountain passes, so the silver cannot remain in Sulaco. On the other side is a more immediate peril. The garrison at Esmeralda has revolted. Under its commander, one Sotillo, it has seized a transport and is heading for Sulaco. The silver must be got out of the gulf before this transport sails in.

When Nostromo appears, Decoud is finishing his letter. The capataz brings Dr. Monygham, for Teresa Viola is dying. She wants Nostromo to fetch a priest for her, but he declares he cannot delay the work of safeguarding the silver. "I am resolved to make this the most desperate affair I was ever engaged on in my whole life."

What is in Nostromo's mind? A foreboding is upon him. He says to Dr. Monygham: "It is as if I were taking a curse upon me. A man with a treasure on this coast will have every knife raised against him." Though conscious that he is a poor man, he is thinking, perhaps, of not much more than the glory to be obtained. He does not take seriously Dr. Monygham's jeering suggestion that the adventure is worth the whole treasure.

The next fifty pages, including the eighth and final chapter of Part Second, are as thrilling as anything out of Scott, Dumas or Stevenson. Decoud and Nostromo set out in the lighter with their extremely valuable cargo—the silver is in the form of bars. The night is windless, visionless; the boat seems to float in space. Nostromo paints a vivid picture of what may happen to them out at sea, standing by for a steamship; he thinks it unsafe to land anywhere with a cargo like this. The night wears on; they scarcely move in the water. And at length a suspicious sound is found to be a stowaway; from the bottom of the boat they drag out the limp figure of Señor Hirsch, the Esmeralda hide-merchant.

Wisdom would drop this hunted animal overboard—Hirsch is a mere fugitive from the terrors of the Three Days. But this is not done. The clouded night has produced one or two little showers on the water, but a new sound, at first judged to be a shower, is soon recognized as the hiss and rustle of a steamship, moving slowly and without lights. It is plainly Sotillo's transport creeping up the Gulf to the capture of the town.

Here are these two blind vessels in a blind bay. There are terribly tense moments. Can they avoid the transport? At length she strikes the lighter a glancing blow. There is a scream from Hirsch, who, catching the first thing within reach of his arms, a wire shroud belonging to the steamship, is swept away. Hauled on board the transport, he serves the very useful purpose of telling Sotillo his story and convincing that adventurer that the lighterful of silver has gone to the bottom of the gulf. So the transport keeps on toward Sulaco. But although the lighter has shipped water badly, with Decoud pumping Nostromo manages to beach her on the Great Isabel. They bury the treasure there, Decoud is left to guard it, and Nostromo starts to sail the lighter back. It occurs to him that he cannot do this; he will be in enough danger from the Monterists and to reappear with the lighter will reveal that the treasure is not sunk and make his life forfeit at once. So he sinks the vessel and swims to shore, to hide, to sleep, to emerge with extreme cautiousness from hiding.

Enough has been given—and at how great length! but it may be with sufficient explicitness—to indicate the scale and general method of the novel. Nearly half of the book lies after the point we have so laboriously reached. It can here be only summarized, briefly. A series of unusual but wholly plausible chances favor Nostromo. He has only tacitly to let people believe that the lighter and its load of silver has been sunk, Decoud drowned, and himself saved by his exceptional strength as a swimmer. He meditates: "I must grow rich slowly." The retrospective method of narrating events, either directly or through Captain Mitchell or some other narrator, continues; it is the only possible device by which Conrad can compose and present the picture of so many events with so many actors in a reasonable compass. The fate of Decoud, after days of abandonment, is suicide. This, not foreseen by Nostromo, is detected by him. It is one of the series of chances that seem to compel him into a certain course. . . . The political events are dealt with in a complete and satisfying summation; it suffices to say here that Nostromo made a famous ride to Cayta, bringing back Barrios, with the final result of Occidental independence, and the beginning of a period of great prosperity out of which emerges a rather modern Sulaco. In particular, Charles Gould and the San Tome mine are on the crest of the wave.

To return to Nostromo: Every now and then he visits the Great Isabel and lifts a few bars of silver. He is become Captain Fidanza, and one Ramirez, a younger man, his pupil, is capataz de cargadores. A lighthouse having been erected on the Great Isabel, Nostromo has secured the appointment of light-keeper for old Giorgio Viola who, with his two daughters, lives on that island. The older girl, Linda, is terribly in love with Nostromo. But Nostromo loves Giselle. Ramirez had been attentive to Giselle, but had been warned off by old Viola. The new capataz is mystified by the discovery that Nostromo comes from the island as late as midnight. The father of the girls, very intent on his daughters' honor, takes to patroling the shore at night with a gun; one night he fires it, as he thinks, at Ramirez, and mortally wounds Nostromo. The old man never knows what he has done, for his mind is failing him. Nostromo breathes out a dying confession to Emilia Gould.

We have now to consider the main aspects of this great and complicated piece of work. In his autobiographical book, *A Personal Record,*[5] Conrad has conveyed pretty adequately an idea of the toil in which he became involved.

> I had not known for weeks whether the sun shone upon the earth and whether the stars above still moved on their appointed courses. . . . For twenty months, neglecting the common joys of life that fall to the lot of the humblest on this earth, I had, like the prophet of old, "wrestled with the Lord" for my creation, for the headlands of the coast, for the darkness of the Placid Gulf, the light on the snows, the clouds in the sky, and for the breath of life that had to be blown into the shapes of men and women, of Latin and Saxon, of Jew and Gentile. . . . There were pages of MS. on the table and under the table, a batch of typed copy on a chair, single leaves had fluttered away into distant corners; there were there living pages, pages scored and wounded, dead pages that would be burned at the end of the day—the litter of a cruel battlefield, of a long, long and desperate fray. Long! I suppose I went to bed sometimes, and got up the same number of times. Yes, I suppose I slept, and ate the food put before me, and talked connectedly to my household on suitable occasions. . . . It seemed to me that I had been sitting at that table . . . for days and nights on end. It

[5] In England the title is *Some Reminiscences.*

seemed so because of the intense weariness . . . the awful disenchantment of a mind realizing suddenly the futility of an enormous task, joined to a bodily fatigue such as no ordinary amount of fairly heavy physical labor could ever account for. I have carried bags of wheat on my back, bent almost double under a ship's deck beams, from six in the morning till six in the evening (with an hour and a half off for meals), so I ought to know.

The only commentary on this is that "the breath of life" is more completely in the people of this book than in any but the few supreme works of fiction. One need not hesitate to involve what is perhaps the greatest novel ever written, Tolstoy's *War and Peace,* in a comparison. If *Nostromo* is less great, it is less only by little. The superb reality of Nostromo, Giorgio Viola, Charles and Emilia Gould, Don José Avellanos, Martin Decoud, Captain Mitchell, Sotillo, Señor Hirsch and a dozen others is not, of course, a thing possible of demonstration in an analysis like ours: it must be sought in the pages of the novel. But it is there, though possibly only an acquaintance with Latins, South Americans, transplanted Englishmen and all the rest fully qualifies a reader to appreciate the full reality.

Conrad has not the difficulty of Tolstoy, in *War and Peace,* with his several subjects.[6] The study of avarice in Nostromo becomes a single, but an integral, part of a large design. But the whole design developed out of this

[6] *War and Peace* will be discussed at length in Chapter VI of this book. For a careful consideration of Tolstoy's several subjects, from the standpoint of one who finds them unsatisfactorily combined, see the first four chapters of *The Craft of Fiction,* by Percy Lubbock.

subject. It is not as if Conrad had begun with one subject and had thought of a couple of others, and had then tried to develop them side by side. He began with his Man of the People, placing him against his background; but as the background took on relief, forming mountains, city, harbor and sea, as its people took on life, beginning to move about the scene, the other subjects disclosed themselves. The scene itself was one of them, a South American scene—what could it be but an epitome of South American history in the light of the Latin temperament? And the stolen silver, the silver of the mine: that would be a subject, too, because it is a mighty mover of human passions. What a cargo of silver might mean to Nostromo, a mountain of silver might mean to a country. The scale did not matter but the meaning must not be lost. And, in fact, Conrad delivers that meaning nine-tenths of the way through his book in a speech of startling prophecy from the lips of Dr. Monygham:

"No! There is no peace and rest in the development of material interests. They have their law and their justice. But it is founded on expediency, and is inhuman; it is without rectitude, without the continuity and the force that can be found only in a moral principle. Mrs. Gould, the time approaches when all that the Gould Concession stands for shall weigh as heavily upon the people as the barbarism, cruelty, and misrule of a few years back."

Mrs. Gould murmurs: "Is it that we have worked for, then?" Dr. Monygham forbears to answer her, but we, who know something of history, may answer. And our answer is affirmative. We have not to be socialists, or any other form of anti-capitalists, to acknowledge that after approximately five hundred years spent in curbing political forms of power—roughly from Magna Charta to the French Revolution—mankind in the civilized states is probably entering upon a few centuries of struggle to curb power in the forms of economic ascendancy.

In the Note inserted as a preface to all later editions of *Nostromo* one may gather hints of what Conrad conveys in the figure of Gian' Battista Fidanza; and it is one of the best proofs of his rôle as an artist in fiction that, although Nostromo embodies these things, speaking of them thus abstractly the author is unable to carry them beyond the hinting stage. Or perhaps he feared to desert Art for Ideas. But we may take our own risks, seeking the concept behind the hero. The moral significance of Captain Fidanza is, to be sure, perfectly plain. It is his political significance that needs a transparent statement. We cannot now know how far Conrad was conscious that his Man of the People typified the fate of the people themselves, of democracy so-called, in political action. He says, of Nostromo:

> In his firm grip on the earth he inherits, in his improvidence and generosity, in his lavishness with his gifts, in his manly vanity, in the obscure sense of his rights and in his faithful devotion with something despairing as well as desperate in its impulses, he is a Man of the People, their very own unenvious force disdaining to lead but ruling from within. . . . With the knowledge of his moral ruin locked up in his breast, he remains essentially a Man of the People. In his secret love and scorn of life and in the bewildered conviction of having been betrayed, of dying betrayed he hardly

knows by what or by whom, he still is of Them, their very own Great Man.

In short, themselves. Inheriting the earth, bewildered in the conviction of being betrayed, hardly knowing by what or by whom, the People, in the sense of political democracy, have only their Present—no Past, no Future.

Turning to the technical side of the novel, we may examine first the liberties with chronology. They make the closest attention necessary in a first reading, but their justification will not detain us long. This immense and crowded canvas cannot be filled in for us all at once; and it is better that the artist should complete the group in this corner before he paints even that important figure in the foreground. Where there are so many characters, reality will greatly depend upon a reasonable concentration on one for a while, to the temporary exclusion of all others; and if this attention involves a passing disregard of time or distortion of perspective, we shall prefer that to a shadowy confusion out of which nothing may finally emerge. Sometimes the instillation of a particular mood or the need of showing a particular aspect determines the artist's hand; in the larger matters, his method with time is dictated by an unfailing sense of drama. It is dramatic, for instance, to save the precise disclosure of Decoud's fate until very near the end of the novel, and to precede it with Nostromo's discovery of the dinghy left on the island afloat in the gulf. Four bars of the silver are missing from the cache, and that is a bloodstain on the dinghy's gunwale. It is dramatic, by means of garrulous Captain Mitchell's discourse to some distinguished visitor, to get out of the way the story of Occidental independence and Sulaco's prosperity in order to clear the scene for the tragic finale of Linda, her sister, Nostromo and the Great Isabel. For of Conrad's several great subjects, only the first, the corruption of character by the incorruptible metal, the silver of the mine, is dramatic in the sense specified for fiction.

Where a narrator is used, it is clearly for the purpose of imparting vividness to events which must be dealt with economically—either this or else, and sometimes simultaneously, to give us the reality of Nostromo and other persons in circumspicious view. Although there is no such isolation of the principal situation as in *The Rescue,* something of the same feat of suspense is accomplished from the instant of Nostromo's return, after leaving Decoud with the silver. The situation is forming; he does not know exactly what he will do, nor are we, who know him a little better than he knows himself, certain what shapes circumstances will assume. We share his suspense, like that of a man on trial who does not know what witness may be called or what testimony be uttered against him—like that of one walking on new-formed ice, whose every step may break through. And when the situation is formed, even then there is suspense, for in it there is no safety. Nostromo has by now walked out, far out. "There is no peace and rest in material interests." It comes forcibly upon us that Nostromo is not the only slave of the San Tome silver. How about Charles Gould? who used to lean so much, in his taciturn way, upon Doña Emilia (she would slip out on the balcony, very early in the morning, to watch the escort for the silver flash by in the still-deserted city, and to wave to her husband) and who in these later years merely manages to send down a message from the mountain: he is remaining at the mine for a few days.

Here in a mere portion of one chapter of a book we make no attempt to exhaust the meanings of Conrad's great landmark in the fiction of the twentieth century. Barely a hundred years had passed when he wrote in which the novel of character had had the maturity to which Jane Austen brought it. If a Voice challenged the fictioner, busy in his pleasant garden, he stammered: "The woman . . . she gave me of the tree, and I did eat." But with Conrad, another wisdom came into the periphery of human consciousness. He had no power to lift the scales fallen over human eyes, to enable mankind to see and resume the God. But he could make men pause, he could make men listen. Under a sky that was a miracle of purity, that extended on all sides, all round to the horizon, that diminished into insignificance even the white Higuerota soaring like a frozen bubble under the moon, he could merge the moment with eternity—could make us know again that the God might come. "The great aim is to remain true to the emotions called out of the deep encircled by the firmament of stars."

Explicit.

IV. WILLA CATHER

A Lost Lady

From a novel of character involving so much else we need to turn to a simpler work in the same large classification—simpler, but if possible no less enriched by beauty of workmanship. We shall find what we ideally want in Willa Cather's novelette, *A Lost Lady*.

The author was born in Virginia but at the age of eight the family moved to Nebraska, then still a great grazing ground and only beginning to be fenced for farms. Willa Cather's most impressionable years were spent on the prairie, in a region populated by European immigrants chiefly, where the nearest neighbor was often ten miles distant and mere existence was an unrelenting struggle. Afterward, at the high-school age, she knew the life of a Nebraska village. From college she went into newspaper work in Pittsburgh, varied by teaching. She was for four years managing editor of a magazine, retiring to write long fiction. Her material, at first almost wholly derived from the early Nebraska days, lent itself to none of the conventional methods of fiction, and for a time she had difficulty in working with it. A fortunate encounter with Sarah Orne Jewett put her on the right track without much delay. It is probable that at least in *My Antonia* and *A Lost Lady* Miss Cather has made enduring contributions to the front rank of American literature.

A Lost Lady is exceptional in her work for its perfection of form—accepted form would be more exact. In all other respects it exhibits her characteristically and well. We may defer the look at these special qualities of her writing until after a sketch of the story on which they are expended.

It is the story of a fascinating woman. Marian Forrester is the wife of Captain Forrester, a retired railway builder who has built a house and settled on pleasant acres close to the village of Sweet Water, Nebraska, in the 1880's. He is a simple, direct, old-fashioned man, of great physical impressiveness and as calm and calming as he is rugged. His wife, twenty-five years younger, a Californian by birth, is not really beautiful, despite her blue-black hair and a skin with something of the crystalline whiteness of white lilacs. But she has charm; something alert and spontaneous, something fresh and young and gently, exquisitely radiant, goes out from her always.

The story is told throughout in the tone of reminiscence, and sometimes in the manner of recollected scenes. A few introductory pages lead to the remark: "But we will begin this story with a summer morning long ago, when Mrs. Forrester was still a young woman, and Sweet Water was a town of which great things were expected." And the first incident, whose deliberate selection is thus indicated, is a picnic of younger boys on the Forrester land—by permission of Mrs. Forrester, who comes down for a moment at noon bringing a basket of hot cookies for the youngsters. With magnificent economy and deftness Miss Cather indicates each of this parcel of youths, giving him a certain individuality; with Ivy Peters, the older boy who happens along, she is at pains to show his vicious cruelty. Niel Herbert, an intelligent and fine-natured boy of twelve, is brought forward with especial clearness. Much of the rest of Mrs. Forrester's story is to be viewed through his eyes.

We advance a few years. Niel is nineteen, studying law in the office of Judge Pommeroy, Captain Forrester's attorney and a man of the same breed. The Judge is

Niel's uncle. One winter afternoon Mrs. Forrester comes into the law office, sparkling and melting like a snowflake, to ask Niel and his uncle out for dinner. Some of Captain Forrester's old friends are stopping with them for two days.

Mr. and Mrs. Ogden and their daughter—whom Neil is asked to entertain—and Frank Ellinger are the house guests. We watch the dinner and the evening through Niel's eyes. He can do nothing with Constance Ogden, who has eyes only for Frank Ellinger's animal grace and strength. Miss Cather's method of unforced narration, of distributing emotional light and shade, shows nowhere to better advantage than in these pages. Against the something coarse and over-virile in Ellinger she places Captain Forrester's simple story of this home, whose site he selected when a young man, and his equally unadorned creed, a faith that "what you think of and plan for day by day, in spite of yourself, so to speak—you will get." When Niel and his uncle have gone home we come upon a dramatic scene—unprepared for, in the ordinary way of fiction. Mrs. Forrester helps her husband divest himself of his frock coat and puts it away for him.

Ever since he was hurt he had to be propped high on pillows at night, and he slept in a narrow iron bed, in the alcove which had formerly been his wife's dressing-room. While he was undressing he breathed heavily and sighed, as if he were very tired. He fumbled with his studs, then blew on his fingers and tried again. His wife came to his aid and quickly unbuttoned everything. He did not thank her in words, but submitted gratefully.

When the iron bed creaked at receiving his heavy figure,

she called from the big bedroom, "Good-night, Mr. Forrester," and drew the heavy curtains that shut off the alcove. She took off her rings and earrings and was beginning to unfasten her black velvet bodice when, at a tinkle of glass without, she stopped short. Rehooking the shoulder of her gown, she went to the dining-room, now faintly lit by the coal fire in the back parlor. Frank Ellinger was standing at the sideboard, taking a nightcap. The Forrester French brandy was old, and heavy like a cordial.

"Be careful," she murmured as she approached him, "I have a distinct impression that there is some one on the enclosed stairway. There is a wide crack in the door. Ah, but kittens have claws, these days! Pour me just a little. Thank you. I'll have mine in by the fire." . . .

Her eyes fell. "Good-night," she said faintly. As she turned quickly away, the train of her velvet dress caught the leg of his broadcloth trousers and dragged with a friction that crackled and threw sparks. Both started. They stood looking at each other for a moment before she actually slipped through the door. Ellinger remained by the hearth, his arms folded tightly over his chest, his curly lips compressed, frowning into the fire.

The scene moves to the next afternoon, to a sleigh-ride which ends at a ravine. We observe Mrs. Forrester and Ellinger directly up to the point where Ellinger says: "Sit still, while I take out the horses." There is a lapse of time—indicated by the blank line of customary use—and our vision is resumed through the eyes of pale little Adolph Blum, one of the two sons of the German tailor. Adolph sees the couple return to the sleigh and humbly and secretively watches the rich, fortunate and privileged Mrs. Forrester. "He had never seen her before when her mocking eyes and lively manner were not between her and all the world."

It has taken about one-third of the book to put us in possession of the situation in such a way as to avoid a complete misconception of Mrs. Forrester. The action of the remainder is simple and continues chiefly pictorial, with only a few dramatic moments. But how they are made to tell! Through an act of integrity to bank depositors, Captain Forrester loses all his money; grows very ill; and dies. The Forresters' visitors and friends gradually fall away from them. One of the most admired of the dramatic scenes is that in which worshiping young Niel Herbert gathers meadow flowers to leave outside Mrs. Forrester's bedroom in early morning, only to hear, on approaching the closed shutters, her delicious laugh followed by another laugh, "very different, a man's. And it was fat and lazy—ended in something like a yawn." But Miss Cather handles with equal effectiveness the scene in which Mrs. Forrester, flushed with liquor, visits the law office on a downpouring night to telephone Ellinger in Colorado Springs. With Niel we listen to her first soft words of congratulation on Ellinger's marriage; with him we take frantic alarm at the woman's swift change to a tigerish tone of accusation and an appalling frankness. With him we cut the telephone wire behind the desk.

Perhaps only women fully appreciate the scene in which the women of the village find at last an excuse to get inside the Forrester house, instituting a careful appraisal of Mrs. Forrester's housekeeping.

The three closing scenes are invented with much care. One is a dinner given by Mrs. Forrester for the young men of the place—less a means of showing the exhaustion of her exterior resources than a way to show the inexhaustibility of her tact and aplomb, her charm and spirit. Then comes the moment when Niel sees the unspeakable Ivy Peters clasp his hands about the lady's breasts. Then one or two brief and ominous reports. The lady disappears; it is supposed she has gone to California. A few words enshrine her in Niel's memory. But with this curtain of distance and lapse of long time we are ready for the final glimpse. It comes to Niel through the lips of another of his playmates who had encountered Mrs. Forrester as the cherished wife of a rich Englishman in the Argentine, lapped in luxuriousness, kindly used, happy. She has since died, but a wave of warm feeling passes over these two men who, as boys, had known her, at the thought that she was well-cared-for "to the very end."

Few works of fiction of its length offer so much material for analysis of method as *A Lost Lady*. Nor is analytical attention more highly rewarded than when expended here. The most important matter is the shifting angle of vision. It will have already been noticed that, although Miss Cather uses Niel Herbert more than any one else, she never restricts herself to his viewpoint. It would be most improbable, if not frankly impossible, that he should witness all the aspects of Mrs. Forrester necessary for her purpose with the reader. Yet he is indispensable; and in asking the reason we come upon a discovery of some dimensions: Miss Cather's subject is not, as we might tend to assume, simply Marian Forrester. Quite as much is it the vision of loveliness in women which is natural to healthy youth and ardent and innocent young manhood. That vision must always incarnate itself in some particular woman whose outward graces seem to token the inner and spiritual grace. Now if we wish to go further in the process of abstraction—one of the best tests of a work's substance—we may push on without hesitation to another definition. We may say, with perfect truth, that the subject of *A Lost Lady* is not merely youth's idealism, youth's vision of loveliness, but the inevitable disappointment of both. Does the subject stop there? No, not quite.

> He came to be very glad that he had known her, and that she had had a hand in breaking him in to life. . . . She had always the power of suggesting things much lovelier than herself, as the perfume of a single flower may call up the whole sweetness of spring.

The subject, then, in a final quintessence and complete abstraction, is the threefold process of youth's emotional education, the vision of loveliness, the disillusion, the properly steeled heart kept in its edge and tempering by the bright particles of memory's treasuring. Mrs. Forrester is merely the instrumentality by which the change is effected.

Yet, in such an illustration of *l'éducation sentimentale*, the instrument is all-important. We may state the subject of a work of fiction abstractly; indeed, we should always endeavor at some point in creative activity to do so; and if the fiction is of a finer sort this abstraction will always be possible. But the undertaking is of somewhat the character of a chemist's qualitative analysis, showing a certain richness of substance by breaking down the substance itself. It is generally impossible for the writer to work from a lofty but abstract theme, finding people to enact it. In the overwhelming number of instances he must be enamored of a literal or pictorial subject, he must see his theme in his actors and their setting, as, no doubt, even Bunyan saw the subjects of *Pilgrim's Progress.* When he has done this, our author may become aware, gradually and afterward, of implications and inner finenesses. As he comes to understand these, he may then bring them out, as a lapidary cuts delicate planes and facets on a diamond. The lapidary cannot imagine the many-faceted jewel and then give it embodiment in the rough he is cutting. Once or twice in a lifetime he may find a rough which will realize the purely imaginative jewel of his abstract conception. The rest of the time he must employ his skill to make the most of the opportunity a given stone affords. It is so with the maker of fiction.

Miss Cather, then, is in a certain sense writing about the *effect* of Marian Forrester on Niel and some others. One of her soundest claims to the rank of an artist lies in her realization that these effects of certain people are her true subjects. Thus in *My Antonia,* it is the effect that Antonia had upon Jim Burden; in *The Professor's House,* the effect Tom Outland had upon several persons, particularly Professor St. Peter; but here the peculiarity of fiction steps in. The more intrinsically a thing is one's subject, the more it must be guarded, the less extrinsically it may be shown, dealt with, presented. The way to show Mrs. Forrester's effect on Niel is—not to write about it. It is to write about *her*—as she appeared to the enchanted boy. Just what is this trick of technique? It is the imposition of an angle of vision on the reader. The reader is unobtrusively placed where Niel Herbert stood and agreeably compelled to see her through Niel's eyes at Niel's age, if he is to see her at all. It is not that the light is cut off from all other sides; the only light admitted is from Niel's side, except where the author chooses to alter the lighting and permit a momentary glimpse from some other angle. Nothing is more fascinating than to follow Miss Cather through this little book and note the compulsion to see Mrs. Forrester as Niel sees her, and the exceptions to this vision, and to ponder the reasons for those exceptions.

We cannot quite do that in our space, but perhaps we can meditate a crucial instance. The most difficult revelation to manage is that which shall show Mrs. Forrester's sexual looseness. Her charm and her spirit must be very firmly established before this disclosure can even be touched. They are. One-third of the book has been devoted to them—and to her brightness, her tact, her kindliness—before Miss Cather essays the hardest task. Now how shall the disclosure come? For once it will not do to have the reader standing in Niel's shoes. The boy is going to be horribly shocked and sickened. That is all right, but the reader must not share his revulsion in anything like the same degree when it comes to Niel. Remember that Niel is as much a subject, the youthful idealist, as his lady. And at this crisis he must emerge as a subject, rather more than she may be. The reader must be advanced in knowledge of life—which specifically will mean knowledge of Marian Forrester—beyond Niel, when Niel shall come to know the truth. Most of the emotion about Mrs. Forrester must be got out of the way so as not to interfere with the emotion excited in the reader over Niel. It is perhaps a little harsh to say that the reader can feel only one strong emotion, or emotion strongly in one direction, at a time; but that is what, speaking practically and from an author's proper principle, the situation amounts to.

This is the explanation of why, after the scene of the dinner party, presented mostly through Niel's vision, Miss Cather somewhat abruptly packs the boy off home with his uncle and shifts no less abruptly the point of view. The shift is very noticeable on re-reading *A Lost Lady*. It would, in other circumstances, merit criticism as a traverse of technique. But it is amply justified by the ends to be gained.

The scene downstairs over the glasses of brandy, dramatically presented, adds drama from the fact that it is not prepared for. In the preceding pages and during the dinner there have been, possibly, once or twice, the merest hints awakening suspicion in the watchful reader. But no "preparation" in the technical sense. Attention may be called to the fact that in this scene downstairs Miss Cather moves circumspectly. By having Mrs. Forrester suggest that the young girl may be watching, she imposes a curb on Marian and Ellinger. One may well imagine that this is a curb imposed for the reader's sake. When the scene is finished, the reader knows some of the truth about Marian—quite enough for his immediate emotional digestion. He does not know all.

The fullness of knowledge comes the next day, during the sleigh ride. Here is the scene:

> Ellinger took off his glove with his teeth. His eyes, sweeping the winding road and the low, snow-covered bluffs, had something wolfish in them.
>
> "Be careful, Frank. My rings! You hurt me!"
>
> "Then why didn't you take them off? You used to."

With those three words, " 'You used to,' " Miss Cather tells us the further thing that we had not known; this is a *liaison* of long standing. Piecing with this what we already know of Marian's temperament, we arrive easily at the conclusion as to this side of Mrs. Forrester: she is shaped for promiscuity. And with this knowledge the ground has been cleared for the revelation of the truth to Niel. It is not long deferred, and has its fullest force.

Two minor points, however. Ellinger's "You used to" breaks the stress of the couple's disappearance into the ravine shortly afterward. And Miss Cather is careful to remind us of the other Marian immediately afterward, by means of humble Adolph Blum, whose respectful gaze beholds her in a soft revery, some psychic transformation of the animal side of her nature. It is the only time in the book when a lowly Blum boy has any actual rôle, but it is pat for Miss Cather's purpose which is to instill or renew in our minds at this wretched juncture the reminder that perhaps, in some mysterious way, creatures like the lovely Marian Forrester are dispensed from the full rigor of those moral laws to which they know not how to give intelligent assent.

V. LABORATORY

The Strain Runs Out

Let us now make our own experiment, or the beginnings of one, in the novel of character. In order not to be vague, we will select a definite subject and at least one principal setting; agree upon several principal characters; and outline the action. It is, of course, rare for one writer to kindle to another's idea; but we shall not be trying, individually or collectively, to proceed with the actual execution of a work of fiction. We shall only be trying to understand how such a work germinates and pushes up to the surface. We shall not be describing the process of creative writing, we shall be watching it. It is not to be supposed that the process is identical in detail with any two novels, even when these issue from the same mind. A gynecologist is not made by attendance at a single clinic. Yet, if one were called upon to deliver a woman of a child, it were helpful to have witnessed just one birth.

It is not birth, however, so much as gestation with which we have now to do. And we must bear carefully in mind that our present concern is with a single broad type of novel—the novel of character, in which the proper study of mankind is held to be man; the finite fiction of yesterday and to-day. In succeeding chapters other broad types of fiction will be dealt with.

For clearness, and to insure progression, let us commit

this piece of laboratory work to assignment under the following headings: Origin and Choice of Subject, Appeal of the Subject, Development of the Subject (Outline of the Novel), and Treatment. The discussion of Treatment can be salient, merely.

Origin and Choice of Subject. Where shall the subject be found? In its core, it must come from life exterior to the author but as it has passed directly under his observation or within his experience. There would seem to be no other trustworthy source, since people and human nature are the true, general subject. The requirement to look outside oneself is a precaution not lightly to be disregarded. A reliance upon subjective material is only too likely to result in a novel of quite different *genre.* Nor may imagination generate the subject, lest the result be as far from finitude as *Wuthering Heights.* The rôle of imagination, in the novel we are now considering, cannot lie in the origination although it may have a considerable part in the treatment. But in saying that the subject must come from actual life, we do not mean, of course, any large or literal transcription; we may mean something as single as one marked trait of character, something as intangible as the sense of relation between several people whom we have watched. Not much, perhaps, but it is quite enough, provided the impression made be sufficiently strong to set our invention at work.

The genesis of our novel is found in the following extract from an imaginary notebook. But although the notebook does not exist and has never existed—being a mere convenient form for our perusal of substance—

everything described is, or was, actual; and there was an actual observer whose account is thus represented.

I think it was in the spring of 1925. I had been visiting in northern New Jersey, not more than thirty miles from the city of New York, and there met Mr. Eugene N——, who had married the daughter of the house. His personal appearance was unusual—rather small, finely-formed, dark, with a handsome face, at once aristocratic and agreeable, and charming manners. One noticed the wrist and ankle and wondered from what beautiful woman of the European nobility they had come. . . .

The next day was Sunday, and Eugene N—— took us out in a car. Ostensibly we were going simply for the drive, of which the culmination was to be the stretch of road high above the Hudson River and built by blasting a circular ledge along the granite side of Storm King Mountain. We did indeed traverse this arc, but it was not the culmination of that ride. Eugene N——, who had brought down seven German airplanes in the World War and to whom the driving of a motor car was a species of second nature, plunged straight from the banks of the Hudson back into the rolling countryside, in the general direction of Goshen. We entered upon a tangle of leafy roads and woodland tunnels. These grew less and less frequented; finally we struck into one which had every aspect of a private road, though not of the sort leading to a millionaire's country seat. A mile or more brought us to a clear space of ten or a dozen acres—and to the house.

It was of field stone, long and low. It had all been constructed in about 1770, and the adaptation of the interior was without any violence to its character. Some kind of heating system must have been installed and one or two smaller rooms had been fitted as baths. But at the side you could see the brick bulge of an old Dutch bake oven and progress from room to room still required a step up here, two steps down in that place. This was Eugene N——'s boyhood home, and his mother was living there at the time of our visit. We did not see her; she was an invalid and remained secluded in one of the upstairs rooms. N——'s two brothers were on hand and we had a jolly luncheon, after which we strolled about the place.

At one side of the knoll on which the house stood lay a small lake, apparently natural but really artificial, made by damming a little brook. On the far side stood a row of four or five tents and boys were swimming in the water and floating in a canoe. One of N——'s brothers—the one who lived with the mother, the other being merely home for the week end—kept this very small summer camp for a few youngsters from good families. He tutored them for college entrance and I suppose exercised some general oversight on their recreation. I remember that he told me that one boy was a Grandee of Spain. At a distance of a quarter mile or more from the house in the other direction lay large stables. It seems that Mr. N——, now dead some ten or a dozen years, had kept a string for the race-track and had bred not a few animals. In the house two things took my attention. One was a great chest in the hall downstairs, filled with weapons. There seemed to be a sample of everything from the Revolutionary flintlock to French and American rifles used in the World War. I know little about swords, but there was a Civil War sabre. Paul N—— said laughingly that if the house were besieged by the Ku Klux Klan, then somewhat assertive and conspicuous, here was material for the defense. The other thing gave real point to this jesting remark. In a room which the boys' father had used as a kind of office and which was now a little library, behind a screen at one end, was a Catholic altar. Not a Catholic myself, I was able to understand that this represented a very special honor to the family. Such altars, with a properly consecrated stone and valid for the celebration of the Mass, are found in few homes in America. The Papal license or permission, and I suppose blessing, hung in a frame on the wall near by.

The little I learned about the family fascinated me. The father, Mr. N——, had been an immigrant to America as a very young man, coming, I think, from Alsace. He was of peasant stock, I judge. He went to work in some importing house in downtown New York. He lived on the East Side and had the chance Tammany Hall gives all its youngsters to make something of themselves in political work. He became his district leader's righthand man. All this while he was studying in night school and he progressed somehow—I suspect mainly by studying at home—through college courses. Then he studied law. I believe he got admitted to the bar, but never practiced. By this time he was very valuable to the importing firm; he left them ultimately to set up his own business of importing French wines and food delicacies.

Then he married. The mother whom we did not glimpse that day was the daughter of a French-Belgian family of great distinction. I am not sure that it has not intermarried with royalty, and it is certainly of the nobility in one or both countries. About the circumstances of that marriage I learned nothing. Perhaps he met her on one of his early trips abroad in connection with the importation of foods and wines. It seems improbable that he could have met her in New York. She was perhaps orphaned; and she was almost certainly penniless—those people are, so often. It must have been the kind of romantic story that Joseph Conrad sometimes handled.

Tammany had made N—— a city magistrate and on the

death of the district leader whose aid he had been, N—— succeeded to power. It was the actual, personal and surprisingly potent authority that a Tammany leader exercises. And it called for a degree of hard work such as only the physician to the poor, or the priest of a poor parish, knows about. N—— would be called out of bed in the night to restrain drunken fathers, to go bail for adventurous sons, to hear the broken whispers of dying women laying a trust upon him. His days were filled with the wails of families threatened with eviction, or actually evicted; with the discipline of gangsters and rowdies; with provision for neglected children. There was much more of this than of high political debate and cautious manipulations, such as the American mind associates with Tammany Hall. But of course there was that side, too—smokebound conferences in the political temple on Fourteenth Street, trips to Albany, state conventions, deadly banquets of aldermen.

Soon after his marriage he was making a good deal of money. Not in politics—that took money, largely in the form of paying the rent for poor families in his district, contributions to party funds, and so on. But he could afford these things and a good deal more. When the first of his three boys was born he decided that a new order of living was called for. He bought this charming old Revolutionary American farmhouse fifty miles from New York, took his wife there, and thereafter made it his home for at least six months of the year. Mrs. N—— was enchanted with this country demesne. He dammed the brook and made the little lake. He built a racing stable. His wife busied herself with carpets and draperies and a vegetable garden and flower garden. She also acquired her servants, a Frenchwoman to cook and a Belgian gardener and some others. And she liked to charm their guests, of whom, first and last, the procession was endless and varied—fat politicians, young swells, priests, business men, including an occasional merchant from Europe. And their wives. I suppose Mrs. N—— had a few women friends but men must have preponderated in that house in the country.

There the two younger sons were born. I think the scene develops as two pictures. One is of the little noblewoman, who had so surprisingly found herself the wife of a Tammany political leader. I see her becoming more and more firmly rooted in this country home in a foreign country—but still the soil, land, acres, trees, a house and servants to entertain with, an orchard, and her sons. It had to be very complete and richly sufficing in itself, for she could have had no society in that countryside except the people imported as their guests. The other picture concerns the boys. What a delightful mixture, their boyhood, of the life of young country gentlemen and the sidewalks of New York! For a few months of winter's severity the family moved into New York, living in a house in N——'s Tammany duchy, a clean, dignified and spacious old residence in singular contrast to all its crowded tenement neighborhood. But this picture of the boys is best expressed in a remark one of them made to me, Paul I think, that day of our visit with Eugene.

"We had ponies," he said, "and in the fall we used to get up very early, before five, eat our breakfast, mount our ponies and ride four miles into town—not very quiet about it and I suspect the townspeople hated us. We'd stable the ponies and board an Erie train, ride fifty miles to Jersey City, cross on the ferry, and take the elevated to Public School Ten" —or whatever is the number of the school in New York he named. "After school was out we reversed the journey. This was the rule two months in the fall and for six weeks or two months in the spring."

The father's death smashed everything, coming while Eugene, the oldest, was in college. He must have met with business misfortunes or else it was one of those cases where one man creates and sustains the whole affair. Perhaps a little of both. The political prestige evaporated at once, the importing business, source of a princely income, could be sold for very little, and the racing stable had to be abandoned. The change from a kind of voluntary imprisonment in the country to an involuntary one probably affected Mrs. N—— little. Eugene finished college and his two brothers were put through after a considerable struggle. I have spoken of Eugene's appearance but I should add that the same aristocratic stamp, in the physical sense, was upon his brothers. And they had the same exquisite manners; only a certain boyish unaffectedness and frankness of manner suggested that they might be Americans. They were evidently willing and industrious and brave enough, but their talents, so conspicuous, were not the most useful, or at least the most successful, in the America of to-day. They had not the valuable plebeian qualities nor the hard early schooling of their father; they would never, all three of them collectively, make as much money as he did without particularly trying to. And the things their mother had been able to give them, which would have been priceless assets in other societies, did not stand them in much avail in the life they must fashion for themselves out of the ill-assorted materials of an industrial democracy. Eugene, except for the episode of the World War, could achieve for himself a position little better than a clerk's. . . . It was all too bad, too wasted. Perhaps if those boys could have been on a ranch in New Mexico or Arizona? or if they could have had careers in public life in Europe? It was simply their ill luck to require a setting, you know. . . .

Appeal of the Subject. The time to fix the title of a work is when the actual, abstractible subject is determined. In the material just spread before us the principal subject is plainly the endowments of the three sons and brothers and its misfit in present-day America. The title should therefore be some phrase of unmistakable meaning embodying this idea—if one can be found. There is a phrase of near enough accuracy; let us call our novel, *The Strain Runs Out.*[7]

The appeal of the work, as nearly as we can determine it, will greatly influence the development of the subject (or the outline we give to the story) and our treatment. In any sufficiently good subject there is more than a single appeal—or perhaps, more accurately, there are appeals to more than one audience. In the case of *The Strain Runs Out* we must now try to settle what these appeals are, and which is to the largest audience.

Now aside from the story-interest, the interest of "What next?" which will depend upon the action we may be able to develop in the next stage, the studies of character will be the greatest interest of the greatest number of readers. It must be so. It must be so not only in this story of ours, but in all stories whatsoever in which the interest of "What next?" is not specially emphasized and

---

[7] The business of selecting a title, fascinating and beset with difficulty, has never been adequately treated and is of an importance greater than most authors will admit. The title should do something to attract the reader, especially where the author is unknown or little known. Needless to say, it must be honest. The reason for an early determination of the title is this: The right title, chosen at the outset, may unify the work. As has been said, it is something like conferring a title of nobility on a man—there is some chance he will live up to it. But if a novel be written and a title then sought, the author is certain to find almost *any* title a makeshift. By that time he is aware of *all* the aspects of his story, and no imaginable piece of string seems sufficient to tie this bundle of sticks. A revolution occurring in the development or writing

in which a sincere effort, however inadequate, is made to present living characters. We remember that character affords that constant appeal to the recognition which is the chief source of pleasure and emotion in the mass of mankind. Thus, although our innermost subject is not the character of the three sons, but its maladjustment to environment, we cannot approach this subject directly. It is of less appeal, less recognition than the boys themselves—it is more abstract, doubtful, less sure of assent. It must remain implicit in their actions and in the course of events in the story in the hope that it may emerge and become explicit at the end.

This is perhaps the point to consider another aspect of the inner subject. One may recognize that the boys are misfits in the America of their hour, and show it, without thereby condemning either the boys or American life as we find it. Upon the degree of detachment in this matter will depend the whole effect of the book. We must ask ourselves immediately: What effect do we want to make? A wide range is possible, from the fierce tract to the dispassionate presentment.

It is possible to view these boys as exquisite, useless

---

of a work may make it necessary to scrap the original title, but that is another matter, and the nature of the change should indicate the new title. Search for the proper title at the beginning is one of the best aids to a clear view and just conception of the work in advance.

It follows that titles consisting merely of the name of a principal character are simply evasions of the title problem. Such books, where not advertised by the author's name and previous performance, make progress in spite of the title.

The fact that every author of a number of novels or stories must often fall back on a title less than ideal should act as a strong incentive. Let him try to multiply the times when he can find the perfect label.

objets d'art. A little difficult, to be sure, in view of Eugene's military record; but possible, sustainable. In this view there has, of course, never been anything comparable with the America of our day. Anything that cannot flourish under the conditions of our industrial democracy is proper for extirpation. This attitude would probably seek reënforcement in a contempt for Old World aristocracy as hereditarily represented in Eugene N—— and his brothers, with their slight physique, their gracefulness, their lack of "drive."

We can also, theoretically at least, for in the case of any given individual author no such breadth of attitude is possible, shape our story as a polemic in precisely the opposite direction. We can heroize, or at any rate sentimentalize, the N——s, and make our novel a powerful "indictment" of contemporary American civilization.

Either course is likely to make a highly popular and best-selling novel, if one may judge by the vogue of several books of this present time. To the formation of either it would be possible to bring many of the excellencies of good fiction—strong characterization, a plausible use of episode, relieving humor, and so on. Since the primary business of fiction is to make the reader feel, an intensity of feeling on our part—regardless of direction—would make our task easier and its chance of succeeding with large numbers of readers very great. Why, then, not be passionately one-sided?

Such a question would usually be answered by moral or æsthetic arguments. These are not very satisfactory, for they merely raise other issues in disposing of the first. *Not* to be on one side is in itself, in the view of many, immoral; and in this conviction they may be careless which side is espoused. They believe in partisanship, if not in parties; and for a literary example from contemporary writers they feel that Mr. Galsworthy is sometimes too busy scrupulously balancing injustices to record the side toward which the scale inclines. Again, while a good deal has been made of detachment for æsthetic reasons, it is by no means certain that the argument is final, or even wholly sound. There are æsthetic defects, very large ones, in the *War and Peace* of Tolstoy, but Tolstoy's extreme one-sidedness with regard to Napoleon is not among these. Hardy is one-sided about God, Sinclair Lewis is one-sided about the American village; but neither *Tess of the D'Urbervilles* nor *Main Street* suffers æsthetically from their respective attitudes.

We cannot be passionately biased for or against the N——s, for or against their environment, because we do not see them like that. This, the simplicity or accident of our perception, the verities of our emotion, is what constrains us—nothing else. It might so have happened that our view was different; it has happened to be as it is—for we are assuming the notebook-keeper's view as our own, in lieu of that personal vision denied us by circumstances. The view is a clear one, almost directly at right angles; though probably not free from distortion it seems to be almost without warping. There is in it no dark shadow and no very high light, no thought of particular blame. It instructs us, our view, that these boys had certain charming and valuable qualities which America cannot use; but that this is no great shame upon America, which could and did use and reward their father, no less worthy. It suggests that America may be at fault in its failure with the boys, but implies quite as plainly that the N——s are defective in adaptability, energy, resilience and tone. The light and shade are distributed almost too faithfully throughout the picture, it may be, to make an instant impression; but the picture is one that repays scrutiny better than many another. It is, indeed, one of those compositions which the spectator does not so much absorb as become absorbed into, on which he comes to dwell with an attention that finds new detail, new matter for emotion and reflection, as it stays in his mind. Such is its final appeal, æsthetic no doubt and with a certain touch of permanence amidst the fluctuations with which the rational faculty treats the theme. And with this appeal in mind, this lingering of the sum of the created impression kept foremost, the story must be treated.

Development of the Subject (*Outline of the Novel*). Now at last on the firm ground of construction, no doubt we can breathe more freely, in spite of the responsibility which weighs us down. It is evident from the nature of our subject that most of the story we shall write is not in our given glimpse of the N——s at all. *That* has served well its principal purpose; and while it is not to be discarded, can be drawn upon only for facts in the background and useful hints. We must first of all decide who is to tell this story. Is it to be the author, or another? Is it to be told in the first person, by one of the characters, or presented in the strictest and most impersonal sequence of dramatic scenes—a method whereby no one really tells the story, not even the author, but it is all, as it were, acted before the reader's eyes.

Or are we, perhaps, to adopt the subtle and most disclaiming method, developed to a high pitch by Henry James, and present (rather than tell) the story in terms of the fine consciousness of some actor or onlooker?

How gladly should we digress, if it were proper, to the thorough discussion of these various standpoints, the merits and demerits of each, the suitability of each for a certain purpose. But such a digression would be far too long, would make a book in itself—and besides the whole matter has been cunningly and sympathetically examined, and is presented with a perfect skill, by Percy Lubbock in his volume on *The Craft of Fiction.* Here we can deal only with his very sage conclusions and their applicability to the case in hand.

For the author to tell the story, from his omniscience, is the commonest way, and everybody is familiar with plenty of instances. Mr. Lubbock shows that the use of the first person, Stevenson's favorite device, is ordinarily the first step in dramatizing the story. Its principal limitation is that we can never see the narrator himself, except as the behavior of the others indirectly yields his likeness, and if he is an actor of importance this is a serious drawback. There is another difficulty, which Mr. Lubbock does not deal with, but sometimes arises: the narrator may be a strongly individualized and even eccentric fellow of whom the reader tires and toward whom he conceives an antagonism that spreads to the whole story.

In both its general and detailed presentation, all fiction is either pictorial or dramatic. This distinction may be applied to single pages or even paragraphs; equally may it be used to designate main divisions of a novel. Thus in a novel of 300 pages the purpose of the first hundred may be wholly pictorial[8] although the method in detail may be quite strictly scenic. It is perfectly possible to write a whole novel in the impersonal and vivid style of drama, all acting itself in front of the reader, with only such description as takes the place of stage directions and stage settings. The story thus offered will frequently be stripped as bare as a printed play although a little smoother in the reading, devoid of the singular jerkiness of plays in print. Very good examples of this effect may be found in most of the stories in W. Somerset Maugham's collection, *The Casuarina Tree.*[9]

This, "the most finished form that fiction can take," in the words of Mr. Lubbock, is evidently

> not a form to which fiction can aspire in general. It implies many sacrifices, and these will easily seem to be more than the subject can usefully make. . . . It is out of the question wherever the story is too big, too comprehensive, too widely ranging, to be treated scenically, with no opportunity for general and panoramic survey. . . . These stories which will not naturally accommodate themselves to the reader's point of view, and the reader's alone, we regard as rather pictorial than dramatic—meaning that they call for some narrator, somebody who *knows,* to contemplate the facts and create an impression of them.

---

[8] Mr. Lubbock cites Balzac as perhaps the best example of the huge pictorial beginning; Dickens, in such work as *Bleak House,* as the example of the vast pictorial effect achieved by many little scenes, *i.e.,* detail dramatically presented.

[9] His play *The Letter,* separately published in play form, was made from the last tale in the book.

The strict succession of scenes is exceedingly hard to maintain throughout a whole novel; hard for the author and very hard for those many readers who seem to require, not an elbow in their ribs, but certainly a touch on the shoulder in order to proceed toward the rational inference or the appropriate emotion, to know whether to laugh or cry. Strict scenic method unduly distends a novel—*Anna Karenina* is the salient instance—and may even defeat its own purpose. For after all, as Mr. Lubbock points out, the dramatic scene is the fictioner's most powerful effect, and if he uses it all the time he squanders its force with a recklessness that will bring sore regret before he is done with his enterprise.

We may well decide against rigid drama, then, for the presentation of *The Strain Runs Out*. Adequately to follow the three boys would entail a great number of scenes —and besides, how are we to do justice to their father and mother in the highly important background, in the vital action which has taken place, presumably, before our story opens? Scenically rendered, perhaps, that must count pictorially in purport and effect. Moreover, it is probable that we shall not be able to rely completely upon the reader's point of view. We are fairly dispassionate in the presence of our spectacle but by no means detached to the point of indifference. Our whole aim, as Conrad says, is to make the reader see, to make him feel; but except at certain moments we may well doubt our skill in evoking the true feeling merely by making him witness from the outside. We, or some one we select, will be needed to "contemplate the facts and create an impression of them," to touch the reader's shoulder.

We may also dismiss, on the whole, the narrator in the first person, not so much because it will be difficult to account for the necessary knowledge of three or more lives at the moment when such knowledge must be offered to the reader as because we can see no gain for us in this method, either dramatically or in narrative authority, that cannot be procured equally well by another approach. This, of course, is the presentation of our story in terms of the consciousness (mainly) of some actor or onlooker—a fine consciousness being indispensable. And at once we inquire where such a consciousness may be lodged. In one of the three boys? Perhaps. In some one standing in an intimate relation to the family or some member of it? That may be. But the difficulty about past action—the story of the father's career, for any fullness—reasserts itself; and we feel already some difficulty in rendering the exact shades of intercourse within the family, between Mr. N—— and his wife, the mother and her boys, for example. We acknowledge that we may want to use this method of somebody's perception and view and knowledge but with large reservations—so large, possibly, as to force us to abandon it except for special effects. Thus are we forced back, as it were, on the "old, immemorial, unguarded unsuspicious way" of auctorial omniscience, for the most part. It may be that we shall be able to vary this viewpoint a good deal; and, indeed, few novelists in a given work are able nowadays to use an unmixed method.[10]

---

[10] Mr. Lubbock is a little too severe on the traditional method, in *The Craft of Fiction*, p. 263, where he says: "And if there is any one who can proceed in this fashion without appearing to lose the least

We proceed to the outline of our story, recollecting that it must probably be only of the most general sort. While in short fiction the writer must almost always have everything definitely fixed, from beginning to end, before writing at all, in longer work this is a bad practice for the majority. The mere writing of a novel takes weeks and months; if, in addition to ordinary fatigue, the writer has any sense of a stereotyped performance his production may be lifeless.

It is also the general experience that invention is inconsecutive. One can sometimes, in the course of a few days or a few weeks, think a short story straight through, testing all the parts and fitting them together in final adjustment. In the case of a longer story the mind does not execute the feat well, at least, not often. The beginning, the sense of the ending and the main trends of the novel must be assured. But when they are, the author need not wait longer to make a start at the writing; usually he will do well to settle down to Chapter One. All the while he is getting his story under way, in the form of an actual manuscript, his mind will be busy with the remoter stretches as well as the passage immediately at hand. Some striking scene will occur to him, some covetable effect in the future, for which the first preparations must be made at the point where he is working. Perhaps

---

of the advantages of a more cautious style, for him the minstrel's license is proper and appropriate. . . . But we have yet to discover him; and it is not very presumptuous in a critic, as things are, to declare that a story will never yield its best to a writer who takes the easiest way with it." It is not a question of taking the easiest way, in every instance, but the way which, on the whole, is subject to the fewest disadvantages. This, in fact, Mr. Lubbock recognizes in several places elsewhere in his study.

it grows out of some discovery he makes while at work, a further penetration into the possibilities of the character, A., an unforeseen obstacle in the circumstances surrounding B. He must know where he is going, but can scarcely know in advance all he will come upon by the way. His skill must make the discovery en route a help toward his destination; and if it cannot help, at least his skill must dissolve it from becoming a hindrance.

Where shall we begin? With a fully-created picture, no doubt, though not with the picture recorded in that notebook which is our source. We might begin, of course, with the youth of Mr. N——, the father, and draw his struggle and success, his marriage and the partial metamorphosis by which a Tammany leader became a country squire. But it will make the book too long; it begins too far back from our real subject. The best we can do for *that*—and quite good enough—will be to begin somewhere in N——'s floodtide, when his three boys were children, himself powerful and happy, his wife still young. That will give plenty of chances to relate or imply all that is significant in the history of the father and mother; it is the real point of departure for the story we have to tell.

As for our ending, that must also be a fully-created picture—the hour or moment when each of the three sons is seen to be fixed in his destiny, if each still lives. The main trends of the novel are the courses of the three, their ups and downs, illusions and defeats, gains and losses. It is indispensable that they have a stamp in common, of character as well as physique, but we shall fail utterly if we do not endow each boy with a decided and differentiated personality. Eugene's is a steady and controlled nature; it is easy to think of him as having a responsibility his younger brothers never attain to. Charles, perhaps two years younger, has none of Eugene's tempered quality; in spite of his grace he is vacuous and weak. Peter—his mother called him Pierre—is more brilliant than Eugene but less controlled, an impetuous, magnificent youth, with enough driving force to succeed as an American among keen, competitive, hustling fellow-Americans. Unfortunately his ambitions are never identified with theirs; their forms of success are to him no success at all. None of these brothers has a "bent" in the English and American sense of the word. None has genius unless it be Peter and his is a genius of personality. He and Eugene have fine taste; but Charles is an example of that curious coarseness of taste often found among aristocrats and which may be nature's rebellion against over-refinement.

The following outline omits the many matters with which we are now familiar. It is outline only; its invention is free, not fixed; and it may well be susceptible of improvement.

The novel opens at the country home of Victor N——, at the particular moment when his wife, Eugenie, emerges from the house to pour tea on the lawn for a garden party, attended by a number of house guests as well as by a few families from the countryside. The week-enders include the leader of Tammany Hall, an up-State Senator or two, young Rutherfurd Bleecker, of an old New York family, a rather vacuous aristocrat and dandy who aspires to political renown, and various others, including wives. Prominent in the scene are the

N——'s three children: Eugene, aged ten; Charles, eight, and Peter, four.

For several chapters we shall be busy with the picture of this family and with the communication of the necessary background. Such incident as is used must be under strict contribution for this purpose. If, in addition, it can be preparation for the later action of the novel, so much the better. For example, we may write a scene (perhaps opening the second chapter) dealing with Senator Tom Twichell, of Adirondack Forge, N. Y. We must show him as a shy, naturally intelligent, not very well educated man who has come out at Victor N——'s invitation, unable to resist the opportunity to see the N—— stables and a fine stamp collection that Victor N—— possesses. We will picture him waking up quite early on Sunday morning, unable to sleep longer, dressing and going downstairs, tiptoeing through the house. He remembers an autographed photograph of President Cleveland, and other mementoes, hanging on the wall in one room. Ranging in their direction, he opens a door and is fairly in the room before he quite realizes what he has walked in upon. Hastily closing the door he rushes outdoors, in much mental perturbation. Through the disclosure of this agitated state of Senator Tom's mind the reader is informed of what he saw. He is thinking about the Roman Catholic Church, and inherited and inculcated mistrust is battling with an observation and contacts that have been, on the whole, favorable to that institution in his mind. What has really happened is simple. Father Dufranne, an old friend of Mrs. N——, a missionary priest, has arrived late the night before, stopping over on a journey from Buffalo to New York. He is celebrating his mass at the private altar and the family is in attendance. But if the net result of his experience is to revive in Senator Tom Twichell anti-Catholic prejudice (founded on the conviction that secret conclaves are held in private houses) we have something of possible use in the story later on.

With the same view to possible future use the scene presenting Rutherfurd Bleecker may be constructed. One or two at a time, Victor N—— conducts the men who are his guests to his sideboard for a drink and such personal conversation as will at least make the guest feel singled out for hospitality. In this fashion he devotes a few minutes to young Bleecker, whose tone of admiration for Mrs. N—— seems quite that he might adopt in praising a thoroughbred in the N—— stable. Victor N—— remains polite, congealing slowly; and a little later, talking privately with the Tammany leader, vetoes the chief's wry-faced suggestion that Tammany run Bleecker for the State Legislature. Bleecker, N—— indicates, will sooner or later be mixed up in a scandal with somebody's wife; that is N——'s reading of the fellow's character; and Tammany wants none of that. It will be possible to use Bleecker's frank interest in Eugenie N—— in a later chapter.

"The sidewalks of New York" have already intruded into this picture of a delightful country life; they must; and these pictorial chapters constituting from an eighth to a quarter of the novel must now show the N——s in the New York scene. The picture must continue to be dramatically treated. Perhaps we shall have a private conversation between Victor N—— and the Tammany chieftain, in Fourteenth Street, in which N—— will nominate as his successor a young Irish aide. Can we imagine N—— remarking: "We take care of our people, all right, but we don't set the feet of our young men on the rungs of a ladder. City jobs, the Legislature, yes; but we've got to do better than that. We must expect to put a Tammany man in the Executive Mansion at Albany —one of our own boys, not just an indorsed candidate. We ought to work on the theory that a Tammany man can get as far as the White House."

Of the young Irish aide, so introduced, it will be possible to make much or little as the book proceeds. There must be several glimpses of the N—— boys at school on the East Side, and at play. Each such glimpse can serve the double purpose of showing their *milieu* and of displaying their marked differences of character and personality. The revelation of these differences must proceed entirely by episode and action, and cannot begin too early.

* * *

Eugene. It is upon his shoulders, not only as the oldest but as the steadiest, that the burden of the family falls after Victor N——'s death. (The funeral of Victor N——, with its touching tributes to his popularity, is worth a chapter; and an effective antithesis might be achieved by a succeeding chapter on the wedding of his aide and protégé, the young Irishman who succeeds to leadership.) The story of Eugene is the story of the devoted and faithful son who stands by his mother. Indeed, young as he is when his father dies, there is little he can do at the time but stand by and see so much that made up life for the N——s vanish forever. The city house, the importing business, the racing stables—all are gone. Eugene finds himself marooned in an extremely rural countryside with a little, delicate woman whose health has been broken by the loss of her husband. There is this house, these acres, and a certain amount of income from bonds. There are his two younger brothers to educate. And Eugene, whose temperament, aided by a vocation, would have fitted him to become a priest, takes vows that bind him as firmly. There is nothing he can do out there, except a bit of farming or something of that sort. He tries that, he tries keeping a dairy herd, he is always trying something and coming out even on it or losing a little money. An exile from society, he never marries, though perhaps he is once in love. When America enters the World War he has his day of glory, but it is short-lived, he returns to the home and his invalid mother, who needs him more than ever now that Charles and Peter are severed from her. And with his return Eugene is again automatically cut off from life, from any achievement possible to him.

Charles. In spite of Eugene's stern attempts at disciplining Charles as a boy, Charles the youngster was untruthful, boastful, gluttonous and—cowardly? Perhaps it was not so much that Charles was a physical coward as that he lost his head so easily. In truth, few more badly muddled brains can be imagined than Charles's. His history inspires alternations of anger, pity and contempt. Its climax comes when, without warning, he marries a coarse girl of the countryside and brings his bride home to meet his mother. What a scene! Eugenie N——, with some of the best blood of Europe in her veins, must sit and smile upon this wench for her son's sake—must stifle her feelings and summon all her courage and composure, if she is not to lose all of Charles forever. (And, of course, she has always been blind about Charles; has always defended, extenuated and spoiled him, from the mother's instinct to do most for the weakest.)

This is not to say that Charles's wife is bad morally. She is a good wife and a good mother, by the standards vouchsafed her. It would be difficult to argue that he deserved a better woman, perhaps. She bears him a son and a daughter, both with her own thick ankles and clumsy wrists, both with Charles's youthful gluttony. It is perhaps nature's rapid adaptation of strains to environment; this boy and this girl may be better fitted to survive, however modest their survival, than their uncles. Where Charles's wife is worst is in her aggressive provincialism, intolerance, and acute jealousy of his mother and brothers.

Peter (*Pierre*). Here is the—comparatively—meteoric career. Peter belongs to the after-war generation and flings himself into the life of New York and Paris. Capable of success in the usual American sense—in person, money and career, a little of all three—he makes a flashing start in business only to abandon what he so easily masters as soon as it bores him, which is always quite soon. He is a cork floating on many waters, but always floating, always buoyant. A succession of well-begun, half-won careers must be invented for him, proceeding out of friendships, need of money, new appetites. A love affair with a girl of the most conspicuous New York society is his first failure; then there is an actress; then, it may be, an older woman with whom he breaks when he grasps that she only wants a *gigolo*. Peter even strays into politics; he goes to the Far West; he returns to New York and ventures into advertising with a more stable fellow. His ultimate destiny is to become a gay old dog, a man about town in spite of advancing years, with his fine apartment, his manservant, his car—financed by devious means that are essential to the picture. When his mother dies, releasing Eugene at last, it is Peter who invites Eugene to come to New York and live with him, and Eugene accepts the proposal. But in spite of Peter's genuine affection their tastes are by now too far apart. It is a lonely but relieved Eugene who finally retires again to the old home.

* * *

The final scene of the novel can be quiet enough, but must be fully significant, must create the whole picture. It may be sufficient to show Eugene and Peter as guests at dinner and for part of the day of Charles and his wife. Mrs. Charles is still upset because the Sevres china, Aubusson carpets and other possessions of her mother-in-law have never been passed on to her. They are Eugene's. Probably this whole last scene must be dramatized by means of Eugene's mind—the method of which Strether, in Henry James's *The Ambassadors,* is criticism's favorite example. But it must be done with care, without preachment; the reader must be completely and unobtrusively surrounded with the spectacle as Eugene sees it. That vision is without any harshness; it is just, whatever its sadness. It sees the practical worth in Mrs. Charles, the high usefulness of her to her husband, and it acknowledges the utility of the nephew and niece in all the circumstances in which they are likely to find themselves. If Eugene's vision is a little emotionally despondent, it is yet free from the wasted resentment and despair of Peter's view—Peter, who has been West, and who breaks out to Eugene in a tirade against presentday American life, comparing it to a desert that swallows up the river that tries to flow through it. "You know, Eugene, we were brought up to beauty and to worship. Our mother, that old place, our beautiful religion—. Our mother is dead, the place is full of ghosts. Even our religion suffers in this damned country. Father Gillis hit it on the head when he said that the visitor to American churches must often feel that he had strayed into the Church of the Holy Chromo." But this is not Eugene's perception. The desert drinks up the river, every last drop, but the water is still there, every drop of it. It is merely underground; and perhaps a way can be found to bring it up. In all the material preoccupations of his countrymen he sees the almost total disappearance, perhaps, but certainly not the extinction of the things of the spirit. His final thought is that all he has—chiefly such money as can be got from the old home, by its sale to some rich man in search of a country estate—shall be expended on the education of Charles's children, unpromising but also unknown. . . .

Treatment. A good deal of the matter of treatment has already been discussed. The following observations, nearly all derived from Lubbock's *The Craft of Fiction,* are purposely kept as general as possible.

The devotion of anywhere from an eighth to one-quarter of the book to picture must not be begrudged. It will be a picture scenically rendered, for the most part—put on page after page directly in front of the reader, acted out before his eyes. But we will not pretend that these scenes, for the most part, are of importance in themselves. It is their total effect that is important.

They must give all we are to get of Victor N——, and nearly all of Eugenie. Her charm, her sweetness, her richly nourished nature and her strength must all be displayed to conviction here. After the death of her husband, her part in the story is inconspicuous, perhaps, certainly almost wholly passive; yet her influence is powerful and her meaning grows with the years. This effect cannot be had unless it is fully created, stored up, in the earlier chapters. It must be there, a rich reserve to draw upon, to appeal to and have the appeal *felt,* through three-quarters of the novel.

Something similar is true of Eugene, Charles and Peter. Insofar as we are able to characterize and individualize them strongly in their childhood, we simplify all our problems with them later on. There are three of them and each must, for intervals which may sometimes be long ones, drop out of sight. This is particularly true of Charles. There may well be opportunity to prepare very little for the scene in which he brings home the girl of his choice. She may enter the story almost as unknown to the reader as to Mrs. N——. A good deal about *her,* in that first apparition, as well as everything about Charles's behavior will depend upon the accumulated impression of Charles—upon what the reader already knows about him from episodes occurring, many of them, years earlier, and apparently of little significance in themselves and at that time.

Eugene's is the best mind in the story, and when we wish to give an impression of the facts we shall do well to use his perceptions. Eugene's mind, indeed, the effect upon him of events, his effects upon them, is a most essential part of the story itself, and must be dramatized with great frequency throughout. But Peter may be used a good deal under the same method; and if this shift of the point of view be found fault with, as subversive of unity, we need not be too much disturbed. Vividness comes ahead of unity. Nor is ours a story in which unity can be pressed too far. It will not do, for example, to try to knot the action too closely, to relate the brothers' fortunes and affairs at every stage, or to make all the characters interdependent. A large effect is sought, a point of view on American life in general, for one thing, and the means of achieving such an end are not, to say the least, abundant. Eugene, for the most part, is cut off from the world; Charles is sunk from sight in the mass; only Peter gets about and can give us much sense of the American scene. And more important, too, than a formal unity is the proper indication of the lapse of time. How much time is covered by the action? The best means of fixing it will be by Charles's children. We wish that boy and girl, in the final scene, to be—shall we say fourteen and twelve, respectively? Charles, in the kind of marriage he makes and in view of his nature, will not be very old when he marries, perhaps twenty-two at the most. If we take him as twenty-three when his son is born, then he is thirty-seven in the final chapter; he was eight when the book opened; and the period of the action is established at nearly thirty years. That is a long time to cover satisfactorily, and from the nature of our story, it tends to seem longer than it is, at the close. But this impression must be avoided; there must somehow be emphasis at the end on the fact that, after all, Eugene is not yet forty, and Peter is only thirty-three. Part of the difficulty of the twenty-nine years can be circumvented, when the pictorial chapters of the beginning are completed—terminated by Victor N——'s death. An abrupt, unmoderated, decisive advance at that point, possibly of as much as six years, may recommend itself. If this plan is adopted, it may be desirable to make the final scene a glimpse from the years beyond those with which the center of the book is concerned, so that in this way the period of the interior chapters may confine itself to not more than fifteen to eighteen consecutive years, say those when Eugene is seventeen to thirty-three, Charles fifteen to thirty-one, Peter eleven to twenty-seven.

Does this seem to call for some recasting of the general outline? If it does, we shall do well to think it all over with care, and make any necessary alterations, although in putting it on paper we were naturally letting our thought stray over the whole lives of the N—— brothers, including a future not compassed by whatever actual story we might find to tell. It is of value that we should take our leave of Eugene and Peter when they are thirty-nine and thirty-three; while we cannot hold out bright futures as in prospect for either of them, it need be no tax upon our conscience if the reader finds a relieving optimism in their ages.

One final word. If ours is not particularly an optimistic novel, pessimism, raging, except from Peter in one of his fits, has no rôle in it, either. We are not to forget our title, "The Strain Runs Out," and that may as easily be the fault of the strain as of conditions which did not create it and are neglectful rather than hostile. We ask no questions, we answer none; we show the picture. We show the picture that has fallen under our eyes, that has raised in us a clear emotion, an emotion that it is our endeavor to communicate, directly, fully, and without weakening. That is all our aim, and in whatever we do we must never be perverted from it.

CHAPTER V

SECOND STUDY IN METHOD. PLOT, ANCIENT STYLE

AS we have seen, the ancient manner of plot was already obsolete when the novel came into existence. Naturally examples of long fiction which employ, or endeavor to employ, plot in that sense are comparatively few. Short fiction, which lends itself more readily to experiments, could easily furnish us with sufficient instances; and for those who would like a perfect one there can be no better recommendation than to a short story by Melville Davisson Post, "The Doomdorf Mystery."[1] Many, perhaps most, of the Father Brown stories by Gilbert K. Chesterton achieve very perfectly the atmosphere of old-style plot.[2] If a particular one be sought, why not "The Oracle of the Dog," in *The Incredulity of Father Brown?* The difficulty of these pieces—and the difficulty of most short work in which some flavor of ancient fiction is preserved for us—lies in the fact that the rationally-inclined reader, like the literal reader, can rest on the merely puzzling story-facts, can sate a checkerboard inclination and dismiss all else. How could Doomdorf have possibly been slain in his inaccessi-

[1] The first tale in his collection, *Uncle Abner: Master of Mysteries,* published by D. Appleton & Company.

[2] Collected in *The Innocence of Father Brown* (1911), *The Wisdom of Father Brown* (1914), *The Incredulity of Father Brown* (1926), and *The Secret of Father Brown* (1927).

ble room? Who could have killed Colonel Druce in his summer house in such circumstances as Chesterton assures? There are people whose only interest is in the methodical answers to these questions and who, at the end, remain interested only in the physical demonstration. Our purpose must be to find and examine one or more examples where this type of mind cannot function; where such readers will either have to seek another kind of satisfaction or remain unsatisfied.

A recent novel, somewhat over-praised, might afford a good example if we could be a little more sure that it would remain unforgotten. *The Bridge of San Luis Rey*, by Thornton Wilder, opens with the death of five persons in Peru, in 1714. A native bridge collapses, and the occasion seems to Brother Juniper, a Franciscan, to offer the possibility of making theology an exact science. Why did these five die at precisely this moment? The answer, no doubt, will be found in an examination of their lives. To this he proceeds. In place of his long-drawn-out reports of the five, the novelist offers us a more direct and essential account of the victims, up to the instant of their taking-off. Unfortunately this interior, this body of the book, is done with too little vitality, with thinness of detail and with too much the air of an intellectual demonstration. A magnificent conception is but weakly realized.

Perhaps the two best examples for our purpose will be Herman Melville's *Moby Dick* and Johan Bojer's *The Great Hunger*. After examining these we shall imitate the constructive method of the preceding chapter in the approach to a novel of this stamp, but wholly original—our own, to work out in our own fashion.

I. HERMAN MELVILLE

Moby Dick

It might be urged that here, too, the matter-of-fact reader can have his way, that he can read *Moby Dick* purely as the story of a whaling voyage with an exciting chase of the White Whale brought to the height of climax, the whole marred or improved, according to his taste, by much lore of the sea and more lore of whaling. This is evidently in the mind of E. M. Forster when he begins a brief discussion with the remark: *Moby Dick* is an easy book, as long as we read it as a yarn or an account of whaling interspersed with snatches of poetry." But, in fact, has anybody ever been able to read it in that fashion? Probably not. The great length of the book, the extent to which it is interpenetrated by fantasy, the nature of that fantasy, make it seem extremely improbable that the rationally-interested or literal-minded ever persevere to the end. Doubtless such readers read skippingly; perhaps the other class of readers also skip, each accepting what the other puts aside. But the difference must be that to the one sort, Melville's book is an exasperating way of acquiring facts about one of mankind's disused occupations; to the rest of us, it is all manner of things else.

So many, indeed, that there is no exact agreement upon them. Mr. Forrester would have it that *Moby Dick* is one of a few specimens to which he attaches the term "prophecy." By this he means a work in which the characters and situations always stand for more than themselves. "Infinity attends them." They conceal nothing, and therefore are not mystical; they are not charged with a special meaning, and hence we may not explain them as symbols. The prophetic novelist is not a reflective creature but a singer; and like the poems and drawings of William Blake the novel of prophecy requires, not that we accept it, but that we lose ourselves in it.

To all this it is easy to assent, but we can scarcely stop with it.[3] Except the tone, all the marks by which Mr. Forster identifies Prophecy are unmistakable marks of ancient fiction. And the tone is easily accounted for—like a bird imprisoned in a cage, the nature made for the ancient freedoms falls back on song in the cage that rationalism has thrust it in. *Auf Flügeln des Gesanges:* its only wings are the wings of song. Mr. Forster distinguishes carefully between Prophecy and Fantasy, Sterne's *Tristram Shandy* exemplifying the latter. Prophecy "is unlike fantasy because its face is toward unity, whereas fantasy glances about. Its confusion is incidental, whereas fantasy's is fundamental." That is to say, Prophecy is, comparatively, a triumph in the situation brought about for certain natures by the loss of Deity; fantasy is a despair, albeit sometimes a humorous despair (half-hearted humor at the best). And sentimentalism, as we noted a long while back, is the so-familiar, unconscious diseased condition resulting from the same malnutritive plight.

Who are the prophets? Mr. Forster names four—Dostoevski, Emily Brontë, D. H. Lawrence, and Melville.

[3] Forster was compelled to stop with it. The matter of his *Aspects of the Novel* was originally a series of lectures at Cambridge in which the lecturer was restricted to English literature and to English literature from Chaucer onward.

Tracing cause and effect from ground denied to him, we may feel a further distinction possible and desirable. Is there not a considerable distinction between Dostoevski and Melville, on the one hand, and Emily Brontë and D. H. Lawrence on the other? The extreme rational mind, called upon to define the difference, might make short work of it by saying that the Russian and the American were more than a little mad, whereas the Englishwoman and Englishman were queer—more than a little queer, no doubt, but still within sanity. We can feel the difference, in a sense less narrow, but our definition can hardly be so glib. Dostoevski and Melville, we may affirm, have nothing whatever to do with realism—do we not feel it to be so? Their ships, rooms, *personæ,* waters and skies, in spite of a certain attentiveness toward the facts of normal vision, are charged with a strangeness of contour, texture, behavior like the strangeness of Blake's art. "Mr. Blake," said his devoted wife, "is always in Paradise." We cannot say that Dostoevski and Melville are always in Paradise, but we are sure that it is because they have not escaped from Hell, or are yet lingering in Purgatory. Dantes, every one of them; they differ from the Italian chiefly in not being cumbered with theological cosmogony, the materials of ordinary life will do. The materials of ordinary life, but distorted by the pressures of truly extraordinary experience, so that when we gaze upon the least thing in the way of furniture in their stories we have the profound uneasiness of Father Brown in one of Chesterton's tales, the deep disturbance because —it may be only a chair or a table—"the shape is wrong."

The shape is always wrong, in the work of these writers, for the procurance of anything like realism in their fiction. But we scarcely feel that this is true of others whom Forster brackets with them. It is not true—is it?—of the background or the foreground in *Wuthering Heights,* nor is it exactly true of much in D. H. Lawrence; the strangeness of *Women in Love* or *The Plumed Serpent* or *Kangaroo* is grounded on a realism with which we have no trouble; it is this realism, in fact, that excessively annoys some readers of Lawrence, for if they could get rid of it, they could be rid of him, they feel.

But the Dostoevskis and the Melvilles have no more realism than children and poets and angels. They are concerned with the invocation of Deity, although they may feel an epiphany to be impossible. Their mood is one of awful certainty even where it is without expectation; they are apocalyptic, tranced. No longer able to instance the *deus ex machina,* they are unforgetful that *deus in machina movet;* and while most of mankind are become unable to see the god for the machine, they can scarcely perceive the machine for the god agitating it, to them visibly and constantly. Their reports of the machine are somehow unrecognizable, their realism is confronted by Reality. And all their fiction moves toward an apotheosis, or a series of apotheoses, of the Divine Will.

There is another test, for Mr. Forster, of Prophecy: the characters of the story must give us the feeling of extension, must seem to join up with all mankind, back of them and after them. We must feel a strong current flowing between them and ourselves, between ourselves and the eternities of pity and love. This is the pure *katharsis* of elder fiction; its intensity varies greatly in the general class of writers under our consideration. In Dostoevski and Melville, to use an electrician's figure, it is "stepped up" to a tremendous degree; in Miss Brontë, in Mr. Lawrence—even in so towering a writer as Tolstoy—the feeling is impressive but by no means terrifying. The extension *they* give us is in finitude, after all, a sense of the antiquity and continuity of the race, of the emotions, pretty nearly covers it. "Infinity attends them"—but it is purely an infinity of the human series. They are realists still.

To them, therefore, in the belief that the distinction we have tried to draw is a real one, we give the name Transcendental Realists—Prophets not without their honor from us—and reserve the discussion of their work for the chapter following this. Our present concern must be with the major Prophets, who, by whatever means, manage always to achieve the *effect* of ancient plot. Among them Johan Bojer may seem misplaced, even with *The Great Hunger,* but the justification of this choice, if any appear, must wait while we ponder *Moby Dick.*

That is not the best choice Melville offers us. For the illustration of his genius *Billy Budd* would be brighter and sharper, but this much shorter story is available only in a collected edition, one that must be supposed inaccessible to most readers.[4] But *Moby Dick* is easily had; it is the most famous of Melville's books; and such advantage as accrues from the selection of an author's best-known book will be procured for us.

---

[4] A brief but brilliant account of *Billy Budd* will be found in Chapter VII of Forster's *Aspects of the Novel.*

There is no satisfactory life of Melville; it is improbable that we shall ever have one, as material is lacking. He was born in 1819, of New England ancestry on his father's side, New York Dutch on his mother's. A whaling voyage furnished him with adventures for more than one book. Two South Seas romances appearing in 1846-47 were popular and—at that time—a source of some sensation and scandal among church people who supported foreign missionaries. One of Melville's few friendships was with Hawthorne, to whom *Moby Dick* is dedicated. A publisher's fire seriously affected Melville's fortunes soon after the appearance of *Moby Dick* (which was in 1851) and all his middle age and old age, for he lived to be seventy-two, were passed in a deepening obscurity. The sense of futility and what may be called human insectitude was vast in Melville. His fame in his lifetime came from things he knew to be ephemeral; it could not be transferred to the work which he put a value upon and he knew this as well. He is one of a number of men who cannot be happy in living, but only in having lived; his posthumous fame, in connection with *Moby Dick* and a few other matters ignored in his lifetime, would be ideally satisfying to his temperament, wherever that temperament may now be indulging its solitary exercises.

It would probably be possible to take *Moby Dick* apart and, without too much far-fetchedness, show its structural relationship with the roots of Greek drama. Of its spiritual affinity with such a source—whether that source be taken to be the Dionysiac ritual or the funeral cult of individual heroes—it would seem that no student could entertain a doubt. Our purpose, however, is not one of scholarship in this manner. We wish to regard Melville's mind, manifesting itself in the ancient ways of fiction; we wish to see, if possible, the means by which he gets certain effects. In order to do this we must first get clear on one or two things which he does *not* attempt.

He makes no attempt at plot in the associations now inseparable from the word. The title of this chapter is "Plot, Ancient Style," but we know how plot has changed down the centuries, and that its modern meaning is almost entirely due to efforts to provide a substitute in ingenuity for the drama of emotion. We know that when plot served great ends it was often loose and formless; but that when those ends were taken away from it, plot had to suffer the cheapening of becoming an end in itself. Now the story of Captain Ahab's pursuit of the White Whale is a simple situation with an indicated climax toward which the story steadily leads. There is nothing unforeseen, unless it be the precise details of the climax itself. We know that Ahab hunts the whale, we are pretty sure he will find him and join battle, else it is unlikely Melville would be writing his book. Suspense attends the outcome of that encounter—and not much else. Suspense, we mean, in the modern "plot" sense; for the modern plot, having to be an end and not a means, must be tightened up, taut-trimmed, insoluble and baffling and exciting. But with Melville all these considerations of the modern plot can be put on one side; *his* plot is still a means—of what we may presently gather.

Not only does Melville discard modern plotting, he puts aside all idea of coherent method. In addition to the usual alternation of picture and scene, he employs the dramatic soliloquy, the strict form of the play for forecastle dialogue, forthright exposition in the manner of an encyclopedia and poetic interludes. We have seen such versatility in our own day, in a novel called *This Side of Paradise,* by F. Scott Fitzgerald, of which Edmund Wilson, Jr., made the truest criticism, saying that it had every conceivable fault of a novel except one—it did not fail to live. Melville does not fail to live, either; and it is sometimes hard, in reading *Moby Dick,* to understand why. Those dramatic monologues! that Brutus-Shakespeare bombast! But in the midst of a fulminating eloquence, the madness of poor Pip with his rig-a-dig-digging and the lunacy of Ahab, and the contortionist vocabulary of the incredible Stubb, there is something else, something that pitches and pursues its intricate song as unbrokenly as the Wagnerian music in *Tristan und Isolde.*

This, the main effect in *Moby Dick,* is quite aside from all philosophies. It does not derive from the human wisdom spilled by Melville in random fashion throughout the vivid and episodic pages of his book. It has its source in a natural ecstasy that imputes personality and meaning to the phenomena of nature. No doubt we all do that. Take this range of mountains off in the distance from where we are sitting. From one standpoint—possibly for our recurrence in a later chapter and another connection—the whole range is a series of minor and accidental contours, verdured or unverdured, with or without snowfields. But we are quite unable to take it like that. We may, indeed, achieve a strictly impersonal interest in the nature of those rocks, geologically considered; we may find coveted metal in them and mine it after the most businesslike fashion. But even then the range insists on assuming an aspect different from a valuable rubbish pile. It becomes personal, the guardian of a treasure house; not all our smokestacks and cars on aërial cables despoil this dignity of the mountain. The mountain, perhaps, is naked; snow never visits it, there is nothing apparently to invest it with beauty or any sort of worth. It is a tawny waste, colorless and forsaken. And yet we cannot leave the subject alone; we insist on personality, we create meaning. Perhaps this smooth flank likens the range to some unimagined animal; perhaps the light catches the slopes in a moment brimming with significance. The very contours become something in our vision, the planes of the mountain, little more in themselves than geometrical surfaces and nearly as abstract, are seized upon by this natural ecstasy of the human mind and appareled for the mind's delight.

But this faculty, which is so feeble in most of us that it does not struggle beyond a strained literalness of "Hog's Back" or "Camel's Hump," exists in Melville as the *droit du poete,* the poet's right, and is possibly the single greatest force of his mind. He shares it with Thomas Hardy, this way of regarding the universe as enactment, and his intimacy is as complete as Hardy's, just as his expressiveness displays the American exaggeratedness of Walt Whitman's.

Hardy proceeded, we know, to the affirmation of purposelessness behind this great theater in which he saw heaths and cliffs exercising a more compelling power than men. Melville sought to affirm nothing but the spectacle.

> The ethical view of the universe involves us at last in so many cruel and absurd contradictions, where the last vestiges of faith, hope, charity, and even of reason itself, seem ready to perish, that I have come to suspect that the aim of creation cannot be ethical at all. I would fondly believe that its object is purely spectacular: a spectacle for awe, love, adoration, or hate, if you like, but in this view—and in this view alone—never for despair! . . . The unwearied self-forgetful attention to every phase of the living universe reflected in our consciousness may be our appointed task on this earth—a task in which fate has perhaps engaged nothing of us except our conscience, gifted with a voice in order to bear true testimony to the visible wonder, the haunting terror, the infinite passion, and the illimitable serenity: to the supreme law and the abiding mystery of the sublime spectacle.

These are not Melville's words, but those of another seaman; but Joseph Conrad might almost have been speaking for the earlier writer.[5] "Narrowed and hardened into words," says E. M. Forster, "the spiritual theme of *Moby Dick* is as follows: a battle against evil conducted too long or in the wrong way. The White Whale is evil, and Captain Ahab is warped by constant pursuit until his knight-errantry turns into revenge"—a statement that he at once proceeds to qualify until,

[5] Chapter V, *A Personal Record,* by Joseph Conrad. (In England the title is *Some Reminiscences.*)

perforce, he very nearly pares it all away. Finally, "nothing can be stated about *Moby Dick* except that it is a contest," he exclaims. "The rest is song." But the more we view Melville's book, the less we shall be willing, possibly, to assent even to this. There is no ethical view, no spiritual theme; the contest—at least insofar as Ahab and the whale are concerned—is remote throughout the book until the actual encounter at the very end. What Melville is interested in is the physical and spiritual metabolism that makes the stuff of primitive religions, animism so-called.

> Creation is a great flood, forever flowing, in lovely and terrible waves. In everything, the shimmer of creation, and never the finality of the created. . . .
>
> The mind is there merely as a servant, to keep a man pure and true to the mystery, which is always present. The mind bows down before the creative mystery, even of the atrocious Apache warrior. It judges, not the good and the bad, but the lie and the true.[6]

"Call me Ishmael." Thus imperiously Melville opens his tale. It is a tale that, despite bizarre instances, might after all become only one of a hundred sea stories. If it is to be distinguished apart from every other fiction using the same material the distinction must be achieved by displaying on every page the rare and powerful mind of the author. Of several ways in which this might be accomplished Melville selects the one that is unquestionably best for his book. He uses the first person—

[6] *Mornings in Mexico*, by D. H. Lawrence. Chapter V, "Indians and Entertainment."

Lubbock's "first step in dramatization." He will not use it rigidly or carefully; he will abandon it utterly for whole chapters, which thus hang suspended in the air 'twixt earth and heaven, as unaccounted-for in origination as their content is unaccountable. But in the main the device of Ishmael telling the story of an adventure he shared will answer. Ishmael, present at the events he describes, will settle the question of authority for the tale. Constantly through his thoughts Melville will be able to inflect the recital of scenes and persons and convert mere prose into the semblance of "creation . . . forever flowing, in lovely and terrible waves." The chief defect—that Ishmael must remain himself shadowy—is scarcely a defect here; it is no more than an inability to see the singer's face when we have an incomparable voice in our ears. We may well shut our eyes and listen, simply.

The book begins with a whimsical justification of life before the mast, at least on occasion. But then, just as we have decided that we have to do with a lusty fellow possessing his own conceits, the first chapter is closed in a paragraph of far different quality.

> By reason of these things, then, the whaling voyage was welcome; the great floodgates of the wonder-world swung open, and in the wild conceits that swayed me to my purpose, two and two there floated into my inmost soul, endless processions of the whale, and, midmost of them all, one grand hooded phantom, like a snow hill in the air.

And in spite of all liberties, lapses and excesses of style and fancy, we are thenceforward in a special environment—for "mood" is too transient a meaning. At once the scene transfers to New Bedford, a New Bedford just recognizably that of the 1840's and whaling days, but no more than that, if even that. For from the moment when Ishmael sets foot on the New Bedford streets, stumbles into a negro church, finds the Spouter Inn and acquires the harpooneer, Queequeg, a cannibal, as his bedfellow, everything begins to go wrong with Melville's realism, by the usual standards. It is warped out of recognition, indeed, by the constant pressures of the special reality he must create for us.

That reality is fashioned out of a hundred strange and appropriate loose ends—Father Mapple and his pulpit and his sermon, Captain Peleg and Captain Bildad, Ahab's toast drunk from brimming harpoon sockets, "barbed steel goblets"; the elaborate and stagey scene in which the foresail is supposed to rise, like a theater curtain, and disclose the crew in song and dance and repartee, verging finally on a brawl that is aborted by the mate's order to take in sail.

And now we may examine in a condensed form a passage in Chapter XL:

> It was not so much his uncommon bulk that so much distinguished him from other sperm whales, but . . . a peculiar snow-white wrinkled forehead, and a high, pyramidical white hump. . . . The rest of his body was so streaked, and spotted, and marbled with the same shrouded hue, that, in the end, he had gained his distinctive appellation of the White Whale; a name, indeed, literally justified by his vivid aspect, when seen gliding at high noon through a dark blue sea, leaving a milky-way wake of creamy foam, all spangled with golden

gleamings. . . . More than all, his treacherous retreats struck more of dismay than perhaps aught else. For, when swimming before his exulting pursuers, with every apparent symptom of alarm, he had several times been known to turn round suddenly, and, bearing down upon them, either stave their boats to splinters, or drive them back in consternation to their ship. . . .

Judge, then, to what pitches of inflamed, distracted fury the minds of his more desperate hunters were impelled, when amid the chips of chewed boats, and the sinking limbs of torn comrades, they swam out of the curds of the whale's direful wrath into the serene, exasperating sunlight, that smiled on, as if at a birth or a bridal.

His three boats stove around him, and oars and men both, whirling in the eddies; one captain, seizing the line-knife from his broken prow, had dashed at the whale, as an Arkansas duellist at his foe, blindly seeking with a six-inch blade to reach the fathom-deep life of the whale. That captain was Ahab. And then it was, that suddenly sweeping his sickle-shaped lower jaw beneath him, Moby Dick had reaped away Ahab's leg, as a mower a blade of grass in the field.

Concerned with more general problems, we make no attempt in this book to consider such elements of prose style as rhythm, assonance and those other subtleties so interestingly analyzed by R. L. Stevenson.[7] But it may be remarked that few prose passages will better repay the most exacting study of this finer detail.[8] But what

[7] In his essay, "On Some Technical Elements of Style in Literature" (1885), included in *Essays in the Art of Writing* (1905).

[8] The second paragraph of the excerpt affords an easy comparison in effect with a passage in Joseph Conrad's *Youth*—sufficiently quoted for the purpose in Chapter I, iii, of this book (see pages 4, 5). Melville, with his "serene, exasperating sunlight, that smiled on, as if at a birth or a bridal" is both compacter and more poetic.

is the predominant value of this superb piece of narration? Its sanity reassures us quite as much as its vigor thrills. It comes after the first of the book's more apocalyptic manifestations, after the soliloquies by Ahab, Starbuck and Stubbs, after the set-piece presenting the crew in song and dance and incredible dialogue. And its power is the peculiar power of lucid and stirring speech from the lips of a man we had suspected of being a little mad—aside from its sufficient power as dramatic picture.

The middle of the work expands in chapter upon chapter devoted to the wonders of the whale. There is an interspersion of incident—Pip, jumping from a whale-boat, is at last taken from the ocean a hopeless idiot; other ships are spoken; the mates kill whales; at last Ahab meets a captain whose arm has been sheared off by Moby Dick even as Ahab's leg. The approach to the climax is perceptible when Queequeg is measured for his coffin and the disused coffin—for Queequeg recovers—is re-fashioned to make a life-buoy. In the interval Ahab has dipped his harpoon barbs in human blood, sacrilegiously invoking the devil's baptism upon them, and corposants have burned at the summits of all the masts and on the tips of the *Pequod's* spars. We come to the three final chapters, the first, second and third days of the chase, with breath held over a wonder as to whether Melville's pen can be equal to the demand his approach has made upon it. It is.

The narrative assumes a movement we have not seen in it before; present action is to be spread on the page. The invocatory nature of Ahab's speeches is not lost but they are shot through with the piteous appeal of breathless and overmatched struggle. Moby Dick himself is painted with such words as few poets have been able to use. There is no sacrifice of picture but drama carries all before it. For the final act of this long pursuit Melville strips prose to its sinews:

> The harpoon was darted; the stricken whale flew forward; with igniting velocity the line ran through the groove; ran foul. Ahab stopped [stooped?] to clear it; he did clear it; but the flying turn caught him round the neck, and voicelessly as Turkish mutes bowstring their victim, he was shot out of the boat, ere the crew knew he was gone. Next instant, the heavy eyesplice in the rope's final end flew out of the stark-empty tub, knocked down an oarsman, and smiting the sea, disappeared in its depths.
>
> For an instant, the tranced boat's crew stood still; then turned. "The ship? Great God, where is the ship?" Soon they through dim bewildering mediums saw her sidelong fading phantom, as in the gaseous Fata Morgana; only the uppermost masts out of water; while fixed by infatuation, or fidelity, or fate, to their once lofty perches, the pagan harpooneers still maintained their sinking lookouts on the sea. . . .
>
> Now small fowls flew screaming over the yet yawning gulf; a sullen white surf beat against its steep sides; then all collapsed, and the great shroud of the sea rolled on as it rolled five thousand years ago.

* * *

Moby Dick creates the emotion of ancient fiction. In part, it is the purge of Greek drama—the bosom ridded of perilous stuff—but in great part it is an emotion more ancient still, that of "truth to the wonder," an exertion to be worthy of the great creativeness going on all about us, a creativeness in which Deity shares the struggle with mankind, in which reason may serve but cannot rule. Primitive animism, if you like, but there are worse religions than this creed of active, utmost being. It has none of the passivity of better, intellectual creeds. Even the best of fiction, old as well as new, has a tendency to vicarious emotional exercise. We are a little too comfortable, no matter how deeply stirred.

We are told of Ahab that after the loss of his leg, while for long months of days and weeks he lay stretched with anguish, "his torn body and gashed soul bled into one another; and so interfusing, made him mad." But it is exactly this interfusion of soul and body, in time of health and not only of sickness or wounding, that Melville and all animists inculcate. It is useless to ask of them what they mean; they mean what they are; and what they are is simply an activity of becoming something else, perhaps merely an extension, perhaps something different. Emotion is an essential of that activity; thought, in the aspect of rationalism, is sometimes a help and sometimes a hindrance. In no sense in which we have come to accept the phrase do they teach us "how to live"; but in teaching us how to be, in showing us the wealth of being, they are magnificent and something more than mortal.

II. JOHAN BOJER

The Great Hunger

Johan Bojer, the Norwegian, first attracted wide attention with his novel called, in English, *The Power of a Lie*. He first came to a large audience of readers, however, with *The Great Hunger;* and it will be more profitable to consider this story because of its open dénouement. Indeed, though there can naturally be no epiphany in a modern work of fiction, no appearance of the god or gods in the Greek manner, the last chapter of *The Great Hunger* shows strikingly how close to the Greek effect the fictioner may still come, and this at the conclusion of a work quite realistic in its simple premises and in nearly all of the incident and delineation—both somewhat frugal, after the general Scandinavian manner.

Peer Holm is the natural son of a charming and beautiful woman. From childhood he has been left with fisher folk in the country. His father, an army officer, treats him generously in the matter of pocket money, and Peer is something of a leader among the boys of the village. Our first look at him is when he captains his fellows in a forbidden enterprise—fishing the fjord with a deep-sea line. He comes into his teens and, obeying instructions, writes to his father, who intends to see to the boy's education. A reply informs him that his father is dead.

He is thrown on the world, but through the friendship of one of his chums, goes to work in an engineering plant, with the design of later becoming a student in the Technical College and an engineer. In his loneliness he writes and invites his half-sister, Louise Hagen, another of his mother's natural children, to visit him. Louise takes him at his word and the brother and sister share Peer's mean room above a stable. The story of their life together, full of pathos and very happy, is among the more beautiful idyls of fiction. Most writers, especially English or American writers, would have spoiled the narration, either by sentimentality or from the mere danger inherent in the use of English with its luxuriant vocabulary. In Peer's necessary absence for a week, Louise dies of diphtheria, and the brother arrives home only in time to fly through the streets, overtake her coffin and follow it to the resting-place.

Peer completes his education and goes forth as an engineer. We lose sight of him for a term of years, and reencounter him returning to Norway. Through a reunion with a fellow-student who has remained in poorly-paid posts at home, Bojer neatly acquaints us with a new Peer Holm. This is a man who has carried through important engineering projects in North Africa and elsewhere—the Nile Dam is specified; who has seen many parts of the world; who has amassed a fortune that is, at least in Norway, very large; and who is considerably disillusioned and deeply dissatisfied.

"To help mankind to make quicker progress—is that nothing?"

"Lord! What I'd like to know is, where mankind are making for, that they're in such a hurry."

"That the Nile Barrage has doubled the production of corn in Egypt—created the possibilities of life for millions of human beings—is that nothing?"

"My good fellow, do you really think there aren't enough fools on this earth already? Have we too little wailing and misery and discontent and class-hatred as it is? Why must we go about to double it?"

"But hang it all, man—what about European culture?

Surely you felt yourself a sort of missionary of civilization, where you have been."

"The spread of European civilization in the East simply means that half a dozen big financiers in London or Paris take a fancy to a certain strip of Africa or Asia. They press a button, and out come all the ministers and generals and missionaries and engineers with a bow: At your service, gentlemen!

"Culture! One wheel begets ten new ones. Brr-rrr! And the ten again another hundred. Brr-rr-rrr—more speed, more competition—and all for what? For culture? . . . It strikes me that fire and steel are rapidly turning men into beasts. Machinery is killing more and more of what we call the godlike in us. . . . No such thing as religious feeling exists any longer. . . . Ask the good people in the great cities. They spend Christmas Eve playing tunes from 'The Dollar Princess' on the gramophone."

In this temper, Peer loiters in Norway, finding his way up into the countryside and idling deliciously at a farm. There, in a fit setting for young and romantic love, which he has never known, he meets Merle Uthoug, of the family of a merchant whose summer home is near by. The two love and marry, and Peer takes a magnificent estate that his father-in-law acquired in a business deal and rehabilitates it. He goes into business with Herr Uthoug but the bulk of his fortune remains invested in a friend's large irrigation enterprises in Egypt. Now he has everything—power, wealth, leisure, a beautiful home, an enchanting wife, a child. And now? Is this enough? The question will keep recurring.

It is brought up again when his two close friends and

fellow-engineers come for a visit. These are Ferdinand Holm, Peer's half-brother—one of his father's legitimate children—and Klaus Brock, the boyhood chum. Ferdinand speaks of an immense project for harnessing the Tigris and Euphrates Rivers; here is work for Peer. But Peer declines.

> "Ah!" Ferdinand Holm lifted his glass to Merle. "Tell me, dear lady, how does it feel to be married to an anachronism? . . . Yes, your husband's an anachronism . . . an an egoist, a collector of happy days. . . . A man has no right to ravel out his life, even though the threads are of gold. A man's days of personal happiness are forgotten—his work endures."

Peer rejects this at the time but its effect upon him becomes manifest after the two friends have gone their ways. A contract for damming the Besna River is offering. Klaus had spoken of this, though Ferdinand had ruled against it as too small for Peer's record and ability. Now Peer goes after the contract and gets it, his father-in-law taking on a fraction of the security that must be furnished. Everything goes wrong with the contract; Peer completes the work, doing a splendid job, but at a heavy loss, and at this time word comes from Klaus that the company in which Peer's fortune is mainly invested has gone to pot. One chance remains to retrieve his fortunes, a mowing machine in which he interests British and American capital, but one small detail has been overlooked, and in the race against time to find a remedy for this fault Peer loses. His fine place is sold. He is penniless.

We seem him now with his wife and three children settling in a very poor little place in the country. He is still weak from illness. He has managed to borrow enough money to keep them all for a year. For long he does little; as his strength returns he fills his time with desperate chores. Once the idea for a small device that will perfect his mowing machine comes to him; he fashions it himself at the blacksmith shop, only to find that an American inventor has hit upon something neater still. Time wears on; there is no improvement in Peer's health or the family's fortunes. First a girl and then a boy have to be relinquished to their rich aunt, for it is unjust to the children to deny them the best opportunity of education. The engineer of the Nile Dam has sunk to a blacksmith in a country parish.

A letter to Klaus Brock closes the book and gives us the dénouement in Peer Holm's own words. After some recital of his condition, Peer tells his friend of his five-year-old girl, Asta. He travels on to the subject of a brazier and his wife, bad neighbors, who kept a vicious wolf-dog. The terrible event itself is summed up in a few lines—Merle's shriek, Peer's rush to the fence, his glimpse of little Asta lying at the dog's mercy. "Merle tells me that it was I that carried our little girl home." The child, her throat torn, is dying; that night is dead. Then follows one of the memorable passages of modern literature:

> I saw a man rush out into the night, shaking his fist at heaven and earth; a madman who refused to play his part in the farce any more, and so rushed down towards the river.

But I myself sat there still.

And I saw another, a puny creature, let loose; a humble, ashen-gray ascetic, that bent his head and bowed under the lash, and said: "Thy will be done. The Lord gave, the Lord hath taken away—" A pitiful being this, that stole out into the night and disappeared.

But I myself sat there still.

I sat alone on the promontory of existence, with the sun and the stars gone out, and ice-cold emptiness above me, about me, and in me, on every side.

A terrible drought that spring was followed by frosts, snow and sleet—but meanwhile people had sown their corn. Peer's neighbor, the brazier, had sown his patch of ground with barley. "Now he would have to sow it again"—or starve—"and where was he to get the seed? He went from farm to farm begging for some, but people hated the sight of him after what had happened about Asta—no one would lend him any, and he had no money to buy."

After a sleepless night, Peer rose, dressed. took of his own seed and sowed his neighbor's plot.

It came home to me that it is man himself that must create the divine in heaven and on earth. . . . Therefore I went out out and sowed the corn in my enemy's field, that God might exist. . . .

We are flung by the indifferent law of the universe into a life that we cannot order as we would; we are ravaged by injustice, by sickness and sorrow, by fire and blood. . . . And yet man smiles and laughs in the face of his tragic fate. In the midst of his thralldom he has created the beautiful on earth; in the midst of his torments he has had so much surplus energy of soul that he has sent it radiating forth into the cold deeps of space and warmed them with God.

So marvellous art thou, O spirit of man! So godlike in thy very nature! Thou dost reap death, and in return thou sowest the dream of everlasting life. In revenge for thine evil fate thou dost fill the universe with an all-loving God. . . .

Dear friend, it was thus I felt. And when the corn was sown, and I went back, the sun was glancing over the shoulder of the hill. There by the fence stood Merle, looking at me. She had drawn a kerchief forward over her brow, after the fashion of the peasant women, so that her face was in the shadow; but she smiled to me—as if she, too, the stricken mother, had risen up from the ocean of her suffering that here, in the daybreak, she might take her share in the creating of God. . . .

The Great Hunger concludes with these words.

The marked correspondence of this ending to the *deus ex machina* is in no need of stressing; if we elect, we can regard it as an epiphany, even as a divine epiphany, without deviating a particle from the standpoint of Peer Holm. He acknowledges the divine, but sees it as a partial and fragmentary, intermittent but undying creation of mankind. What are the differences between such fiction as *Moby Dick* and *The Great Hunger?*

Both belong to fiction in the ancient mode, but within that mode, hundreds, and generally thousands of years, divide them. The animistic spirit of *Moby Dick* exalts being, utmost being, creativeness as we have said. But it is not the "creating of God" with which Peer Holm comes to rest. It is self-creativeness. The animist lets

God look after Himself. He, God, is busy about His own creation; the animist has no idea of contributing to that. It is enough for him, as a man, to be ever more fully Man—and even ever more fully his own particular type of man, of his own race, tribe and lineage. If he is Ahab, let him be Ahab to the utmost; or if he is not human at all but a whale, then he serves his ultimate end by being, or striving to be, as redoubtable as the White Whale.

Christianity might never have come into existence and in every essential *Moby Dick* would be the book we have to-day. But *The Great Hunger* could not have been written if Christianity had never happened.

It rests, Bojer's novel, upon an assumption which Christianity first brought into the world. This is the return of good for evil. The religions that were in existence when Christianity developed held no such premise. To do good was sometimes part of their teaching; the best of them held strictly to the view of justice in affairs human and divine; none insisted upon the efficacy of such an act as Peer Holm's.

But, it will be objected, *The Great Hunger* is not a Christian book. At first glance, this seems obvious and true. Peer Holm has no use for the church, and there is more than one allusion implying disbelief in and indifference to the Christian faith. So far as we know, this attitude is unchanged at the end of the story and remains without change during the rest of Peer Holm's life. But the fundamental facts are that Peer Holm acts upon a principle uniquely Christian, and that he *acts;*

for not only did Christianity inculcate the return of good for evil but taught that the return must be an active, not a passive one.

This is to say that Bojer is writing in a world in which Christianity has been highly potent for a great many centuries—a world so saturated with the Christian ideal that even the rationalist may not escape its pervasiveness. It does not matter that Peer Holm's attitude is the inverted one, that he sees man creating God rather than God creating and inspiring man, since the mechanism or mode—good for evil—is identically Christian, and since human action is indispensable. The point, for us, is an historical one: Two centuries after the triumph of rationalism, and nearer five hundred years since the extinction of Deity began, Deity reappears in a work of fiction in precisely the ancient manner and with all the antique force. That the reappearance was of some moment is testified to by the translation of Bojer's work from Norwegian into English—possibly into other languages—and the sale of many copies of *The Great Hunger* in England and the United States.[9] So far at least as America is concerned, knowledge of Bojer and interest in his work began with *The Great Hunger,* extending back into earlier books, such as *The Power of a Lie,* and forward into subsequent books, like *The Last of the Vikings.*

Technically considered, *The Great Hunger* is not with-

[9] The English translation by W. J. Alexander Worster and C. Archer has been relied on in this discussion and the excerpts quoted are from that text, published in England by Hodder & Stoughton, and originally in the United States (1919) by Moffat, Yard & Company. The American edition had gone into nine printings in a year.

out instructive aspects. From one angle the whole novel is simply preparation for the drama of the final chapter. Although the novelist may wish to indicate Peer Holm's quest of God through many years, he cannot do so directly without the greatest apparent irrelevance. Wisely, he does not try. Peer is first represented as lonely, with no one to love, none to love him. Work and the acquisition of knowledge, then the companionship of Louise, satisfy him. The death of Louise makes the first dreadful breach in his life. But he is led on by the goal of knowledge, then by mastery of power and the attainment of riches. God, in the forms known to Peer, has been erased from his life. His quest for long takes the shape of a recurring question: "And then? What then?"

It is necessary for the novel's significance that he should become powerful and rich, but these temporary solutions can be elliptically treated; and so Bojer does not present them directly. There is undoubtedly some loss; many a reader would like a glimpse of Peer as the master of men and the engineer of the Nile; but the loss is more than compensated, it may seem, by the gain in compactness of the book as a whole and the increased movement. When it comes to the solution of love, ellipsis is not to be thought of; the reader must see directly and circumstantially just what Peer's marriage means to him. And in the same way the culminating picture of him pleasantly sated with every good thing that life has to offer must be clearly and amply shown.

For upon the evidence thus offered to us, the impression in this way fully created the force of the remainder of the story wholly depends. A restlessness in Peer has carried him through successive stages to a satiety which is not its cure. He is to lose his wealth, then lose his power (not merely through its non-exercise but by actual destruction of his physical health); even his gain of knowledge is to be neutralized. What is left? The unselfish love of ripened marriage and parenthood. But surrender of two children tears at this possession. The last third of *The Great Hunger* is a strong instance of the point made by Percy Lubbock in discussing the method of Balzac. He says, in *The Craft of Fiction:*

> Balzac's care in creating the scene is truly economical; it is not merely a manner of setting the stage for the drama, it is a provision of character and energy for the drama when it begins. . . . *Eugenie Grandet* is typical of a natural bent on the part of any prudent writer of fiction, the instinct to relieve the climax of the story by taxing it as little as possible when it is reached. The climax ought to complete, to add the touch that makes the book whole and organic; that is its task, and that only. It should be free to do what it must without any unnecessary distraction, and nothing need distract it that can be dealt with and despatched at an earlier stage.
>
> . . . The process of writing a novel seems to be one of continual forestalling and anticipating; far more important than the immediate page is the page to come, still in the distance, on behalf of which this one is secretly working. The writer makes a point and reserves it at the same time, creates an effect and holds it back, till in due course it is appropriated by the page for which it is intended. . . . It is the art of rendering an impression that is found to have been made, later on, but that evades detection at the moment.[10]

[10] Chaps. XIV and XV.

Why is the final chapter in the form of a letter to Klaus Brock? It can be made veritable only if we have it from Peer's own lips. No one else's account of what happened to him will have due weight. The point of view must be shifted for this chapter and the shifting must not abuse credulity. A certain eloquence is needed —the eloquence of utter sincerity, nothing more—but that Peer should be able to command that in speaking to some other person is not very likely. It is probable, however, that he might command it when putting pen to paper in a letter that we may easily suppose to have been managed with long pauses between some of its sentences. Note, however, that Bojer tries to prepare us for even this shift or device by presenting a short letter from Peer to Klaus several chapters earlier.

Putting aside the theological and even the ethical view of the substance of that ultimate chapter—with which we are not concerned, except historically—we are bound to consider the nature of Bojer's *deus ex machina,* his God from the steel and fire that obsessed Peer Holm until he felt himself their plaything. Peer, like most men of his time and ours, is too much imbued with the pride of the rational faculty to achieve a religious selfishness.[11] With his personal self reduced to a cipher, the racial self became more and more dominant and unyielding. "So marvelous art thou, O spirit of man! So godlike in thy

[11] The Greeks would have said that this intellectual arrogance, as manifested at its height in the eighteenth century and not uncommonly since, was a form of *hubris* (or *hybris*), the certain punishment of which is death. To wax too strong and to presume upon that strength was to commit the sin of *hubris,* or Pride, entailing a heaven-sent blindness and pointing straight to a fall.

very nature!" But there is another point, personal to Peer, involved in the manner of his finding God. It rests on the utter destruction of his personal creativeness. He has lost that power. The engineer, the artificer, is no more. The inventor has perished. Even parenthood, it seems probable, is ended. And who shall say how much the need of a recovery of personal creative power influences the form which his discovery of Deity takes? One can only assert that rational arrogance, racial persistence and individual frustration all irresistibly weld together to make the desired engine for his action, as if the emphasis had passed from the *Deus* to the *machina,* from the spirit to the apparatus. Perhaps it has.

And still, it is the spirit that tells. In a final report, rendered as readers upon whom a desired impression, a particular effect, is sought to be created, we need not hesitate to avow the fullness of our emotional satisfaction nor our indifference to the machinery used to evoke it. Electricity is electricity, whether it falls as the bolt of lightning or is elaborately produced by coal, boilers, steam and dynamos. The latter give us the illusion of creating electricity, just as Peer Holm's return of good for evil gave him the illusion of creating God. The supremely important thing is the affirmation, either way, that electricity is, that God exists. Subjectively, the overshadowing thing is the emotion, intense and undying, which is our way of compassing that Being. Fiction, it may seem, cannot elude the task of bodying forth that emotion.

The gods, too, die, alas!
But deathless and more strong
  Than brass
Remains the sovereign song.

III. LABORATORY

A Wink Toward Heaven

Origin and Choice of Subject. Unlike the novel of character, fiction in the ancient style may be almost wholly subjective in its origin. Where it has its basis in actuality, subjectivism transforms the nucleus by successive emotional and imaginative layers not unlike those which convert the unconsidered speck of sand into the lustrous pearl. Perhaps the only parallel in the arts lies in the literature of music, where the accident of a few notes has sometimes meant the miracle of a symphony. As it happens, we stumble upon our "subject" in a medical textbook devoted to the maladies of pregnancy, in the pages discussing *toxœmia gravidarum.*

A very general, and possibly inexact, summary will suffice. It occasionally happens that a pregnancy will seem to go wrong from the start, and from no specific cause, but merely because some kind of toxic effect or poisoning seems to take place in the mother. In the more baffling type of this disease, the toxic agent is as yet unknown. Early in the pregnancy the patient becomes unable to retain any kind of nourishment, even water, and is speedily in danger of starving to death. In obstinate cases the only chance of saving the mother's life is by surgical intervention that sacrifices the life of the child if, as most often happens, the infant life is not viable When the mother can be sustained through seven months, the child may be saved; but in the graver cases of *toxœmia gravidarum,* or "pernicious vomiting," the crisis is reached at the end of three months' pregnancy.

In many instances, according to medical experience, the child must be sacrificed if the mother is to be saved. In these cases, let it be clearly understood, no real choice exists. The situation is not in the least like that of a difficult childbed, where some alternative of saving mother or child may exist, or seem to exist. So far as human knowledge goes, an acute form of *toxœmia gravidarum* early in a pregnancy presents only the following courses:

1. To empty the uterus, a course which nearly always results in saving the mother and need not preclude subsequent attempts at child-bearing—often successful.

2. To endeavor to keep the mother alive until the child is viable, which nearly always results in the death of the mother as well as the sacrifice of the infant life.

Moral or personal and religious scruples, or religious faith, may elect the second course, and not infrequently do. According to the teaching of some Christian bodies, consent to the first course is a sin, no matter what may be the force of medical opinion in its favor as the only means of saving the mother,—a sin provided the child is not viable or cannot with certainty receive while yet living the rite of Christian baptism. The principle involved is, of course, the sacredness of human life, which Christianity was the first faith to insist upon. The insistence had to be extreme, in early Christianity, and the theological positions arising from it were very carefully worked out. They are logically quite unassailable.

But where they lead, in their practical and individual application, to what in any other view must appear to be the deliberate albeit passive sacrifice of a woman's life, as well as the unborn life, it is natural that they should be furiously challenged, give rise to unreconcilable points of view, and lead to the gravest consequences in the spiritual life of the individual. It must, however, be kept in mind that moral and personal decisions, quite as much as religious principles, may dictate the passive and fatal course for the mother.

Life, it may be thought, holds few more terrible dilemmas. Whichever solution is adopted, the sensitive soul may incur life-long suffering as the result of the decision. The only persons in any degree fitted to bear the responsibility at stake are the physicians and, if he chances to enter into the affair, the priest. But having said so much, we do wisely to say and think no more of the matter from the uncertain ground of objective truth, beset by the rash attempts of scientists, sociologists, and persons with ideas about everything to be solely heard. Ours is the method of fiction, which disregards ideas, preferring always to listen to and look upon an experience.

Appeal of the Subject. It is as an experience that we must enter into the quest for those meanings which have a validity denied to objective truth. And the moment we envisage this thing as an experience, all its aspects alter. The perplexity, the poignancy and the anguish remain; indeed, they intensify; but the vexation of controversy is dissolved quite away; the sitting in judgment is put out of mind; in the abysses that open before our feet we see something springing green that has manifestly the living water at its roots. The living water of that love which, in the declaration of Dante, moves the sun and the furthest stars.

Our first impression is that this is the mother's story, and so strong is this feeling that modification comes only gradually. It may, of course, not come at all. But let us reflect a little. There is a father, as well as a mother; and if his concern with the unborn child is still weak, since in most such cases the child is to him yet without reality, his relation with the mother is as full of intimate anxiety as hers with the life within her. If, then, he can have his will, unconstrained by forces outside himself, the mother must be saved; and his determination is likely to be strengthened in circumstances where her preservation may appear alone to be possible.

A conflict of wills is only too likely. The appeal of the subject, dramatically, lies here, no doubt. In what other respects can we assert it to be appealing? None, perhaps, at least until we begin the development of an action, when, if we are fortunate, this and that appealing aspect, or glancing significance, will press constantly upon us, forcing our invention along a given path, less by any direct propulsion than by shutting it off from all other possible paths. And whatever the path we take there must be the incessant welling up of emotion, never fouled, never dried, never flooding, always controlled.

Development of the Subject (Outline of the Novel). We start with a young woman and a man at least comparatively young. They have been married less than a year when the toxæmia manifests itself. The course adopted in this crisis will depend on themselves, their education, and the circumstances in which they are placed. These must be settled at once.

It is easy to imagine a brilliant and controversial treatment by Bernard Shaw—perhaps a *Patient's Dilemma* to set beside his *The Doctor's Dilemma.* Or John Galsworthy might have incorporated the situation somewhere in *The Forsyte Saga,* showing the exquisite anxiety of a Forsyte where property rights are involved. There is, indeed, a page in *Arrowsmith,* by Sinclair Lewis, where the whole *impasse* arises, demanding and receiving a sentence or two by way of plumbing its agony, and requiring a few more sentences for its effective dispatch. Eugene O'Neill would construct a drama markedly different from Shaw's. The course of surgical intervention would be adopted off-stage between a Prologue and the first of a series of acts or scenes, and the heroine would go through the remainder of the play with her thoughts audibly dwelling on her misfortune. Barrie, no doubt, would fashion us a story in which the mother would be seen living with and nurturing the Child-That-Could Never-Be-Born.

There are, evidently, any number of effective treatments in the "modern" manner, where the young wife should be a complex, highly civilized creature like a finely-made watch, with not less than nineteen jewels and adjusted to five positions. In such a story the husband might require to be less finely tempered, of simpler mental habit and more primitive in his allegiances. But an outstanding disability assails us on the threshold of any such conception of the story: the mixture of rationalism in unstable combinations with the emotion we wish to evoke. It is all very well to assert that we shall bring a just intellect to the performance; no doubt we shall; no doubt our treatment will sprinkle ideas as judiciously as a good cook works raisins into a cake. But the raisins may all go to the bottom of the cake and we have no such control over the mind of the reader as the cook has over her oven.

The author or playwright makes the cake, the auditor or reader bakes it. We have not forgotten, have we, the mind of the reader, that most vital of all the human relationships which fiction involves? And the theater, it must be admitted, is a much safer place for the drama of ideas than a novel. In the first place, the auditor is not alone in judgment; he is influenced by those others seated all around him even when they laugh and he is disposed to cry. In the second place, and far more importantly, the playwright's ideas can scarcely dominate the emotion of those actual human beings with their bodies, faces, gestures and tones of voice. In fact, they are lucky if they survive them.

Why, the thought may occur to us, did Thomas Hardy choose the peasants of Wessex as his actors and the simplicities of heath, crags and moorland for his theater? Without prohibiting other explanations or weakening the force of what was probably an instinctive preference, we may well believe that he understood the necessity of so simplifying his treatment as to make his subject seem entirely general of mankind and the application of its issue universal. He could have elaborated as much as he pleased on Eustacia Vye and Tess and Jude, but the result would have only been to delimit, qualify and confuse. He had to do with life and death and immortality, with these things and essentially these only, whether by affirmation or denial. A few physical forms in their relation to the surrounding meadow or plain and the overarching heaven were his subject. Their small gestures must be isolated, they must seem as diminished as ants at one moment and as real as self at others, and always they must appear in a right perspective and a right lighting, despite the continual manipulation of light and distance, of which, so far as possible, the observer must remain unaware. Naturally Hardy did not always succeed; there are times when his people appear staged; there are more frequent times when they seem as puppets and we feel that they jerk and dance at the end of twitched strings—though this effect, indeed, was a portion of the author's purpose, since he proposed a theory of mannikins senselessly handled by a blind Will.

Nevertheless in his method there is much to our purpose, perhaps the more because we have no edge of rationalism to whet. We have in fact no ax to grind, no philosophy to expound, no remedies to offer. We have merely an experience to share; and we leave the reader untroubled in his attitude toward birth control and in any and all of his ideas, prejudices, opinions and arguments upon love, marriage and racial propagation. We cannot so leave him unless we shear away all those particulars of background and environment which serve to introduce such confusions. The woman and the man of our fiction must have both the remoteness, and the nearness in humanity, of Hardy characters. They must be of the world and yet in a world apart. In a sense, they are to exist for a space suspended between earth and heaven; and we may well feel that the seacoast and a lighthouse are the fittest setting for such an existence as theirs.

In such a setting, it is unlikely that we should ever find any but a girl or woman of simple and uncomplicated feelings. But it is very possible that we might encounter a man of sophisticated experience, even a quite young man, whose sickness of the world had had the effect of driving him into a self-imposed exile from it. And his marriage with the young girl more or less native to that spot would not necessarily be compassed in cynicism; a touching faith in the power of her youth, her freshness, her artless goodness to restore his own soul could lead him.

The nationality of these two people is of some importance. A racial psychology well-known in its outlines and luminously expressed in behavior is to be sought for; and this will seem to exclude English or American nationality and, except we were a Bojer of a Chekhov, Scandinavian and Russian. This may seem pretty well to fix the choice upon the Latin peoples, but Latins are what we really want from the psychological standpoint. Italian, Spanish, French? Each is brightly possible, but the French psychology is, if not less idiomatic, more generally understood. Our lighthouse stands on the seacoast of France, then, possibly where some river meets the Atlantic. Everything else is abandoned for a time, while we wander up and down the French coast in an array of books, while we dip into the article on "Lighthouses" in the Encyclopedia Britannica (on maritime subjects the British authorities are amplest and best), and while we discover that French engineering has contributed much to the science of *le phare*. We visit a lighthouse, continue to read, forget what we have read and go back to our story.

It is a return, for the present, to those two people, and somehow, we do not quite know how, the action has advanced while we were completely inattentive to *that*. But this is the way of such an affair. The difficulties into which the creative process leads are rather often not to be surmounted directly. One refuses the impossible obstacle, strays off in some other direction, browses on this or that bit of succulence, taking unconscious steps hither and yon—and looks up to find oneself on the other side of the hedge or stone wall, not at all aware of how one got there or what gap one has strayed through. So far as we can detect the process we seem to have inferred that our young girl would be quite incapable of consenting to the course that would almost certainly save her life; a natural passivity, a horror of the unknown, a feeling of sacredness for the first-born and a clinging to delusive hope all conspiring to fix her attitude. Her husband, of so much more worldly experience, to whom in these few months she had become everything, would hesitate at nothing which offered the prospect of her recovery. But he would have to sit by her bedside through days and nights and weeks and see her die.

And immediately the conviction is strong upon us that the rest is his story. She was a girl without a history, apart from the simple annals of the poor, when she came into our story, whereas he had a history like that of a Joseph Conrad hero, coming into our vision for the first time with "the secret of his moral ruin locked in his breast." She has been his brief and complete redemption, and now the redeeming agent is taken away from him after a protracted and terrible struggle in which his hands have been shackled while he was compelled to look on. Peer Holm in *The Great Hunger* confronted no deeper tragedy.

It might seem that the effect would be to induce him to fling himself from the balcony that rims the beacon in that lofty tower. But there is a residue of health and strength in nerves and mind. The attempt at suicide was made years before, when his moral ruin appeared complete, and ignobly failed. The result of that failure, where the essential fiber is still sound, is to erase suicide as a possible means of escape thereafter. Possibly some force of superstition or some notion of fatality is the cause, but the evidence from actual life seems to be fairly conclusive on the point.

He does not kill himself, nor does he go mad. He searches for a meaning. That life in those years before his self-exile to the pharos had many times seemed meaningless. And then he had come here, had found *her*, and significance had flowed into his life, had inundated all that dismal past, as if he had existed only to run a course that might bring him hither, to find her waiting for him. He has had this short time with her, and now she has been snatched from him in a fashion utterly senseless and still scarcely credible. What has happened? And to whom? To him or to her? Sometimes he fancies it has befallen them both, and that he is dead with her—or rather, since he cannot find her, that she is living somewhere but he himself is dead.

All these wild and torturing fancies pass from him and still the meaning is not found.

His mind is taken up with a variety of images growing out of his surroundings. There is the light that he tends, not of the fixed type but a flashing and piercing ray that sweeps in a kindling arc for a few seconds and then expires. A wink toward Heaven, a mighty effort by man, but far too feeble to rank as a gesture. The bland white unseeingness of fog, the black abstraction of the midnight skies, the restless tossing of the indifferent ocean in its sleep close down upon the tiny gleam. Man has made a tremendous attempt, assembling and focusing with anxious care millions of candlepower, and perhaps he has signaled successfully to some fellow-man close by, and perhaps he has not. But God? From God there is no tokening.

This lighthouse is very old. A pharos of some kind has existed on these wave-washed rocks through many centuries. Even in the days of the Merovingian kings, a sort of raised platform had been constructed here on which bonfires were lit at night for the guidance of ships seeking the mouth of the river. This primitive beacon was later replaced with a stone tower; and in the time of Saint Louis the tower was enlarged, and a tiny chapel was incorporated in it. But the great transformation came in the reign of Louis XIV. The tower was entirely rebuilt; above the rooms of the keeper a tiny royal suite was fitted up, exquisitely luxurious. Louis Quatorze slept in the bed one night, and after that the suite was occupied at intervals, for short periods, by this or that one of the King's favorites. A Cardinal or two stayed briefly in the tower, celebrating mass in the chapel; and a mass for seamen is said annually at the altar down to this day.

The tower itself is called after Saint Christopher and the beacon known as the St. Christophe light.

Once, quite early in his young wife's illness, the husband had fetched a priest for her, and after the visitor had comforted the sick girl, those two men had talked—the husband fiercely, the priest with a firm sadness. Almost the only other visitor during that time had been the attending physician, in whom could be seen a conflict of feeling—impatience to intervene and save the mother, contempt for what seems to him to be her superstitious refusal of help, admiration for her resolute endurance, a kind of awe of the thing that can sustain her. But ordinarily the keeper is alone at the lighthouse with his wife and an old French peasant woman, their servant—a somewhat gross, comfortable creature and yet in some respects a little girl at heart. Her name is Thérèse, and she cherishes a dog and a cat; it is impossible to recognize in her the thin child with dark eyes who once in a mountain village, dressed all in white with a veil and a handful of flowers, walked at a measured pace with other girls, fingers joined and eyes kept rigidly downward, to make her first communion.

The story is building, but the issue for that man, the keeper, remains obscure for us—as obscure as for him while he searches the sea and the heaven for a meaning in what has befallen him. And at length that also appears.

The meaning is love. He looks upon a world which for centuries has witnessed the forms of cruelty and the death of saints. He has made the mistake once made by a very great poet, who sought "to justify the ways of God to man." On the other hand, any attempt at justifying the ways of man to God is impossible. Only love can be felt, only selflessness can be practiced. It was because she felt the one and exercised the other to the utmost that this young girl whom he had married placed herself among the very greatest. There are many rites of death, but there is only one rite of the ever-living, only one assertion that the Divine is really present on earth and among men. He spends one night alone in the little chapel, for he has asked to be relieved of his duties at the lighthouse. In the morning he goes ashore, to commence his studies at a seminary of the Benedictines.

Treatment. A great deal of nonsense has been written about literary style, but it is certain that *A Wink Toward Heaven* cannot avoid the problem of style. Let us, therefore, consider the point a moment, with sanity and without dogma.

The style of the outline just given, if indeed it can be said to have any, is not for a moment to be regarded. But something as to the possible verbal treatment may be learned from a re-perusal of such fiction as Walter Pater's *Marius the Epicurean,* Joseph Conrad's *Victory,*

Flaubert's *Madame Bovary,* and Hardy's *Tess of D'Urbervilles.*

No one can doubt the necessity of a kind of atmosphere which must begin to be created by the first sentence of the book and which must be sustained, without faltering, until the last. Within this envelopment all the other effects of the tale are to be wrought, this and that emotion is to be struck and the sound of it allowed to die, the pitch of emotion is to be extremely altered, there are to be deafening *forti* and whispering *pianissimi,* and a long crescendo culminating in the death of the young mother is to be succeeded by exhaustion without the least sense of anti-climax.

She is not the subject, only part of it, and this determines at once the point of view. The case is somewhat like that of *Madame Bovary,* so brilliantly examined by Lubbock in *The Craft of Fiction,* where we are accustomed carelessly to assume that Emma is the story's all-in-all, but where the fact is quite different. In any one who seriously proposed to reveal the young wife's mind during her profound and fatal adventure, we should not know whether chiefly to applaud the courage or the rashness. It is not easy to imagine how such a revealment could be made convincing; it is even harder to suppose that its nature could be satisfying to the reader, whose simplicity of mind might be equal to hers but who would then almost certainly expect from her, in the circumstances, mental grandeurs dazzling to his own brain. But, of course, unless we were two or more times violently to shift the point of view, *her* mind would not serve, since it could give us *his* experience neither before nor after those few months allotted them together. The point of view throughout is the husband's.

No one will suppose that the first personal form is meant. That is much too unlikely, and it unduly circumscribes our vision of the whole history. And for our purpose the conventional form of auctorial omniscience is a little cold, a little too undramatic, somewhat too lacking in the suspense which an author may legitimately create by demanding that the reader merely watch his character and judge him by his behavior. The "dramatization of a mind," as Lubbock terms it, is the ideal method for *A Wink Toward Heaven,* ideal meaning, as Lubbock explains, that method which makes the most of the subject's possibilities while incurring the fewest disablements.

This way of narration is fully discussed in *The Craft of Fiction,* where the study of its use is taken from Henry James's *The Ambassadors* and his *The Wings of the Dove.* Only the consciousness is offered to the reader; the depths of the mind, where vital purpose is slowly forming and the fundamental alterations of attitude proceed, is shut off from view; the novelist does not assert his knowledge of that, partly, no doubt, as a matter of credence, but much more because suspense and drama are promoted by the abstention. The reader becomes the character around whom the action takes place and through whose eyes it is viewed—whose mind is dramatized—and knows fully what that one is conscious of, but no more. It is a way of bringing the reader directly into the tale and is, at its best, unquestionably what Lubbock declares it to be, the acutest form of dramatization in the novel. To overcome the disabilities of the method, resort is had, whenever the action moves into scene, to shutting off the view of that mind. In a conversation we know no more of the thoughts of our chosen character than we do of the thoughts of the others present, and thus the chosen character is to a partial degree objectively established. The view of his mind may also be withheld from us at other moments, but the point is that we do not then adopt another pair of eyes, nor enter even momentarily into some one else's mind. And where it is necessary the point of view may be almost imperceptibly shifted without any disturbance of the general effect, as in *Madame Bovary,* where Flaubert opens Emma's mind and then abandons her view, offering another instead, his own, from just behind her shoulder.

The method is not to be confused with the more recent "stream of consciousness" manner of realism. If the special qualities of Henry James make the study of method in his novels too difficult and distracting, one may, perhaps (though only perhaps), find this form of dramatization more comprehensibly shown in many passages from Marcel Proust. Here is an all-too-brief one from the second volume of *Swann's Way:*

These new manners, indifferent, listless, irritable, which Odette now adopted with Swann, undoubtedly made him suffer; but he did not realize how much he suffered; since it had been with a regular progression, day after day, that Odette chilled towards him, it was only by directly contrasting what she was today with what she had been at first that he could have measured the extent of the change that had taken place. Now this change was his deep, his secret wound, which pained him day and night, and whenever he felt that his thoughts were straying too near it, he would quickly turn them into another channel for fear of being made to suffer too keenly. He might say to himself in a vague way: "There was a time when Odette loved me more," but he never formed any definite picture of that time. Just as he had in his study a cupboard at which he contrived never to look, which he turned aside to avoid passing whenever he entered or left the room, because in one of its drawers he had locked away the chrysanthemum which she had given him on one of those first evenings when he had taken her home in his carriage, and the letters in which she said: "Why did you not forget your heart also? I should never have let you have that back," and "At whatever hour of the day or night you may need me, just send me a word, and dispose of me as you please," so there was a place in his heart to which he would never allow his thoughts to trespass too near, forcing them, if need be, to evade it by a long course of reasoning so that they should not have to pass within reach of it; the place in which lingered his memories of happy days.[12]

This example, it should be noted, is a pictorial or summarized dramatization of Swann's mind; it recapitulates a recurring situation. It might, of course, have been scenic and particular, and then we should have seen Swann on a given day edging elaborately away from the cupboard while his consciousness made a similar circuit of his spirit's wound.

But exactly this manner of pictorial dramatization in the young husband's mind is our perfect means for traversing his history in the days before he came to the

[12] *Swann's Way.* Volume II. Translated by C. K. Scott Moncrieff. The American edition consists of English publishers' sheets bound and issued by Henry Holt & Company (1922). Pp. 144-145.

lighthouse and to *her*—for traversing that history without its taking too much room or too much delaying the advance of present event. Honest notice to the reader and the binding requirement of atmosphere almost certainly dictate that we shall begin the book at the lighthouse, probably with our man's arrival there to take the post of keeper, at which time, very likely, he first meets that young girl (who is or might be the now homeless daughter of the former lightkeeper, not long dead). But as soon as we fix on this entrance into the story, we have the problem of all our man's past—no new problem in composing a novel but often, as here, a serious one. The easy and rather slip-shod solution is to drop back for a whole chapter or several, and by a consecutive narrative bring the matter up to date. This can be improved upon in our instance; no doubt some pieces of our man's history must very likely be given soon after we have begun, but they can be comparatively small tracts, not an unwieldy load flung down whole upon the reader's attention so soon as the first chapter is off. Let us resolve to make them always the dramatization of his mind, and as far as possible to give them occasion in the present. Some word or sight or look or gesture will be enough to make his mind stir over the past, and that brief movement, recorded by us, will be a bit of the necessary documentation that must be got before the reader.

While on the subject another and excellent method of putting the reader in possession of essentials ought to be spoken of. It is a scene involving conversation, reasonable in itself yet so constructed as to "place" one or more of the characters. In his critical preface to *The*

Ambassadors, Henry James calls attention to the way in which a conversation between Strether and Maria Gostrey, near the beginning, "puts the reader in possession of all the past facts of the situation which it is necessary for him to know." As Mr. Lubbock points out, "a *scene* thus takes the place of that 'harking back to make up,' which is apt to appear as a lump of narrative shortly after the opening of a story."

What should be the general proportioning of the book? After as mature consideration as we can give to this in advance—for some drastic alteration of structure not seldom appears during writing—we may conclude that the three parts, or natural divisions, should be of about equal length. The divisions make themselves, though they need not be marked off in the book itself unless we deem fit to mark them. The first extends to the beginning of the illness, including all or nearly all of the retrospective material; the second begins with the illness, or more accurately, with the discovery of its nature, or at least of its seriousness and the premonition of its nature. It continues until the young wife's death, or death and burial. The third division is our man's after-history. This would naturally be conducted to the door of the seminary; it need not exclude some glimpse of him in the years of his service as a priest, by way of a coda; and such a coda might have a special value, as showing that the whole substance of our novel was but the threshold of a renowned career—something sunk into the background and even unknown, so far as the world went; and we could give a sight of an effect admired by those about the man but proceeding from a cause to them unknown.

It might appear at first that our story ought to move as rapidly as could be managed in its early part. Our first thought is naturally that it scarcely begins until the toxæmia has become manifest. That, we hurriedly conclude, is the "situation." But we are not dealing in situations primarily, and our real drama is a goodly portion of a man's life—goodly in the sense of intensity, of the "life by values." If we do not spend time, words and pains on the circumstances of the marriage, and the changes in our man's life resulting from it even in a very few months, we lose much of the power and significance that ought to be apparent as he stands looking upon that wasted face on the pillow, as he argues vehemently or entreats, and as he kneels in an agony of love and despair by the bedside of that girl who fears death yet stays to meet it.

We must convey the rapturousness of those few months of an unmarred union. They are to have all the idyllic quality of those months passed by Hardy's Tess at Talbothays, on the dairy farm in the Froom Valley, when she was wooed by Angel Clare. The retrospections should have a value of enhancing our man's sense of the perfect bliss into which he has fallen. He has crossed intellectual deserts and has struggled in sensuality's quicksands, to come at last into this green oasis and this pleasant place. How well we can see these two in their tower, which might be of ivory or something yet more precious—thick-walled about, as if they lived in a marriage ring, or standing together, clinging together on that circular balcony which lifts a tiny security two hundred feet above the beating surf.

Coming to the second division of the book, we shall as a matter of course inform ourselves, by consulting medical texts and by conversations, with some fullness on the matter of toxæmia; yet almost everything that we learn in this manner will be discarded. We cannot afford anything remotely resembling a realistic study. There must now and then be the actuality imparted by a touch of physiological detail, but that is all. These touches must not be technically stated. Insofar as they are not derived from our man's own observation, they may well come from the lips of old Thérèse, that blend of inquisitiveness, gossip, kindness and superstitious solicitude who is the young wife's only nurse and attendant in most of that ordeal. It is of great importance in this stretch of the book to indicate both the real and the exaggerated perception of time. From the first serious illness to death will scarcely exceed a month, since there is complete starvation the whole time, but to those watching most anxiously the fatal course of the malady the time appears much longer. To the husband it is as years of life.

In the last part of the story, after her death, we shall find it a wise expedient—and a perfectly justifiable—to shut off with a yet more scrupulous care all glimpses of the depths of our man's mind. At no time, to be sure, do we propose to go below the level of his consciousness, but in such periods of great suffering the consciousness becomes lighter, more limited, more than ordinarily superficial. A part of it is either numbed or else goes about its harder business in a kind of secrecy. One cannot say that it is temporarily added to the subconscious but that is the practical effect. What remains as consciousness is more than ever mere surface, mere sensory perception with weakened responses or even lack of any response. The customary stir of life passes before the eyes, is caught by the ears, moves under the fingertips and is almost automatically noted or recorded, but the nervous centers are indifferent.

The conscious mind is a mere rim around a vast woe, and must be so represented. It is a magnified case of that avoidance which we just saw described by Proust in the quoted passage from *Swann's Way*. Although our pages dealing with our man after his wife's death may turn out to be as numerous as those in either of the preceding divisions of the book, their character will be quite apart, and their length will be constituted, very largely, by aimless and even meaningless little accidents from day to day. The exact method may be seen in some chapters in Henry James's *The Wings of the Dove,* and it is beautifully described by Lubbock.

It is the superficial play of thought that is put before us. The light stir and vibration of Milly's sensibility from hour to hour is all that we actually see; for the most part it is very light, very easy and airy, as she moves with her odd poetry and grace and freedom. . . . She is a rare and innocent creature, receptive and perceptive, thrown into the middle of a situation in which she sees everything, excepting only the scheme by which it is proposed to make use of her. Of that she knows nothing as yet; her troubles are purely her own, and gradually, it is hard to say where or how, we discover what they are. They are much too deeply buried in her mind to appear casually upon the surface at any time; but now and then, in the drama of her meditation, there is a strange look or a pause or a sudden hasty motion which is unexplained, which is portentous, which betrays everything. Presently her great hidden facts have passed into the possession of the reader *whole,* so to speak—not broken into detail, bit by bit, not pieced together descriptively, but so implied and suggested that at some moment or other they spring up complete and solid in the reader's attention. . . .

Not to walk straight up to the fact and put it into phrases, but to *surround* the fact, and so to detach it inviolate—such is Henry James's manner of dramatizing it.[13]

Similarly, we shall see our man as going about the routine of the lighthouse with only now and then the strangeness which betrays his trouble. Involved some evening in the advanced mathematical computations which are the basis of lighthouse engineering, his mind will slip off into the metaphysical inferences, and the pen in his hand will attempt to put down on paper unknown but not unimaginable equations. Our task will be only to note what he writes down and his look as he pens it. To old Thérèse, perhaps, he will not appear very different—a little more noticeably kind, a little absent, and not eating properly.

For how can we pretend to know what is going on in that mind which does not itself know its processes? Toward the end, no doubt, the final decision will "pass into the possession of the reader whole," as it seems to pass into his own consciousness, so that when he leaves that tower for the last time and bends his steps in one certain direction no explanation of any sort will be neces-

[13] *The Craft of Fiction,* Chap. XII.

sary, it will be a natural thing, like sitting down to a meal, or lying down to sleep, or rising after one wakes, or drawing a fresh breath to take the place of the one just expelled.

CHAPTER VI

THIRD STUDY IN METHOD: TRANSCENDENTAL REALISM, OR "PROPHECY"

WE TRIED, in the preceding chapter, to distinguish between novels which endeavor to achieve the effect of ancient fiction and those others which are transcendental without the loss of finite aims. The distinction is loose, like all the divisions one sets up in the arts. Literature cannot be sorted and placed in pigeonholes; the fewer classifications we attempt, the fewer generalizations we venture upon, the better for us as we come into increasing touch with books old and new. But certainly between the novel of character with both its feet on the ground and works like Melville's *Moby Dick* there is a great gap or gulf. It will scarcely seem arbitrary or excessively meticulous if we essay to fix a point somewhere around midway between the two extremes. The novel of character abates not a jot of its realism for the sake of emotions that realism cannot evoke; at the other extreme any demanded sacrifice of realism is cheerfully made in the interest of emotion that may be at once lofty, strange and unstinted. There is obviously a class of novels in which a limited surrender is accorded, novels with one foot on the ground, so to speak; and it is these that we have now to consider.

The examples chosen may not be the best for the purpose and no effort will be made to force them into line. The purpose of our study is not dogmatic, but suggestive merely. Assertions may be looked upon as generally no more than the "Resolveds" with which a debate begins —some form of statement or assertion being essential in order that the discussion may take form.

Wuthering Heights, by Emily Brontë, is possibly the first enduring example of what we are calling transcendental realism. Its importance is that it followed the so-called Gothic novel, of the type of Horace Walpole's *The Castle of Otranto,* and secured to the full the heightened emotional effects which the Gothic novel strove for. The method of that striving had been about equally ridiculous and pathetic—gloomy castles, dismal sounds, ghosts and so on. The whole effort had perished, and Jane Austen had satirized it in *Northanger Abbey,* and about thirty more years had passed by. The romantic movement, extending from the French Revolution, and destined to culminate politically in 1848, was nearly over when *Wuthering Heights* appeared. It was in no sense, of course, intended to be a satire on Miss Austen or the reply of an ancient spirit to the novel of character's self-satisfaction and complacence in finitude. Yet in a certain view it is just that.

Tolstoy's *War and Peace* is possibly the most discussed novel in all literature with the single probable exception of *Madame Bovary.* There may be nothing new to say of it, but it must be considered here because of its preeminence among the novels that blend realism with transcendental effects.

For a very recent novel, E. M. Forster's *A Passage to*

India has been chosen; and also because the realism is more scrupulous than in either *Wuthering Heights* or *War and Peace*. Of the three, Miss Brontë's novel is least realistic, so that our study will progress a little away from transcendentalism and toward realism.

Lastly, as heretofore, we shall conduct our own laboratory experiment in the fusion of these two qualities of fiction.

I. EMILY BRONTE

Wuthering Heights

If as we read *Wuthering Heights* it seems an incredible performance for a secluded young lady who died of consumption at the age of thirty, we are prompted to the reflection that everything about the Brontë sisters is incredible. A north Irishman called Patrick Prunty, born in a thatched cabin in County Down, the son of a Protestant weaver and the Roman Catholic village belle, raised himself to be a Cambridge scholar and parson—Patrick Brontë, new style. He married a gentle Wesleyan girl from Cornwall who soon died, leaving him with five little girls and a boy.

"One can imagine the family society," comments Rose Macaulay, in her Introduction to the Modern Library edition of *Wuthering Heights*, "even more sufficient to itself than are most large families—the five motherless, clever, delicate little sisters (the two eldest died under twelve) and the one bad little brother, growing up together in the charge of a queer father and a bored Cornish aunt, reading anything they could lay their hands on, discussing politics and public affairs in the nursery, led by the amazing eldest infant, Maria (who, if at the age of eleven she really talked like Helen Burns in *Jane Eyre,* perhaps did well not to survive it), walking through the moorland country in the appalling Yorkshire weather, forever scribbling, as little girls will, stories and poems."

The three sisters surviving childhood, Charlotte, Emily and Anne, first published a book of poems, under the pen names of Currer, Ellis, and Acton Bell (in which it will be noticed, the initials of each are preserved). Of their work, from which they were cut off so terribly soon by death, *Jane Eyre,* by Currer Bell, or Charlotte Brontë; *Wuthering Heights,* by Ellis Bell, or Emily Brontë; and some of the poems of Emily Brontë (Ellis Bell) are perhaps all we care about to-day.

Through the delays sometimes incident to publication —more common then than now—*Jane Eyre* was given to the world before *Wuthering Heights,* which in some quarters was taken to be an earlier book by the author of *Jane Eyre.* Partly on this account, but only partly, there was a general failure to do justice to *Wuthering Heights;* and Emily Brontë dying in a year had no time to see the change which should come about—a change which has put her novel far above Charlotte's. Indeed, eighty years have passed over Emily's grave and her book lives on, its strange power unweakened.

That power excites wonder and awe, of itself, but has always seemed the more marvelous because Emily Brontë lived in virtual retirement from the world. This condition explains a good deal, no doubt. It explains why she should make a housekeeper talk like a woman of much better education. It also explains, to a degree, why she could create a figure like Heathcliff, of inhuman cruelty; as her sister Charlotte tells us, Emily heard all the stories of the countryside and they fed an imagination unchecked by personal intercourse with the people of whom they were told. But when all the circumstances, including Celtic blood, have been duly weighed, the explanations fall quite short; we are driven back upon something that is outside the action of cause and effect as we understand it. Emily's own line suggests something:

> He for whom I wait thus often comes to me.

And Charlotte, in her preface to *Wuthering Heights,* puts it honestly:

> The writer who possesses the creative gift owns something of which he is not always master—something that, at times, strangely wills and works for itself. . . . Your share in it has been to work passively under dictates you neither delivered nor could question.

Wuthering Heights is often called faulty in construction; it is not so easy to say how it could have been bettered. Joseph Conrad had a liking for subtitles and one of his books is described as "a novel between two notes." Emily Brontë's work is a novel between two glimpses. We open with a good look at, and an experience at the hands of, Heathcliff—"we" being the reader and one Lockwood, the tenant at Thrushcross Grange. The look and experience includes Heathcliff's odd household in the dwelling called Wuthering (Yorkshire for Weathering)

Heights. A churlish young man named Hareton Earnshaw, Heathcliff's daughter-in-law, and two servants, comprise the lot, unless we include the dogs that set upon visitors.

Mr. Lockwood tells us of calling on Heathcliff to introduce himself. In spite of a most inhospitable reception he resolves to call again; this time for tea. He meets with unparalleled rudeness from every one in the house. A heavy snowstorm rages, the dogs knock him down and maul him, and at last he is grudgingly quartered for the night. In the room to which the housekeeper conducts him the names "Catherine Earnshaw," "Catherine Linton," "Catherine Heathcliff" are scrawled on the paint. He picks up an old Testament from a heap of mildewed books and reads from what is apparently a diary kept by Catherine Earnshaw as a child—a spirited child engaged with Heathcliff, in rebelling against her brother, Hindley. At length Lockwood dozes off into a dreary dream of an endless sermon, half wakes to the scratching of a fir-bough against a window, and sinks into a nightmare—one of the few whose full terror has been prisoned in a piece of writing.

This time, I remembered I was lying in the oak closet, and I heard distinctly the gusty wind, and the driving of the snow; I heard, also, the fir-bough repeat its teasing sound, and ascribed it to the right cause: but it annoyed me so much, that I resolved to silence it, if possible; and, I thought, I rose and endeavored to unhasp the casement. The hook was soldered into the staple: a circumstance observed by me when awake, but forgotten. "I must stop it, nevertheless!" I muttered, knocking my knuckles through the glass, and stretching an arm out to seize the importunate branch; instead of which, my fingers closed on the fingers of a little, ice-cold hand! The intense horror of nightmare came over me: I tried to draw back my arm, but the hand clung to it, and a most melancholy voice sobbed, "Let me in—let me in!" "Who are you?" I asked, struggling, meanwhile, to disengage myself. "Catherine Linton," it replied, shiveringly (why did I think of *Linton*? I had read *Earnshaw* twenty times for Linton); "I'm come home: I'd lost my way on the moor!" As it spoke, I discerned, obscurely, a child's face looking through the window. Terror made me cruel; and, finding it useless to attempt shaking the creature off, I pulled its wrist on to the broken pane, and rubbed it to and fro till the blood ran down and soaked the bedclothes: still it wailed, "Let me in!" and maintained its tenacious gripe, almost maddening me with fear.

In the end, Lockwood lets out a shriek that brings Heathcliff; and Heathcliff is quite evidently perturbed or worse; it seems that no one has business in *this* room. Without explanation he orders Lockwood to take his own bed.

I obeyed, so far as to quit the chamber; when, ignorant where the narrow lobbies led, I stood still, and was witness, involuntarily, to a piece of superstition on the part of my landlord, which belied, oddly, his apparent sense. He got on to the bed, and wrenched open the lattice, bursting, as he pulled at it, into an uncontrollable passion of tears. "Come in! Come in!" he sobbed. "Cathy, do come. Oh, do—*once* more! Oh! my heart's darling; hear me *this* time, Catherine, at last!" The spectre showed a spectre's ordinary caprice: it gave no sign of being; but the snow and wind whirled wildly through, even reaching my station, and blowing out the light.

Back at Thrushcross Grange, away from that house where the reality of daytime is hardly less terrifying than the nights—for Heathcliff is of violent temper, quite ready to strike his daughter-in-law—Lockwood is unable to rest until he knows who these people at Wuthering Heights may be. He finds a perfect mine of information about them in his housekeeper, Mrs. Dean. With a few slight and unimportant interludes, the rest of the book is her story, until near the very end.

Wuthering Heights had belonged to the Earnshaws. Mrs. Dean's mother had been their servant and Mrs. Dean as a child had played with little Hindley and Catherine Earnshaw. Returning from a three days' journey to Liverpool, Mr. Earnshaw had brought back, bundled in his greatcoat, a dirty, ragged, black-haired child, big enough to walk and talk, found starving in the city streets. The waif was ill-received, but after some days was treated as one of the family and named Heathcliff, after a child the Earnshaws had lost. Almost from the first little Catherine became fond of the stranger, while Hindley hated him. Heathcliff seemed a sullen, patient child; Mr. Earnshaw took his part against Hindley's truculence; a lasting feud was set afoot; and when Mr. Earnshaw died, Hindley brought a wife home with him and Heathcliff was degraded to work with the farmhands. Under his wife's influence, Hindley used his sister badly also. The attachment between Catherine and Heathcliff was naturally only made stronger.

At that time the Lintons lived at Thrushcross Grange, and two children were there, Edgar and Isabella. In their contacts with Catherine and Heathcliff, Heathcliff is always put in the wrong, punished by Hindley Earnshaw and made an outcast. Hindley Earnshaw's wife gives birth to a boy, Hareton, but dies soon after, leaving her husband quite indifferent to the child in his loss. From now on Hindley Earnshaw begins to sink into the evilest ways; Heathcliff is neglected utterly or treated in a fashion to make a fiend of a saint. Catherine remains loyal to him, but can do little.

A little later, and Edgar Linton is seeking to marry Catherine Earnshaw, a quick-tempered, imperious girl. Mrs. Dean, our narrator, is in the family as Hareton Earnshaw's nurse—Nelly, they call her. One day Catherine talks with Nelly about Edgar Linton and Heathcliff. Acknowledging that she loves Heathcliff, she declares that she is going to marry Edgar Linton. Heathcliff is "more myself than I am; whatever our souls are made of, his and mine are the same." But Hindley has utterly degraded him. Catherine does not intend to be separated from Heathcliff. "Edgar must shake off his antipathy, and tolerate him, at least." She and Heathcliff would be beggars, "whereas, if I marry Linton, I can aid Heathcliff to rise, and place him out of my brother's power." And when Nelly calls this the worst of motives, "it is not," retorts Catherine, "it is the best!" And she continues:

"The others were the satisfaction of my whims: and for Edgar's sake, too, to satisfy him. This is for the sake of one who comprehends in his person my feelings to Edgar and myself. I cannot express it; but surely you and everybody have a notion that there is or should be an existence of yours beyond you. What were the use of my creation, if I were entirely contained here? My great miseries in this world have been Heathcliff's miseries, and I watched and felt each from the beginning: my great thought in living is himself. If all else perished, and *he* remained, *I* should still continue to be; and if all else remained, and he were annihilated, the universe would turn to a mighty stranger: I should not seem a part of it. My love for Linton is like the foliage in the woods: time will change it, I'm well aware, as winter changes the trees. My love for Heathcliff resembles the eternal rocks beneath: a source of little visible delight, but necessary. Nelly, I *am* Heathcliff!"

Up to a point, the point where she says that it would degrade her to marry him, Heathcliff has overheard this conversation, as Nelly becomes aware when she catches a glimpse of him stealing away. He totally disappears, an event which provokes in Catherine serious illness. After her recovery she becomes Linton's wife, and Nelly goes with her to Thrushcross Grange to live.

Some years have elapsed since Heathcliff's disappearance, not so much time since Catherine's marriage, when Heathcliff reappears. Catherine is wild with delight and Edgar Linton is more or less constrained to receive Heathcliff civilly. The latter frequents Wuthering Heights on a new footing; what that is does not transpire at once. But gradually Nelly comes to know that Heathcliff has a definite hold on Hindley, now a gambler and sot, and is corrupting and coarsening young Hareton.

Matters between Edgar Linton and Heathcliff are not long in coming to a head. Edgar's sister, Isabella, fatuously falls in love with Heathcliff. Catherine cruelly tells her secret to Heathcliff in Isabella's presence. Heathcliff's response is brutal indifference. In the crisis between Edgar and Heathcliff, Linton strikes the other. Catherine is thrown into convulsions of fury, threatening her mind, such is her weakness since Heathcliff's disappearance gave her brain fever. There is, besides, another complication, for she is pregnant.

To strike at Linton, Heathcliff runs off with Isabella and marries her. Catherine dies giving birth to a daughter, Catherine Linton. Heathcliff had imprisoned Isabella at Wuthering Heights, whence she escapes to London or thereabouts, remaining there till her death, when she leaves a boy of above twelve, her son and Heathcliff's.

In the course of a lifetime, Heathcliff assembles the materials for a complete revenge and is able to put it into gradual execution and to bring it to utter fulfillment. He sees Hindley Earnshaw, his ancient oppressor, live through years of ruin and disgrace and finally die. Wuthering Heights and every penny of Hindley's is at last Heathcliff's. But possibly more important to Heathcliff is the fact that Hindley's son, Hareton, is devoted to himself, and he has been able to treat Hareton with every bit of the degradation *he* had once suffered. Hareton, for example, though now grown, can neither read nor write. Heathcliff has also been able to spoil the life of Edgar Linton's sister. But the completion of his revenge is involved in a match between his feeble and girlish son, Linton, and Catherine Linton, Edgar's daughter. Fortune favors him in this project, one calculated to give the final torturing twist to Edgar Linton, who dies unhappy. Young Linton is a doomed consumptive but keeps alive long enough for the marriage. After his death the household at Wuthering Heights settles into the composition that Mr. Lockwood found when he went to pay his polite tenant's call—Heathcliff, the younger Catherine, Hareton Earnshaw and two servants. Heathcliff has added by inheritance Thrushcross Grange and all Edgar Linton's property to his own.

So much for the story of the housekeeper, Nelly (Mrs. Dean). Another direct glimpse of the surviving actors and the situation is afforded by Mr. Lockwood's next visit. An interval of about nine months passes and we have Mr. Lockwood's account of a passing visit to Wuthering Heights. Heathcliff has died. Mrs. Dean gives Lockwood his account of all that has happened. The younger Catherine and Hareton Earnshaw have come through enmity and difficulty into the relationship of lovers, and Catherine has gone a material distance toward civilizing and educating Hareton. The picture that makes the profounder impression and lingers in the mind is that of Heathcliff, gradually declining, dying of no ordinary mortal illness, but of a strange condition, one would think. The strangeness seems partly to consist in a surfeit of revenge and a turning of revenge upon the revenger in the fancy that Hareton more and more resembles the lost Catherine; and partly Heathcliff's strangeness is plainly the result of a growing belief that he can reach to his dead love. He haunts the moors, in those last days, and if one can believe the story of a boy found out there sobbing with fright, "Heathcliff and a woman" were on the moor after his death.

This, in poor substance and pale outline, is Emily Brontë's book. Thirty years after Jane Austen came *Wuthering Heights,* with all the effect, if without any of the intention, of saying:

"Fiction is not to be tamed. In its origin it was coextensive with human nature, and we need to keep it so. To confine it to a sweetly reasonable treatment of the more plausible aspects of human nature is a terrible mistake. There are emotions never exhibited in the parlor and they are still at least as influential as those aroused over the tea cups. The Gothic novel was absurd, no doubt. But it recognized forces that are not deprived of their existence by ignoring or denying them. They are forces in human lives, moreover. You tell us, 'Man is a rational creature. Let us have novels of character, that he may become more rational, more civilized.' Very well, we will deal in character—and when we have done you shall cease shuddering, and not before. We won't make the mistake of assigning to old castles and ghosts and gruesome sounds the effects we wish to make; they shall be created by flesh and blood, by men and women whose general humanity you will not be able successfully to impeach. You shall see that your novel of character has changed nothing—nothing! Novel of character, indeed! What you mean is not human character, with which fiction has dealt since time immemorial, but the I-bury-my-head-and-do-not-see-these-things-and-therefore-they-no-longer-have-existence ostrichism of a particular age, a passing mode of thought, a narrowed society."

The limitless power with which *Wuthering Heights* is written has led most critics to emphasize its transcendental side. Thus Rose Macaulay declares that "the chief figures in the drama . . . are not actual men and women as we know them, nor as we should know them lived we ever so long with Yorkshire farmers, but neither are they . . . false men and women; simply they move in an alien dimension." And E. M. Forster says:

> The emotions of Heathcliff and Catherine Earnshaw function differently to other emotions in fiction. Instead of inhabiting the characters, they surround them like thunder clouds, and generate the explosions that fill the novel from the moment when Lockwood dreams of the hand at the window down to the moment when Heathcliff, with the same window open, is discovered dead. "Wuthering Heights" is filled with sound—storm and rushing wind—a sound more important than words and thoughts. Great as the novel is, one cannot afterwards remember anything in it but Heathcliff and the elder Catherine. They cause the action by their separation: they close it by their union after death. No wonder they "walk"; what else could such beings do? even when they were alive their love and hate transcended them.
>
> Emily Brontë had in some ways a literal and careful mind. She constructed her novel on a time chart even more elaborate than Miss Austen's, and she arranged the Linton and Earnshaw families symmetrically, and she had a clear idea of the various legal steps by which Heathcliff gained possession of their two properties. Then why did she deliberately introduce muddle, chaos, tempest? Because in our sense of the word she was a prophetess: because what is implied is more important to her than what is said; and only in confusion could the figures of

> Heathcliff and Catherine externalize their passion till it streamed through the house and over the moors. "Wuthering Heights" has no mythology beyond what these two characters provide: no great book is more cut off from the universals of Heaven and Hell. It is local, like the spirits it engenders, and whereas we may meet Moby Dick in any pond, we shall only encounter them among the harebells and limestone of their own county.[1]

It is of interest that Forster should make the comparison with *Moby Dick,* for *Wuthering Heights* is a piece of animism quite exceptionally like Melville's story—in this respect. But in the respect Mr. Forster claims? If he is right, or even partly right, it can only be because Emily Brontë *does* achieve that intense personal and individual reality in character which we traditionally associate with Jane Austen. In other words, Miss Macaulay must be wrong.

That can wait a moment while we examine Mr. Forster's other assertion, that Miss Brontë deliberately introduced muddle, chaos and tempest. We are likely to conclude that this statement is utterly without foundation. It is inconsistent with Mr. Forster's own showing as to her methodicalness, and it is inconsistent with his own notion of prophecy. There is, if we understand his view, nothing deliberate or intentional in the prophetical quality; the prophets cannot help themselves. Whatever the nature of the peculiarity distinguishing their writing, it is not deliberate or even voluntary. Mr. D. H. Lawrence, for example, can write in no other way; nor could Melville; nor Emily Brontë. The "sound more impor-

[1] *Aspects of the Novel,* Chap. VII.

tant than words and thoughts"—an expressive and truthful phrase—is innate. Miss Brontë inherited with it a practical strain much more marked than one can usually discover in the same person; and this practical strain warred pleasantly against the gift of song, insisting that if she *would* sing she must at least enunciate clearly. "Muddle"? "Chaos"? These are not discoverable features of *Wuthering Heights*. The intricacy of the tale offered difficulties of narration, and the reader has some clambering to do, but the path becomes easier and the retrospect is clear.

Miss Macaulay, we may feel, is wrong; yet she comes brilliantly near hitting the nail on the head when she asserts that Heathcliff and the elder Catherine "move in an alien dimension." If she had said that they add movement in an extra dimension to their movement in our familiar ones, we should perfectly agree. For that, in effect, is just what they do. In their passion for each other there is an extension, emotionally, beyond every normal boundary of human nature.

"Infinity attends them," as Forster says of Dostoevski's characters, but it is an infinity of perfectly-known and "logical" human emotion, a projection of something we know all about though here we cannot measure it, seemingly. But that is a limited kind of transcendancy; we are likely to decide that the emphasis has been misplaced in discussing Emily Brontë's novel, and that what should be stressed is its firmly realistic foundation. It is, after all, an attempt—one of the few outstandingly successful ones—to give to the novel of character, firm in its outlines, finite in its observation, realistic in its *per-*

sonae and settings, a provision of energy and an outlet of emotion somewhat approaching the tremendous effects that ancient fiction so easily achieved.

But it shows up sharply, in the point we have been considering, the distinctive feature of transcendental realism—extension, entrance into an *n*th dimension, not in a slyness of confusion and a mood of despair, which produces fantasy, but in the confidence and assurance of prophetic hopefulness. But the realist is conjoined with the prophet in the same author; whereas in fiction like Melville's and Dostoevski's, the prophet is ascendant, and will compel any necessary or suitable sacrifice of realism, in natures like Emily Brontë's or Tolstoy's the realist rules. The distinction seems clear; it even appears to offer certain marks by which we can determine the emotional scope of a modern work of fiction. On the authority of *Wuthering Heights,* then, it could be deduced that (1) in a work of transcendental realism, the realism is predominating, (2) there is an extension, emotionally, into some unknown dimension, (3) the thing extended is realistic and normal in itself, that is, known to us all, (4) the purpose—or effect, for volition has not much to do with it—is an assertion of the Unknowable. Not a manifestation of Deity, in the ancient manner, but simply a statement of the unknown and incalculable; a declaration of the possible infinity of the finite, as it were.

These conclusions—deductions, rather—may not be final. We shall know better about that when we have considered Tolstoy's *War and Peace.* It remains to round out our impression of *Wuthering Heights.*

In its careful structure as story, elaboration of Heathcliff's revenge, and characterization generally it must have taught a vast deal to Wilkie Collins; even Dickens may have learned much from it. Hardy's Wessex, perhaps, owes something to Emily Brontë's Yorkshire, and George Meredith, for all his Welsh blood, may have acquired from *Wuthering Heights* some notions of emotional intensity. What perhaps has not always been perceived is that the realism is quite as much responsible for the book's power as the clearly limited transcendentalism—limited especially in the ending, where a softening of so much harshness comes incongruously upon us. Heathcliff is dead; Catherine Linton and Hareton Earnshaw promise a happy marriage, with a restoration of Earnshaw property and happiness all around. Here the weakness of a transcendentalism that is self-limiting shows clearly; poorer books have come to a complacent close without giving us nearly so much the disagreeable sensation of a happy, or happified, ending. No, the thing is a compromise; and more than ever the doubt may come over us as to whether any real compromise in the objects of fiction is possible. There is something about the spectacle of the younger Catherine and Hareton that thwarts the effect Heathcliff should produce; something—not much but quite evident—has not been purged away and the sentimental jaundice clouds the complexion at the close. There is no question of excuse or forgiving toward a work which offers us so much; a truly great novel. But when we come to the abstract question of fictional philosophy, the lesson is there.

II. LEO TOLSTOY

War and Peace[2]

Heretofore we have generally recounted, perhaps needlessly and tediously, the action of a novel under discussion. With Tolstoy's immense work such a course becomes impossible. We can only fix a few principal landmarks on the page; possibly pick up and examine this or that thread or scene; consider the masterpiece as a whole from one or another point of view.

We recollect that the story opens in July, 1805, in Petersburg—St. Petersburg, Petrograd, Leningrad. The scene is an evening reception and the name "Bonaparte" occurs in the first sentence, part of a lady's speech to a guest. At this reception, and in the succeeding chapters, various persons and families are brought to our attention, nearly all of the Russian nobility. Bezukhoi, Bolkonsky, Rostof are family names that gradually fix themselves in our minds. We have become thoroughly interested in at least a half dozen figures when the scene is abruptly transferred to a Russian army quartered in Austria; but in a few pages this shifting appears quite natural, for Prince Andrei Bolkonsky, the most arresting person in the chapters we have read, is now serving as adjutant to the commander, Kutuzof.

The fortunes of war are followed from now on. Besides Prince Andrei, we spend much time with young Nikolai Rostof. But a good deal of our attention is asked for some bits of fighting, the movement of troops,

[2] The discussion is based upon, and the spelling of names is followed from, Nathan Haskell Dole's translation—four volumes now published in one by Thomas Y. Crowell Company.

for tactics and for strategy against Napoleon. After a while the battle of Austerlitz is impending; is imminent, is fought under our eyes. Prince Andrei is perhaps mortally wounded. We have had a look at Emperor Alexander of Russia through the ardent perceptions of Nikolai Rostof. Now we have a glimpse of Napoleon.

Volume II. The story returns to the life of Moscow and Petersburg, with certain scenes in the country, principally at the estate of Prince Andrei's father. There is little about army life and all that has to do with international affairs is mere discussion, except one scene. A direct view of the Peace of Tilsit is given us and we witness the meetings of Alexander and Napoleon through Nikolai Rostof's presence on an errand. But our main interest is probably confined pretty well to three persons whose fortunes are followed in chapter upon chapter. These are Count Pierre Bezukhoi, the illegitimate son of an old grandee of Catherine's reign, who has inherited an enormous fortune. Pierre, clumsy and nearsighted, an ardent idealist, intellectually inclined, weak-willed, infinitely kind-hearted, is snared into marriage with a beautiful, sensual and hard woman, Ellen Kuragina. After a duel in which he wounds the man who compromises her, Pierre leaves Ellen, only to receive her back later on when she makes up to him. At one time Pierre plunges into Freemasonry and we follow his adventure there with the disillusionment in which it was bound to end.

We are even more absorbed by the history of Prince Andrei, Pierre's friend, a man of quite different character, able, even brilliant, reclusive, profound, not so much generous as just, old for his years, which are not many, and a man's man, as the expression goes. Given up for dead, he returns home almost at the very hour of his son's birth and his pretty, childish wife's death. He sinks himself in country life, finally emerging to become of importance in political circles in Petersburg. There the breath of spring comes upon him in the person of Nikolai Rostof's charming sister, the young Natasha or Nathalie, of whom we have already had many views and with whom we are all in love, long since.

Prince Andrei engages himself to Natasha but, respecting his testy old father's prejudices, postpones the marriage for a year. During that time he is abroad. Toward the end of it, when his return is imminent, Prince Anatol Kuragin, Pierre's brother-in-law and a seducer of women, captivates the utterly inexperienced Natasha (she is only sixteen or so) and an elopement of the most terrible sort is barely averted. Pierre has the lame offices of a friend to perform in the finale between Prince Andrei and Natasha; and in the concluding scene it is plain that Pierre is more than half in love with this pitiable girl. As Pierre rides home, bursting with emotion, the white and brilliant comet of 1812 is noticeable in the winter sky.

Volume III. Abruptly, Tolstoy gives the stage directions for the great drama of Napoleon and Russia. From now on, this holds the center of the stage; the personal fortunes of a half-dozen characters are followed in asides, as it were; they are subordinate to, and to some extent developed from, the event of the war and the French advance on Moscow. In particular Tolstoy delivers himself explicitly of certain theories of history and human action, in the manner of a serious essay or treatise inserted in the pages of a novel.

Very attentively do we watch Count Pierre Bezukhoi in his honest, confused spiritual quest. Pierre's trust in Freemasonry has turned out to be almost wholly a repose upon the man who brought him into the fellowship. Distracted by this idea and that, it is largely chance what will sink into his mind and influence his action. At one time a cabalistic significance of the letters in two phrases, "the Emperor Napoleon" and "the Russian Bezukhoi," suggests that he, Pierre, is to be a means of Napoleon's overthrow. In the end, this fantasy recurring after his presence on a battlefield, leads Pierre to arm himself with some notion of killing the French Emperor. With characteristic ineptitude and futility, he only gets himself arrested and disarmed by the French before coming anywhere near their leader.

Prince Andrei is in active service. As the French advance on Moscow, his very old father finally dies and it is Nikolai Rostof that circumstances send to the rescue of Prince Andrei's sister, Princess Mariya. The marriage of these two is foreshadowed. Prince Andrei, terribly wounded at Borodino, is among those wounded men lodged in the Rostof's Moscow house and carried out of the city with the family when evacuation takes place. Natasha Rostof learns of Prince Andrei's presence, visits him at night and asks his forgiveness, though there is no need of that, though he greets her with affection.

Before that, while lying wounded after the battle, Prince Andrei had heard the piteous outcries of a man near him, whose leg had just been cut off by the surgeon, and had recognized in this victim the foppish Anatol Kuragin, who had been discreetly keeping out of Prince Andrei's way ever since the attempt to seduce Natasha.

The capture of Smolensk, the battle of Borodino seen principally through Pierre's eyes, the occupation and burning of Moscow are Tolstoy's great external subject; his principal inner subject is the complicated chain of force and circumstance in which Napoleon is only one link, Kutuzof, the Russion commander-in-chief merely another. This demonstration of fatality and refutation of historians' accounts—which he views simply as posterior explanations—occupy Tolstoy's attention for chapters at a time.

Volume IV. Countess Ellen Bezukhaya, Pierre's wife, who had toyed with Roman Catholicism and the idea of divorce in an effort to decide between two attractive lovers, is dead. She has been ill and has taken an overdose of medicine. The retreat from Moscow has begun and Pierre, with other prisoners, is carried with the French. Tolstoy describes the flight of Napoleon and his army both in large perspective and by means of roadside scenes and Pierre's adventures. Bezukhoi is set free by a Russian raid. Prince Andrei, nursed by Natasha, dies. The military drama and its actors recede into the background, just as the French gradually erase themselves from the soil of Russia. Natasha and Pierre are seen to be destined for each other.

Epilogue. A few short political chapters introduce this glimpse, seven years later (1820). Natasha and Pierre, Nikolai Rostof and his wife, the Princess Mariya, and the children of each, including Nikolenka, Prince Andrei's son, are amply illustrated in family scenes. Natasha is the completely domestic mother and has disciplined the wayward-minded Pierre. Rostof has turned out to be a capital landowner with an unusual gift for handling the peasants. The fortunes of both families are in excellent shape. The last scene of the story is of Prince Andrei's Nikolenka, lying wakefully in bed, dreaming of the day when he shall be grown and do great things. Having finished his novel, Tolstoy devotes a dozen brief chapters to a concluding dissertation on the questions (1) What is Power? and (2) What force moves the nations?

The faults of this giant work are not few, and they are easily apparent. As the book proceeds and Tolstoy inserts whole pages and chapters of argumentation, the reader's impatience often mounts until he rejects the idea that this is a novel: it is an illustrated lecture, and of the didactic sort at that. As Percy Lubbock observes, "wherever 'the historians' are mentioned he knows that several pages can be turned at once." It was, of course, Tolstoy's business as an artist to embody his convictions about historical truth and the nature of human action in scenes of a high plausibility. This he is able to do, to a considerable extent, in the case of Kutuzof, the Russian commander; his failure to do it with Napoleon is signal. He cannot command the necessary evidence from the French Emperor's deeds and words, but nevertheless Napoleon must bear out his, Tolstoy's, doctrine; and so the novelist has recourse to the eloquence of a lawyer summing up before a jury. The final argument (Volume IV, Part Two) is not, properly speaking, a part of the novel at all. Yet had Tolstoy elided from the earlier pages all the dreary tractarian passages, this thesis at the end, in spite fiction in which analysis replaces mere impressionism, Percy Lubbock takes *War and Peace* as the point of departure for his keen study of fictional method. He demonstrates in what seems as we read a very convincing manner that Tolstoy, apparently unconsciously, was writing two novels simultaneously, two novels which do not fuse in any fashion nor at any place. One was the epic of Youth and Age, the other the drama of War and Peace; and Mr. Lubbock believes that Tolstoy had done better to have chosen either than to have combined the two in a work where one lies, unmixed, on the other like oil on water. But then Mr. Lubbock goes on to an examination of *Madame Bovary,* the artistic acceptance of which is universal, and from a careful scrutiny of Flaubert's method in respect of the point of view he deduces what Flaubert's subject really is—it is not simply Emma Bovary, as we unthinkingly tend to assume. But if it is necessary to analyze the method of Flaubert in order to come to a complete view of his subject, should not the same process be applied to Tolstoy, even though the Russian is by comparison asymmetrical, lacking in architectonic, and even clumsy? It would seem proper to make the attempt.

The point of view, always the traditional one of the author's omniscience, affords only a negative clue. We may note one peculiarity: With the possible exception of Thackeray, no one ever intruded himself more decisively into a novel, we may feel. The intrusion is, of course, different from Thackeray's—much more impersonal, blunter, arbitrary, deific rather than auctorial. Not that this entrance of the author is everywhere; Tolstoy had a his wife's death, his eremitism, his enchantment with Natasha (which quite makes him over), his misanthropy following their breach and the serene and gentle vision of love vouchsafed him while he dies by inches. Yet in this instance, as in all the others, Tolstoy's comprehension of the fundamental character is so firm and delicate that all the shapes of rounding-out, all the changes of attitude and intention, impress us as not only perfectly consistent but absolutely exclusive of any alternative development. Oh! if we look long enough we shall find flat characters, no doubt; Anna Pavlovna Scherer is one, Prince Vasili Kuragin, Ellen's father, is virtually unchanging. . . . Napoleon, of course, is not flat but flattened.

There is not much of the famous difficulty of Russian character in the people of *War and Peace*. We mean that different relation between thought and action which seems to come as an obstacle to the understanding of the novelist's creatures in so much of the fiction of Russian writers. In this sense, perhaps only Pierre, in all the book is "Russian"; even so, he is, for fullest comprehension by the Western reader, not a patch upon Raskolnikov in *Crime and Punishment*, or the Karamazovs in that other masterpiece of Dostoevski's. Pierre from moment to moment offers perplexities to us of the West; Pierre in his general contour is a figure by no means unfamiliar to us if a little rare. Moreover, Tolstoy reduces him to a practical basis in the end; wived by the transformed, domesticating Natasha, our spiritual pilgrim has become a happy and particularly harmless specimen of the absent-minded professor type.

In his *The Craft of Fiction*, one of the few books about

great gift for strict drama, for scenes put squarely in front of the reader, and in presenting these he can efface himself completely. Usually he does, except where the reader might misinterpret a look or a gesture; then he bares that actor's mind in a phrase or sentence of quite crystal clearness. But when we leave the scene to what, time and again, do we pass? Sometimes to pictorial, summarizing passages, but these are generally short; almost as often to abstract discussion, expository pages, in the style of a lecture or an essay. Against these we have just uttered our grievance, but having uttered it, we ought to reflect a little. After all, is Tolstoy so poor an artist that this abruptness and abandonment stands for the best he could do with the stuff he had to work? We may well pause over the question; but our answer can only be negative. He is a very great artist, as any examination of his fiction will show. It is at least a fair presumption, therefore, that this didactic method is an intentional performance. It may be less good than it should be; there may be a better method than Tolstoy could put his hand upon, and the result he aimed at, whatever its nature, may achieve but poorly. But it is intelligent to assume that an artist of his powers knew what he was about.

And we who read him must know. Let us look again for a moment at the point of view on which, as Mr. Lubbock makes us understand, so much depends. In the novelistic portions of *War and Peace* the author is conventionally omniscient. He gives the scene, he allows us to glance into the minds of his characters from time to time, he sometimes dramatizes the mind of Pierre or Andrei or Nikolai Rostof or Mariya or another. There is the astonishing freshness and immediacy of which we have spoken, but otherwise the method is simply usual and traditional. But the argumentative passages, the historical lectures? There the point of view is certainly different from any to which we are accustomed in a work of fiction. Perhaps it is an historian's—a rebel historian's—some heretical Macaulay or devastating Gibbon? Well, hardly; there is something too impersonal, often something contemptuous about it. It is bigoted; it refutes dogma with dogma. It is destructive for the most part, until we come to the second part of Volume IV, and it is often unconcerned. As we reflect upon its strangeness we fall back on the word used before, the word "deific." A god—not, evidently, the Christian God, nor the Jewish Jahveh nor the deity of any familiar religion—is on duty, observing, commenting, demonstrating, demolishing petty human conceptions, even disregarding. Perhaps it is Thomas Hardy's Immanent Will and perhaps it is Bernard Shaw's Life Force; or it may be neither; or it may be the wind from the Russian steppes. We do not know and Tolstoy does not tell us. Whoever this god may be, he is imperfectly deific; the voice of Tolstoy can be heard in his tones and the limitations of human reason are often apparent in his terms. But he is godlike for all that, and not least in his manner of consistent brushing aside of human explanations and his scorn for human constructions of meaning.

The name "Bonaparte," as we have noted, occurs in the first sentence of this novel of many hundreds of thousands of words. Why? Not to fix the time, defined a few sentences later as a July evening in 1805. Not to lead into the immediate personal story—a possible match for Prince Vasili's son. Simply because the real motif of the work must be sounded at once, distinctly, in the manner of a classical symphony, to be received perhaps inattentively, to have no significance attached to it at the moment, but to be recalled in the turbulence it will produce later.

Of all men who ever lived, Napoleon has undoubtedly seemed, at one time or another and to the greatest number of mankind, most nearly godlike, and this whether a god for good or evil. There is plenty of fiction to deify such heroes, very little to keep them within bounds. It was the desire of Tolstoy to keep Bonaparte within bounds, and in order to do it he invented his double method and his special viewpoint. Only a god could make the godlike hero seem humanly small; what Tolstoy possibly overlooked, or more probably intended, was that the god's vision might run as far to excess in the counter direction as the human and worshipful view exceeds.

The Woolworth Building rises some nine hundred feet from the New York sidewalks. Shall we view it from the ground, aided by a little distance, or shall we look down from an airplane two miles above the city? It is not possible to say that either view is inaccurate, although one makes the skyscraper a towering edifice, the other reduces it to a mole-hill a little larger than its neighbors. At most it can only be said that the view from beneath is the ordinary and everyday one, with which we have generally to reckon; but in the same breath it could be urged as every one's duty to see the structure at least once in a lifetime from the infinitely vaster depths of the sky. Tolstoy's Napoleon, deifically looked down upon, is no Napoleon that ever moved across the face of the earth from the angle of human vision; it is a Napoleon non-existent to men; and everybody should see it for an instant—an instant snatched out of eternity and to be rendered back as soon as it has fleeted.

This is why, when E. M. Forster has been reading for some time in *War and Peace,* "great chords begin to sound," chords whose source he cannot exactly locate, although elsewhere he decides that "Space is the lord of *War and Peace.* But in this he is wrong; no doubt to Europeans the sense of vast distances in connection with the scenes of Tolstoy's novel is very impressive, but Americans are quite used to distances as vast, and even vaster than any involved in the movement of *War and Peace.* It is the transcendental point of view which Tolstoy slips into and out of, and into again, with his abrupt arbitrament and his crude force, that produces this effect; and of the various transcendental qualities which the novel exhibits, this is easily the most important.

We must not neglect to notice the others. The peaceful and reconciliative visions of Prince Andrei, dreadfully wounded and dying, and the spiritual adventurings of Pierre are borderings upon the infinite, proceeding with naturalness and beauty out of their fine souls. But a more subtle transcendence comes from the roundness—in Forster's sense—of most of the characters. There is something about the development of the people in Tolstoy's novel that joins them up with humanity as a whole in a fashion to make another author despair. They reach back to universals, as Forster would say, though not simply to the universals of emotion, to transcending pity and transcending love, in the way of Dostoevski's Karamazovs. Much more is it a reaching back to the universals of normal and healthy human existence, to such universals as family affection, comradeship in army life, the affinity of friends, a quite simple love of country, pride, vanity, cowardice, courage, mating love and the joy of children. One is never unconscious of the human clay; one sees it take adorable shapes; one watches it find its final shape in Nikolai Rostof, Mariya, Natasha, for chief examples —a final shape far less exquisite, no doubt, but good and sound and true, the best shape for durability. And, with a stir and a sigh, the conviction is profound that in this spectacle one has touched hands with the race.

> The simple nameless herd of humanity
> Have deeds and faith that are truth enough for me.

And over all, in all, throughout all, forever after all the great movement of a tide is felt, the movement of a tide at the bottom of deep waters, such a tide as is perpetual, gentle and remorseless. It depends upon no planetary force or external attraction, this tide, or action of the sea. Those whose business it is to attempt the lifting of sunken ships have a name for the force: they call it *scend,* and they know its habit. One may stand on the bottom of the ocean and be unaware of any movement, but the movement is there and, in fact, is going on all the time. With its noiseless stealth it picks up the sunken vessel, of such stupendous weight, and moves it a few inches; to-day a few inches; next week a few feet. The scend toys aimlessly with this enormous mass of steel; lifts it imperceptibly and lets it fall; and in this way it grinds the steel to matchwood and crumples the iron to tinfoil. Without visible action the leviathan is reduced to rusty flakes and a little powder lost in the sands of the ocean, which are the sands of time.

So with *War and Peace*. It, too, has scend. In spite of the firmness of its realism, the brightness of its scenes, the vitality of a hundred chapters, the undimmed loveliness of young Nikolai and Natasha, the beauty and the truth, a secret action goes on within it, something that holds the reader at its mercy like the clutch of life itself. It is in its force, which Tolstoy perhaps invoked but of which he could be nothing but the medium, that *War and Peace* differs from all other works in the history of fiction. And if, while this force, this scend, was passing through him, subjecting him to its unheard-of pressures, his hand trembled and he wrote strange passages, his head dizzied, and he forgot what he was writing, or where, or why, are we so cool and collected, under the lessened impact, that we can treat his failures with judicial calm and critical detachment? We are not. The scend grips us, too—that transcendent force which we used to deify, which we no longer invoke, which creates, uncreates, and creates again in all eternity—which caught us up out of nowhere and will presently relinquish us to nowhere but, now, for our snatched lifetimes, holds us firmly, in a grip unrelaxing, and will not let us go.

III. E. M. FORSTER

A Passage to India

Ours is the age of large-scale, the reënacted entrance into one of those periods of megalopolitan civilization to which a German philosopher-historian has drawn forcible attention.[3] On this account a certain danger attends the citation and discussion of such a novel as Tolstoy's *War and Peace*—the danger that with our special size-sense we may confuse dimension with effect. It is therefore useful and even almost necessary to follow *War and Peace* with some consideration of a novel of the same fundamental type in which the scale is quite dissimilar. E. M. Forster's *A Passage to India* affords a striking and recent example.

At first examination, Forster's story will scarcely appear to have anything whatever in common with *War and Peace,* except that from our own special viewpoint it is a book about a race or races psychologically strange to us. But if we keep our eye closely on *method,* the precise thing we are watching in this chapter, we shall discover that both Tolstoy and Forster (in this book) are substantially alike. Both are realists, both use their realism for something more than its own sake; both edge away from it and constantly seek to transcend it in a kind of total effect. We often speak of the "impression" that a book leaves upon us, using a modest word—though a word pretentious enough where most books are

[3] See Oswald Spengler's *Untergang des Abendlandes,* translated as *The Decline of the West,* and published in England and America (New York: Alfred A. Knopf, Vol. I in 1926, Vol. II in 1928).

concerned. But fiction of a high order leaves more than an impression; its effect is palpable and is the settlement or treaty or new *modus vivendi* concluding the Wars of the Emotions. The "impression" left upon us by *A Passage to India* contains none of the rich realism with which the book is saturated; a clear rinsing has taken place; the book has perhaps dyed our minds, but evenly and indelibly.

The book really resembles a dyeing process. There is not much "story"; there is no plotting or artifice. A group of people—Mohammedan, Hindus, and English—are presented to us, awash, bobbing about in a fluid atmosphere which is modern India. Without haste a single episode is introduced, much as a tablet of dye might be slipped into a steamy vat of water. The one technical expedient of the novel is that we are not allowed to see the exact dropping in of the tablet; it is done in an instant when our eyes are directed elsewhere. Hardly conscious of the fugitive look away, we see the nebulous spread of angry color up through the water; we see it seize on every character of the book, producing in him or her a characteristic reaction plainly due to nationality. Then, as if an Indian conjuror's trick had been performed before our eyes, we see all the color retreat, vanish. The vat is clear.

Mrs. Moore has come out to India as an escort for a somewhat "queer, cautious" girl, Miss Adela Quested, in whom Mrs. Moore's son by a former marriage, Ronny Heaslop, is interested, and whom Ronny will probably marry. As yet there is no affiancement. Ronny is City

Magistrate in Chandrapore, already thoroughly imbued with the viewpoint of the ruling race.

Soon after Mrs. Moore's and Miss Quested's arrival, the older woman escapes from the tedium of amateur theatricals to the shadows and silence of a mosque. A Mohammedan, Aziz, accosts her there, at first on a point of etiquette: he fears she has not taken off her shoes upon entering. Enough conversation develops to found acquaintance. Aziz is a doctor on the staff of a local hospital—under English superiors, of course.

In a succession of chapters various groups of people are skillfully induced into self-dissection. All is scene —social incident, conversation, race reaction. The strict scenic method is varied only by descriptive touches. Set descriptions are rare and for all their finish, have an informal atmosphere. Along with much realism, a lyrical feeling invades the writing and there are frequent phrases, sentences, that are quite perfect poetry. The most admired instance occurs in the set description which introduces Part II. Forster is painting the caves in the Marabar Hills and writes:

They are dark caves. Even when they open towards the sun, very little light penetrates down the entrance tunnel into the circular chamber. There is little to see, and no eye to see it, until the visitor arrives for his five minutes, and strikes a match. Immediately another flame rises in the depths of the rock and moves towards the surface like an imprisoned spirit: the walls of the circular chamber have been most marvellously polished. The two flames approach and strive to unite, but cannot, because one of them breathes air, the other stone. A mirror inlaid with lovely colours divides the lovers, delicate stars of pink and grey interpose, exquisite nebulæ, shadings fainter than the tail of a comet or the midday moon, all the evanescent life of the granite, only here visible. Fists and fingers thrust above the advancing soil—here at last is their skin, finer than any covering acquired by the animals, smoother than windless water, more voluptuous than love. The radiance increases, the flames touch one another, kiss, expire. The cave is dark again, like all the caves.

The tablet of dye is about to be slipped into the vat. Dr. Aziz has arranged a most elaborate and extravagant party in honor of Mrs. Moore and Miss Quested, to show them the Marabar Caves. While separated from the others, he leaves Miss Quested for a moment; he returns to find that she has entered one of the caves, but which? Here are twelve together, exactly alike. He searches, shouts, and fails to find her. In the end he concludes that she has gone back to town in an automobile, with friends; he is no longer much disturbed about her.

On himself returning to Chandrapore he is put under arrest charged with having attacked Miss Quested in the cave which she visited.

As the reader knows, the charge is false. Aziz has been continuously under reader vision during the time in question. The accusation profoundly excites Chandrapore, and we see the blood of the several races clotting, for even the Hindus are stirred. So carefully has Mr. Forster composed his group of characters that every shade of opinion—or mostly, of feeling—is represented in this crisis, from the weathered English official whose face wets with tears over the "English girl, fresh from England," to Fielding, also English and principal of the

Government College, who is convinced of Aziz's innocence and will face ostracism to defend his friend; from Mohammedan partisans, frothing at the mouth, to the obliquities of the Hindu, Professor Godbole, too slightly immersed in the realm of matter. Fielding is talking with Godbole, who states:

". . . Dr. Aziz is a most worthy young man, I have a great regard for him; but I think you are asking me whether the individual can commit good actions or evil actions, and that is rather difficult for us." He spoke without emotion and in short tripping syllables.

"I ask you: did he do it or not? Is that plain? I know he didn't, and from that I start. I mean to get at the true explanation in a couple of days. My last notion is that it's the guide who went round with them. Malice on Miss Quested's part—it couldn't be that, though Hamidullah thinks so. She has certainly had some appalling experience. But you tell me, oh no—because good and evil are the same."

"No, not exactly, please, according to our philosophy. Because nothing can be performed in isolation. All perform a good action, when one is performed, and when an evil action is performed, all perform it. To illustrate my meaning, let me take the case in point as an example.

"I am informed that an evil action was performed in the Marabar Hills, and that a highly esteemed English lady is now seriously ill in consequence. My answer to that is this: that action was performed by Dr. Aziz." He stopped and sucked in his thin cheeks. "It was performed by the guide." He stopped again. "It was performed by you." Now he had an air of daring and of coyness. "It was performed by me." He looked shyly down the sleeve of his own coat. "And by my students. It was even performed by the lady herself.

When evil occurs, it expresses the whole of the universe. Similarly when good occurs."

Before the incident at Marabar, Ronny Heaslop and Adela Quested had quarreled once or twice slightly, drawn together again, and became engaged. There was physical attraction between them but not love, and Adela, unlike most girls, somehow understood this. Her mind was intensely preoccupied with her situation in relation to young Heaslop when Aziz left her and when she stepped alone into one of the caves. "There was this shadow, or sort of shadow, down the entrance tunnel, bottling me up. It seemed like an age, but I suppose the whole thing can't have lasted thirty seconds really. I hit at him with the glasses, he pulled me round the cave by the strap, it broke, I escaped, that's all." She had fled precipitately down a hillside, falling, rolling, and hundreds of cactus spines had to be picked out of her flesh. With shattered nerves, touched by the sun—for the hot weather was beginning—tormented by an echo, it is several days before she can be considered out of danger.

A moment or two has come to her before the trial begins in which she comprehends and acknowledges Aziz's innocence—but then the moment goes. She has lost all accommodation with reality. It is not finally restored to her until she is on the witness stand in the crowded courtroom. Over the question about Aziz following her into a cave she hesitates, asks for time, frames a negative answer and finally destroys the whole case with the words: "I withdraw everything."

And now we watch the dissipation, in threatening and

subsiding swirls, of all that angry color which has filled the vat of Chandrapore. Part III of the novel, really a coda, takes place two years later, after Miss Quested has returned to England and the Marabar case is mostly a painful English memory, a native suspicion, inert but alive. In England Fielding has married Ronny Heaslop's half-sister; he comes out again to show his wife and her young brother something of India; he encounters Aziz, of course, and the possibility of friendship between Mohammedan Indian and liberalized Englishman is tested out. This concluding section of the story opens with one of the *tours de force* of the modern novel, a marvelous exposition of Hindu religion by means of the dramatic scene observed with a Western eye and recited with subdued ironical inflections, but made intimate by the use of Professor Godbole's consciousness while he takes part in and supervises a festival of great importance.[4] The concluding words of the book are a fine example of Forster's power to make us see all his realism *sub specie æternitatis*. Aziz and Fielding have been quarreling violently about the future of India:

"Who do you want instead of the English? The Japanese?" jeered Fielding, drawing rein.

"No, the Afghans. My own ancestors."

"Oh, your Hindu friends will like that, won't they?"

"It will be arranged—a conference of Oriental statesmen."

. . . Still he couldn't quite fit in Afghans at Mau, and, finding he was in a corner, made his horse rear again until he remembered that he had, or ought to have, a mother-land. Then

[4] The climax of this scene-description has already been quoted; see Chapter I of this book.

he shouted: "India shall be a nation! No foreigners of any sort! Hindu and Moslem and Sikh and all shall be one! Hurrah! Hurrah for India! Hurrah! Hurrah!"

India a nation! What an apotheosis! Last comer to the drab nineteenth-century sisterhood! Waddling in at this hour of the world to take her seat! She, whose only peer was the Holy Roman Empire, she shall rank with Guatemala and Belgium perhaps! Fielding mocked again. And Aziz in an awful rage danced this way and that, not knowing what to do, and cried: "Down with the English anyhow. That's certain. Clear out, you fellows, double quick, I say. We may hate one another, but we hate you most. If . . . it's fifty-five hundred years we shall get rid of you, yes, we shall drive every blasted Englishman into the sea, and then"—he rode against him furiously—"and then," he concluded, half kissing him, "you and I shall be friends."

"Why can't we be friends now?" said the other, holding him affectionately. "It's what I want. It's what you want."

But the horses didn't want it—they swerved apart; the earth didn't want it, sending up rocks through which riders must pass in single file; the temples, the tank, the jail, the palace, the birds, the carrion, the Guest House, that came into view as they issued from the gap and saw Mau beneath: they didn't want it, they said in their hundred voices, "No, not yet," and the sky said, "No, not there."

"But," objects the possible reader, "I never *do* know exactly what happened to Miss Quested." No, unless the reader is a physician, even his conjectures are likely to remain vague. It is a triumph of Mr. Forster's realism to leave the occurrence in the cave where life generally leaves such things—big newspaper headlines one day, rehash the next, then a paragraph or nothing. It is an interesting circumstance that he who cries loudest for realistic fiction is most captious when he gets it. One is reminded of the lines of W. S. Gilbert in *The Mikado:*

> His taste exact
> For faultless fact
> Amounts to a disease.

By realism, such a reader means rationalization. Although it may be impossible to overcome his objection by metaphysics, can he not be brought to see that what happened to Miss Quested is irrelevant? Perhaps.

What—to attack soundly after Percy Lubbock's fashion—is the subject of *A Passage to India?* The moment we ask the question poor Miss Quested recedes rapidly into a limbo of forgettable and forgotten characters of fiction. She is not much more, really, than a few passes of Mr. Forster's hands, busy with an Indian conjuring trick. It is obvious that the novelist is writing about the racial and social three-ply existing in India to-day; his persons exist only for the scenic presentation of his subject, and have vitality to just the degree that each contributes directly to such presentation. Thus Aziz is perfectly and constantly alive; Fielding is alive; Heaslop, a stereotype, is alive; even Professor Godbole, who has nothing directly to do with the action, is excessively alive, far more so than the "English girl fresh from England," who is simply a device. She is essential, Mr. Forster takes great pains with her, and like all necessary bits of mechanism she yields the minimum return for painstaking.

The great distinction of *A Passage to India* lies in the way the author has made a minute, rapid, nervous and realistic continuum of scenes *express* (in the old sense of "squeeze out") something that could probably only be thus derived, something which would probably be lost in any attempt at direct statement. This something is *not* the peculiarities of Mohammedan and Hindu and English colonial minds—which are constantly and frankly illustrated and underlined—but the thing that assumes either Meaning or Unmeaning (significant either way) according to how the individual observer reads the riddle of the universe. If it is Meaning, then the observer is most aware of the sentience in all this spawning of human emotion, all this fretful and intricate activity of human lives. If it is Unmeaning the consciousness ignores the sentience and emphasizes the senselessness. As one reads, one views the thing as a chemical experiment; the realism, color, smell of mixture and changes is nearly all, the implications of what is going on are only faintly disturbing, rarely intrusive. As one reflects after reading the chemical experiment vanishes and a fable takes its place.

Since this novel was published the Thames, and one or two other rivers, have been set on fire by the appearance of a work of non-fiction, *Mother India*, by Katharine Mayo. *Mother India* may perhaps be not unfairly described as an indictment, with many specific counts, brought against native India, and by consequence a justification of British rule. The instance is worth attention for the comparisons it affords between fiction and non-fiction. *Mother India* is a deadly array of facts—the factualness of some being disputed. It depends upon documents and verbal witness, more or less controverted. Its point of view is that of Western civilization, Western morality, Western ethics, sanitation, hygiene. Its effect can only be to insulate, confirm prejudice, arm intolerance.

A Passage to India is not a discontinuous array of facts, so-called, but an integrated serial of impressions, partly external, largely intuitive, sympathetically derived. It is ironical, poetical, tender. If it has moments of harshness toward the East, it balances them with harsh self-judgments: ("India a nation! Last comer to the drab nineteenth-century sisterhood! She shall rank with Guatemala and Belgium perhaps!") But in general it respects, with a genial twinkle, what it does not pretend to understand. It avoids the treachery of statistics, the pathetic fallacy of a declared exactitude. No vain controversy started over Mr. Forster's book, the only effects of which have been and can be to disarm and bring together.

Yet practically everything that *Mother India* so horridly offers is present in or implied by *A Passage to India*. Is it any wonder that while man's science and "truth" perishes from generation to generation, man's art of fiction remains immortal?

IV. LABORATORY

Sangre de Cristo

And now for an attempt, with suitable material, at a laboratory experiment in transcendental realism.

The material, genetically, is found in a personal letter

from which the following passages may be quoted, as being germane:

> . . . Certainly the one book to read about this country is Willa Cather's "Death Comes for the Archbishop." That is, if a single book is in question. I could name you dozens, but most of them are unsatisfactory in one way or another. There is a lot of good stuff in Mary Austin's "The Land of Journeys' Ending"—too much, in fact—but it is the kind of book that is best enjoyed as a rich memoir of things seen. Miss Cather's novel probably comes as near as a book can to creating pictures for one who has never been in New Mexico; it can't be done, actually.
>
> This is true in general, despite the fact that she is writing of the years 1850-1888. It woudn't be true anywhere else in the U. S. nor of everywhere in New Mexico; but from 1888 to 1928, or nearly, time has in most respects stood still in Santa Fe. Pleasantly still. Certain changes are now going forward owing to the development of tourist business and the crystallization of a small colony of painters and writers; but the scale of change is little and the rate of change is not rapid. Personally I feel a conviction that nothing can prevent this State from going backward; if it goes forward in one direction it will retreat in another; and I find this satisfies something in my soul—I am weary of Progress in most parts of my country.
>
> It is the Spanish people, of course. You may call them Mexicans, if you prefer, though they are entirely different from the people of Mexico (whom they do not like). The race south of the Rio Grande is 85 per cent. Indian blood or thereabouts. The people in and around Santa Fe, and to the north, have very little Indian admixture. As everybody else out here is crazy about the pueblo Indians, and as I like the

Spanish people enormously, I will try to tell you about them.

They are for the most part very poor. Large families. I have an idea that the situation here is somewhat analogous to that in the Province of Quebec with the proper substitutions. The older people have, some of them, beautiful manners. There are a few families of proud descent and careful tradition; some of these are still very rich in sheep and lands. Yet most of the fine old names, such as Chaves, Baca (originally Vaca, descendants of Cabezo de Vaca), Otero and so on are now so widespread that both extremes are to be found in them of wealth and acute poverty, high honor and utter worthlessness. Also these names are now so common that in some cases, according to Spanish custom, the surnames of parents are joined, Ortiz y Pino, just as we have Hamilton-Jones or Mapes-King.

Although the youngsters speak English, many of the grown people do not. My neighbor, a man of thirty-three, speaks a little, but I think chiefly because he was incorporated in the army in 1917-18 and even got as far as a military camp near New York. His sister, no older, speaks not a word. Many children do not learn English until they go to school. A knowledge of Spanish, though not necessary, is extremely handy. I should add that to the natives all of us are "the English," i.e., English-speaking, regardless of blood or birth, except in the case of a person distinctly non-American, perhaps, and obviously Italian, German, or something transatlantic.

I can give the picture most aptly by telling you about my servant, Frances or Francisca. She is a woman of thirty-seven, of good family. Her mother died in giving her birth and Frances was brought up by her grandmother. Her father, who seems to have had more than the average education and intelligent opinions, assisted in this upbringing of his daughter, or at least looked benignantly on. The grandmother was a personality. She ran to epigrams. "If a man wishes to stay in my kitchen, let him put on my dress." Frances was an extremely pretty girl—the traces are unmistakable. She has a very white skin, there must have been a pink color in her cheeks, her features are small and of the extreme regularity to be noticed in some Spanish faces; her face is oval but not so long as Spanish faces tend to be. Brown eyes, brown hair with plenty of red in it. She must once have had quite a lot of very small, faint orange freckles. Average height or less; slender—now, poor girl, wasted away, so that her arms are painful to look at. What pretty arms they must have been, and a pretty ankle. She has ruined her feet by wearing shoes with run-down heels, so that all day long while at work she is standing and walking on the outside edge of her foot. I give her better shoes but she will not wear them while there is still wear (as she sees it) left in these tattered abominations.

Her English, for working purposes, is very fair indeed; she was sent to the Sisters' School and they taught it to her. When twenty-one or so she was courted by a young man bearing one of the better family names. She fell in love with him—I sometimes think the more carefully a girl is brought up, the less able she is to withstand the madness of physical attraction. Her grandmother and father were dreadfully disturbed, for the young man was quite worthless, as they well knew. They tried to discourage the match but did not succeed. Both lived long enough to see the marriage turn out an utter failure, so far as Frances was concerned. Before dying, the grandmother said grimly, of Frances's husband: "This man puts his foot where I cast my eye," meaning that he ground down with his heel on an object she worshipped.

He gave her no money, which obliged her to go out to work; he took her money; he was drunk all the time; he struck her and the children. After fifteen years, Frances took the three children (one child had died) and left him. The oldest was a boy of eleven, the youngest a baby a year old; she was working out by the day. Three months after she left him she came home from a day of scrubbing floors and cleaning to bear her fifth child. It was Easter Eve. These people are kind to each other and one or two of the neighbors stayed with her. The child, a boy, was born Easter Day, and named Leopoldo—always referred to, according to custom, as El Niño ("the little one"; a girl would be La Niña). Frances is very proud of the fact that all her children are very white-skinned and blond; I think the only exception is Antonia, who is a little brown, not much. El Niño has blue eyes; so has the other boy, the oldest.

Since coming to work for me Frances has had an easier time, and much she needs it. I shouldn't call it very easy now, for she is up at five in the morning to give the children their breakfast and get the big boy off to school. A neighbor (paid) looks after the younger ones through the day and gives them their meals. Frances cleans up a beauty shop between seven and nine and then comes to me, works here all day, goes home at half-past seven or so, quite a long walk, rounds up her children, climbs a steep hill (and you just want to trying climbing here where the altitude is 7,000 feet and your breath is gone in no time), builds a fire, unless it is summer, and puts the kids to bed. Then up at five.

She has two rooms in an adobe house on top of this hill, in a cluster of houses occupied by three generations of one family. An old man named Montoya owns the hill and his children and grandchildren populate it. At the foot of the hill, in a fine house and gnashing his teeth, lives that one of the local artists whose paintings enjoy the most celebrity and the best prices. He wishes to buy the hill but old Mr. Montoya won't sell. The artist can get only some kind of unsatisfactory option. Meanwhile it has been discovered that the soil in the hill makes beautiful bricks. The prisoners in the local penitentiary just love making bricks, with or without straw, and the further side of the hill is being excavated. Mr. Montoya is growing rich; he may have the trouble of moving on a truly patriarchal scale but he will have the means to do it with. But the artist? His hill! What is to console him for the loss of the goal of a lifetime? It is improbable that the sight of cheerful penitentiarians or even of thousands upon thousands of bricks in orderly arrangement will appease him.

The hill kneels at the feet of the Sangre de Cristo range of mountains. The eye lifts over the poplars and cottonwoods and the silver dome of the State Capitol, over the sunken garden of the city, charming and insignificant, the Royal City of the Holy Faith of St. Francis; the vision makes nothing of miles of the mountain plain, lava beds, extinct cones, mesa, mirages. The sight goes straight and arrowy to the westward, over the ribbon of the Rio Grande and on to a long blue battlement of lofty mountains, the fastnesses of the Jemez, buttressed by hills of black and gray that have a skin as smooth as an animal's and that contain caves, cliffdweller ruins, prehistoric Puye and shards of pottery—but the detail of all these hills is lost to the eye, marsupially pouched in the blue wall along the horizon.

It is a magnificent view. Frances tells me: "I never see it."

The view to the east is equally impressive. The Sangre de Cristo mountains rise steeply and consist of an arrangement of planes, like a modernist *decor*, but with a slight effect of concavity. The noticeable thing about them is the bounding edges of the planes and the high and skilful degree of composition in the surfaces and edges. The summits are from

11,000 to 13,000 feet, so the range appears to be practically all forested. There are great areas of aspen—shimmer of dull silver—and the rest is evergreen, pine, Western spruce, and so on. The patterns of pine and aspen are large and sweep in charming lines. From November to May there are snow fields; the planes are more sharply defined and the New Mexico sunshine on the snow produces a dazzling whiteness seen through crystalline air under a blue heaven. The name of the range comes from five minutes at sunset when a clear rose color (better when the snow is on) lies over the whole barrier. Blood of Christ; the legend is that a Franciscan friar was reminded of the Most Precious Blood and gave the name.

I gather that Frances occasionally looks at the Sangre de Cristo towering above her mud house, but that the others on the hill never give a glance that way. They are all taken up with family squabbles. The life of a family like these Montoyas is communal rather than domestic. Frances relates all the news to me while I ponder the necessary reduction in butter and sugar to adjust my cake recipe for high altitude cookery. Most of the occurrences are trivial, sordid or amusing. Now and then drama supervenes. As, for instance, the other night, when the husband of one of the grandchildren came up the hill, drunken and boastful. His young wife gave birth to her first child less than a week before and was still in a serious condition. The husband insisted that he would sleep with her. The whole hill was aroused; he was persuaded to leave on the pretext that the evening was still young; finally old Mr. Montoya heard of the affair. The grandfather (or great-grandfather), a bent old man, loaded his shotgun and sat all night outside the door of his granddaughter's house, intending to shoot the young husband if he returned and attempted to carry out his boast. Mr. Montoya said that no woman of his family had ever been treated in such a fashion;

he would not have it. As it happened, the young man stayed downtown drinking.

There is a great deal of drinking, mostly of very bad home-made liquor, white mule. It will express the situation in this respect and in general if I tell you Frances's favorite refrain: the appropriate moment for it occurs in three-fourths of her stories: "Well, you know how the men are."

Certainly she knows!

But I must stop this interminable letter. I meant to tell you that I saw Sandison the other day. He is not looking well at all. T. b., of course. How acutely lonely he must be out here! No wife, children; nobody. It is perhaps as well, though, if he is going the way I think he is going, and as fast as I think. . . .

Here is material for fiction, assuredly, and for fiction of more than one kind. It is easy to see, from these people in this setting, realistic and perhaps brutal stories such as Blasco Ibáñez wrote at first (*The Cabin,* for example); or it is easy, in a romantic mood, to limn a New Mexican equivalent for Verga's "Cavalleria Rusticana." The letter writer infers a gentler side of existence among them than that she describes (Frances, her grandmother, the exquisite manners of the older people), so it might not be alien soil for a tale as idyllic as Louis Hemon's *Maria Chapdelaine.* A fertile genre; but there is one contrast which ought to make a particular impression upon us because it has the values of a simple and memorable symbol. This is the human antheap at the foot of the uniquely beautiful mountains. The very name of these mountains, the phenomenon of the rose color occurring briefly in evening light, underline the contrast with a significance which it would not be permissible to invent. For we are not now dealing with a project like a fable or an allegory, but with a novel having serious realistic pretensions for a generation, or epoch, dedicated to a certain literalness in the transcription of life for the exercise of emotion.

Before going further it should be worth our while to digress for a moment and consider what happens to *form* as distinguished from *function* in the realms which we speak of collectively as the arts. The function, or intended function, is always the same, whether the medium be architecture, sculpture, music, painting, or in the case we have been watching, fiction. The function is emotional fulfillment; but the form will vary according to what has been called the morphology of a culture.[5] but what may perhaps not inaccurately, and more simply, be described as man's age in his cycle. There have been various cultures—Chinese, Indian, Arabic, Classical, Western; intermediate ones, like the Mexican, that we know less about. Each has gone through the same life-cycle—infancy, youth, manhood, maturity, old age and death or decay. Each that has been named has had its completion except our own, the Western culture, now entering upon its final stage. Certain highly special and characteristic fundamental conceptions, unrelated and indeed unrelatable, such as those of time and space, are embodied in each culture. But the process of embodiment is always the same. It might be summarized as Simplicity—Complexity (Efflorescence)—Simplicity, with the distinction that the initial simplicity (infancy, youth) is accretive and growing, while the final simplicity is

[5] Oswald Spengler: *The Decline of the West,* Vol. I *passim.*

rather a *simplification.* Thus in painting we have the naïve beginnings of perspective in the work of artists of the Western culture. This is developed into the glories of Rembrandt and Velasquez. Later simplification sets in, with a violence sometimes too sudden, like the chill premonitions of senility that disconcert later middle age. Instead of painting a room, Picasso produces whorls and stabs of color in a tight pattern of exact decorative value; and at first we do not see what he is about. Then we discover that he has taken certain objects in the room—a fan, a piece of pottery, a brocade and so on—and has arranged them ideally and according to some inner necessity they bear to each other, of structure, texture, color. The *function* of his picture is identical with that of an Italian Primitive painter—emotional fulfillment, but the *form,* although a return to simplicity, is quite different. To take an example from literature, we do not know and can never know the true form of the fable or allegory, because it has been lost by the time when, in any culture, literature has been reduced to a language of some general acceptance in a written glyph or alphabet; whatever that form may be it exists only as speech or signs—perhaps only as thought. The first book of Genesis, we may say with no very serious exaggeration, is a Picasso account of Creation.

It follows that to insure the function of an attempted work of art we must conform with some care to the form acceptable at that stage which a given culture has reached. And fiction, or more specifically, the novel, in our present consideration, has scarcely reached the point where we can practice simplification with a Picasso-like directness. We cannot, as yet, spread the fan, snatch toward us the vase and crumple up the piece of brocade behind them, saying: "This is my room—essentially." We cannot, in the case before us, say: "Here is an ant heap shoved down at the foot of mountain majesty for the functional value of human insectitude; rose color, Sangre de Cristo, the idea of Christianity, for the functional value of the immortality of the human soul." We cannot at present go much further in this direction than Mr. Thornton Wilder has managed to do in *The Bridge of San Luis Rey,* which is possibly an intermediate novel, of mixed form, on the path toward the fiction of the future. And, although the gifted and the daring may press ahead—to our applause —we must gait ourselves more slowly, or even lag a little. We shall reach toward transcendentalism but within the now old, wholly familiar realistic perspectives.

Sangre de Cristo, that is the title of our novel, whose subject is human littleness and human glory. We must seek a point of view other than that of the people of the hill, who never look up at the range above them. Yet our observation must be directed from some point close to them, in close contact with them. It must filter through an intelligence superior to theirs. Its emotional expressions must be closer akin to ours than to theirs. It so happens that a device is offered, ready to our hand, in the very letter from which such long quotation has been made. It is Sandison, the lonely sufferer from tuberculosis—the doomed sufferer in the judgment of our correspondent. The connecting link is the simple and natural one existing with the hill, the servant, Frances. We have only to transfer her from the employment of our anonymous informant to that of Sandison.

Sandison, fighting his solitary and losing battle in the sight of those divine mountains; lifted from his miserable thoughts of himself by the vision to eastward; dragged back to the pettiness of humankind by the daily relations of the dispassionate and disillusioned household servant, but to a pettiness not his own, to miseries with no tinge of self-accusation, to the appeals of a pity that is not self-pity. That is what we have, a substance relentlessly woven in realism but with unimaginable color hidden in its drab. We could ask for nothing better.

In our laboratory experiments of the preceding chapters we have each time, for good reasons, rejected the narrative in the first person; here we shall find it superior to any of the other points of view. In the first place, with Sandison as narrator, we can impart the greatest possible vividness to Frances and her people, a vividness that must be almost completely lost in any use of the third person. We see this in the example of our letter from New Mexico—it is not so much Frances, as Frances seen through her employer's eyes that counts. The chief disability of the first person in fiction occurs when the narrator is also a considerable actor in the affairs he describes; his inevitable one-sidedness is then awkward to circumvent. But in our case Sandison is scarcely an actor, almost purely an onlooker. We see that he can give us the immediacy and freshness of the "I" with almost nothing of its drawback; the truth being, of course, that our story will be largely the case of first-person in externals and third-person actuality.

Largely, but not wholly; for it is inconceivable that we should not give Sandison himself a rôle, either directly, by way of some intervention into the Spanish life, or separately, by way of a story of his own (not his past, which has its place, but no values in present function). Sandison, too, must go forward to something, and it is not simply death from disease, it is life in its interior and exquisite experience. It may be externally active, it may be outwardly passive; that is immaterial. For the chief advantage of the first person, in antithesis to its handicap of the single viewpoint, is its power to authenticate events. "I was there; I saw, heard this, and did that." So we must study to make Sandison as much of an actor as may be accomplished with the least possible restriction of the point of view; thus he authenticates for us; while at the same time we strive to subdue and lessen his participation at all points where detachment is observed and commentary is of paramount need. We must struggle to accommodate conflicting purposes; it is hard; but that is art.

One or more simple diagrams will clarify matters and save many words. The following establishes relationships:

```
                              Reader      Author
                                 .           .
                                 .           .
                               ________________
                                       .
                                       .
Montoyas ——— Frances ——— Sandison
```

Probably the antitheses of the triple list following could be extended indefinitely; the list is presented to show the position and value of Frances in the scheme of the novel:

Montoyas	*Frances*	*Sandison*
racial past	racial and personal past	personal past
minimum of personal life	personal life partly amputated; some replacement from communal life	maximum of personal life
life by rote	life by rote, varied by individual exploratory effort in great crises	life wholly by individual exploratory effort
no personal or conscious destiny sense	half-conscious, confused and troubled destiny sense	acutely self-conscious, wholly personal destiny sense
oblivious to Sangre de Cristo	aware of but quiescent toward Sangre de Cristo	instant and incessant challenge felt in Sangre de Cristo
God as friend	God as asylum	God as foe

For an image of the action of the novel we must resort to astronomy. Sandison, on a straight path, passes near Frances, is slowed down and brought within an alien field of influence; certain transformations take place in him; he proceeds to his destiny. But the point is that

Sandison draws the reader with him; the reader experiences corresponding transformations, going on, after Sandison has fulfilled his end, to a separate, further, individual destiny.[6]

In this simple form of action it would be possible to produce a great variety of complications. Other gravitational forces may exert themselves upon Sandison (who, we must bear in mind, exerts a specific and, it is likely, a highly magnetic force himself). There is always the possibility that some one, something out of Sandison's past will come thrusting into the arc he is traveling—it is an arc, so far as we know, not an orbit; but if we can indicate it as part of an immense orbit, how great will be our accomplishment! But so definite is the *frame* of our story, so decisive the bounding edges of the blank canvas before us, that to introduce something from Sandison's past into an active present will probably be a mistake. How can it be convincingly incorporated in the picture? That is hard to envisage. No, present and future are the sense of what we must attempt.

And the effectiveness of what we create will depend almost wholly on its culminative intensity. The form of a diary, or a diary and letters, at once suggests itself. By such means we can induct the reader immediately into Sandison's personal drama of loneliness and mortal struggle with disease. It will act as drama under the

[6] The methods of infinitesimal calculus could be applied with much profit to the analysis of human relations for the purpose of fiction. One might start with the Fermat theorem and its equation: x^n plus y^n equals z^n as a simple form of statement that "within a domain of variable images there exists a relation such that from certain alterations certain other alterations necessarily follow."

reader's eye—the semi-recovery, the decline, the desperate rally, the crisis. All that is withheld will be withheld legitimately; the suspense will be real, for it is Sandison's own suspense; and the deception as to his true condition will be sincere as only self-deception can be. His inattention to himself, in what he commits to paper, will be a trifle strained, and not a little piteous. There will be about what he writes the sad transparency of the conscious confessional.

A good deal of intellectual comedy relieves the story. There is the artist at the foot of the coveted hill, helpless with rage as it is shoveled away for brick-making; there are Frances's *mots* (she appears one morning with the news that "the lady who is living with my husband" has had a baby); there is, no doubt, hovering in easy view the girl who has "got the West" and who thinks the Indians are all just too darling and who finds any other costume than a cowboy's simply too impossible for her wear. There is an immense mystification in the art of the local artists, whose delineations of the countryside sometimes require for their just appreciation a formula of extreme mental fearlessness, say $\sqrt[n]{-1}$.

Some crucial episode, like Miss Quested's experience in the Marabar cave and its consequences nucleating Forster's *A Passage to India,* there may well need to be in our *Sangre de Cristo;* it were foolish to try to invent it out of hand and before beginning to write the book. We should be far too likely to be caught in the gins and pitfalls of remembered "stories," finding ourselves in the windup with Sandison cured of his malady and blissfully holding the hands of the young woman who had just made a similar recovery from her attack of the West. Six months in Santa Fe is perhaps a minimum of time in which to gather sufficient material. And now our paper work on *Sangre de Cristo* is finished, except for some practice pages, which follow. They will either be entirely rewritten or scrapped.

From the first chapter:

Here, then, is where I have got to live, in a house that appears to be as shaky as my own body but is, I suspect, much more solidly built. Walls three feet thick; the front wall of the house appears to sway outward, viewed from the street, but this bulge, which would denote a fatal structural weakness in any other house, matters not at all in this one. There is a living room forty feet long, twenty wide, twelve high. It gives, on the side away from the street, on a *portal* or veranda the floor of which is flush with the ground. A roof supported on little round beams covers the *portal*, which is fifty feet long, twelve wide and brick-floored. It faces south. I sit on it bathed in the sunshine. I am exactly like a mollusk perched in a tiny cave at the bottom of an ocean of sunlight. Or perhaps a weed growing in the cave. The sun, the light press upon me with the uniform pressure of water in the great deeps; the rarefaction of dry air at this altitude gives me a certain buoyancy and makes the pressure supportable. If I were a weed I should wave gently. . . .

The *portal* excludes those mountains. Steamer-chaired at the mouth of my cave, I have no responsibility except the apricot tree on which a limited amount of fruit is trying to convert its green into red and gold. Frances tells me that the apricot blossoms earlier than any of the other fruit trees and regularly gets frosted every year after the blossoms are out. I consider its companionship entirely suitable.

From an interior chapter:

The artist, Merina, has taken a new wife. This is his third. His children (by his first wife) are great chums with his second wife and her children by a former marriage; they are seen about the Plaza all the time, laughing and joking, evidently having the best of times together. Merina is painting better all the while; the wives are mere domestic arrangements that have to be moved around from time to time like the furniture in a room, or added to, or discarded (one need not be vicious about it). It is important that the world should have his pictures and it is important that the children should have some adult companionship and looking after.

Frances tells me of each occasion on which she runs against her husband; he now watches her carefully, knowing that she is making good money, and being slightly dissatisfied with the woman he is living with. Frances expects his overtures for a reunion any day. She is resolute not to go back to him. "I know how the men are." But she will be horribly disappointed if he does not sue for peace.

From an interior chapter:

She sat there, this daughter of one of the best Boston families, in a rig which no self-respecting Santo Domingo Indian would have worn. I itched to tell her to go wash her neck, and then her face, and lastly her hands. Instead I gave her cigarettes and listened with every external symptom of sympathy.

"Well," I said at last, "why didn't you marry him."

"You don't understand," she said. "I'm afraid of marriage." And for a moment I thought she was going to cry. The thought disturbed me quite a lot, as a few watery trickles on that dust-coated countenance would, I felt, make it more than I could bear.

"You goose, we're all afraid of marriage."

What I really felt like telling her was to get over the worst of it in some way, even if it involved sleeping with a cowboy. I hold, perhaps wrongly, that she might then, ridded of her obsession, go back to Boston, marry her Cabot or her Lowell, and live happily ever after. I have seen one or two such cases.

I have also seen—any one out here can see—a case that developed logically out of the path she is treading. There is a boy in this State who is now an undergraduate at Yale or Harvard, I forget which. His mother is the wife of a Taos blanket Indian. She has a good deal of money and there is a very fine house. Perhaps the stepfather keeps out of the way when the son brings home with him a few friends from college.

The lady had really no intention of marrying the Taos chap, but the Federal Government was about to prosecute her on a charge of subverting the morals of one of its wards, so she decided to make a good woman out of herself.

From an interior chapter:

Not so well to-day. One of the Franciscans trudged up the hill and visited Frances. Her husband had been to the Church in an attempt to bring pressure to bear on her to return to him. Frances explained—and when I say "explained" I mean that I gather she concealed nothing. The priest was very gentle with her, said it was very sad, ascertained that she looked duly after the welfare of the children, made no attempt to persuade her to return to her husband, and gave her a little homily which, he probably realized, she does not exactly need:

"You do not have men to this house, my daughter?"

Frances blew up. When she had subsided, he said:

"You must live quietly here with your children."

"No! No! You do not understand; all I want is to live quiet; I do not want the men; I know how the men are."

He apologized and soothed her; said he would report to the Archbishop and thus prevent the making of any more trouble for her by her husband, so far as the Church was concerned. Frances's husband had evidently represented that she had divorced him, but all she did was to get him before the police magistrate who made him promise not to annoy her.

From the final chapter:

Now that it is certain I am to die, and quite shortly, I cannot bear to be out of sight of the Sangre de Cristo. They used to pierce me with their challenge, but now I feel them very friendly. There are, I suppose, no sacraments for me to take at the outset of a new journey and it is too late for me to embrace a particular creed; I should feel like a hypocrite. I cannot "die in the faith"; I can only live in the sight. Goodbye.

CHAPTER VII

CRITICISM: MORALITY: TASTE: ART

IN fiction, as elsewhere, the philosophical inquirer will accept things that lie hopelessly entangled in the confusion in which he finds them, not vainly endeavoring to tear them apart—that is the reformer's zeal—but trying to distinguish them a little in their inextricability. Thus, although we constantly speak of "criticism," "morality," "taste," and "art," these are not wholly independent entities. Average notions of criticism are more or less bound up with ideas of morality, with standards of taste, and with conceptions, usually vague, of art. It is best to acknowledge the fact, and discuss the four together.

Not one of the four is of fixed meaning. Perhaps the two best-known definitions of criticism are Anatole France's, "the adventures of one's soul among masterpieces" and the canon of Benedetto Croce: "What has the artist tried to do? How far has he succeeded in doing it?" In both instances the critic is subjective and impressionistic, and this considerable element of subjectivity, of impressionism, can never be wholly eliminated, for the reason that one is dealing with a work of art, or of attempted art, and art is a means on the one hand and the degree of success achieved on the other.

Art, we have seen, may only be defined by defining its purpose, which is the adaptation of the truths of life to men's physical and emotional needs, by certain means. What means? In the case of fiction, arrangements of words so managed as to present life by values, by intensities, in a semblance of the way we live it inwardly. But this only leads to more questions, quite unanswerable ones, such as: "What arrangements of words? Of two arrangements with the same intention, which is better?" and so on. Even in given instances we can frame no specific or decisive reply.

We may watch, but only in a general way, the practice of method by certain writers, their technique; and we may develop roughly the method of each. But as far as we go—as far as any one *can* go—travels only to the edge of the writing itself, and there comes upon a parting of ways quite innumerable. The same passage or scene may be written by two or more craftsmen with the same exact and definable intent; and the results may honestly divide expert opinion. There are degrees of art; there is undoubtedly good art and bad art, though the latter is a contradiction in terms; there is no best art, nor even any final art. And always the jurisdiction is under challenge, the allegiances shift about. As if there were not enough difficulties in arriving at emotional evaluations, man's pet hobby, the rational faculty, is constantly being brought into the confusion to set the house in order. And when we have given reason full charge the house is indeed swept and ordered, but lifeless; we find we cannot live in it any more.

As for morality, we know that morals are the widely accepted customs of a particular period; unwritten social laws of voluntary assent by the majority. What is the relation of morality to art? Well, we easily conjecture that where the sense of morality is outraged, art is largely or even wholly nullified; beyond that, no relation appears. The artist is not bound to respect the prevalent morality, but if he too flagrantly ignores it he risks all that his art attempts *with the immediate audience at the immediate time.* On the other hand, conforming suitably to the current morality, he may excite the condemnation or contempt of the future, when moral codes will have changed again.

What do we mean by "taste"? Not anything clearly bound up with prevalent morality—and not, of course, the variations of individual preference or prejudice—nor a question of means, like art. Of all the four indefinite subjects we are discussing, taste is the least definable, the quickest sensed. It is the classic line in the execution of a work of fiction, not merely in the literary style but in all the connected phases of treatment; it is not a style at all but a shapeliness and symmetry felt as a structural force, something on which mere style is imposed afterwards, as the dressed stone facing is hung on the steel girders of a modern skyscraper. It makes itself felt as a force, just as in the Greek vase, for which the term "dynamic symmetry" has been coined. If we could analyze it in a work of fiction as tangibly as in the Greek vase or a Beethoven symphony or the Rheims Cathedral, we should likely discover that in fiction, also, it has a mathematical basis, depending on certain relations between dimensions, the affinity of certain numbers, the coherency and even the cohesiveness of particular curves and tangencies. No doubt by patiently looking at a great novel, again and again, we may sometimes be able to isolate the force of taste that is exercised in it; but in general we scarcely get beyond the sense of a centripetal power that pulls the work all together, unifies and poises it, launches it on its flight before our charmed eyes—a force that is alive but inert, that is constantly and capably and gracefully bearing the strains and stresses to which each character in the book and every scene and even the setting forever subjects it. But morality has nothing to do with taste, which may at any moment brush morality aside; art is subdued by the force of taste and becomes a mere handicraftsman employing itself discreetly under the directions of a genius, a spirit. And as for criticism, there is nothing palpable it can lay hold of; in the presence of taste it is reduced to admiring ejaculations and silences as loud with admiration.

The presence of taste rather than that of art is the evidence of what we call genius. Art is consciously exercised; taste has its roots deeper down. We sometimes speak of "instinctive art" and generally mean—where we mean anything—the functioning of taste. A writer's art may be faulty and perfect taste may overcome, in the sense of more than offsetting, all defects of his art. There are in the writing of fiction occasional problems artistically insoluble, or susceptible only of compromise. Where these are encountered, fine taste may make them merely technical failures. Thomas Hardy and George Moore offer plentiful illustrations.

Good criticism of fiction is itself a fiction about a fiction. For its production there are necessary (1) a fairly considerable knowledge of fiction, past and present, not for the purpose of writing down comparisons but so that the appraisals may be both pliant and sound; (2) some experience in writing fiction, or attempting to write it. The degree of success is usually unimportant.

What is important, and what can ordinarily only be furnished by the personal attempt to write fiction, is an intelligent penetration of aim in the work criticised.

"What has the artist tried to do? What are the means he has used? How far has he succeeded in doing it?"

Criticism, of course, has almost nothing to do with the so-called book review. That is, or should be, a well-balanced reporter's account of a new work. It does not need and it should not use any of the paraphernalia of criticism. Critical attempts upon a work of fiction cannot ordinarily be safely ventured in less than a decade, and a longer perspective may be necessary. And this arises from no cautiousness of the critic, but from the impossibility of estimating direction and distance, of analyzing such paramount matters as the true subject and the application of the point of view, or isolating the qualities of taste displayed by the work. In short, there can be no criticism of new fiction in the common meaning of that adjective. At best only the earlier work of contemporaries is eligible; even there, criticism moves only to tentative conclusions.

Tentative from the operation of the same causes; for the death of a fictioner is always the occasion, if not the immediate one, for a process of revaluation, however assured may have seemed the verdicts reached in his lifetime. As this is written, Joseph Conrad is silently undergoing such a reappraisal, the results of which cannot possibly be forecast. It seems likely that much less of him will survive to pass into the great tradition than almost any one would have confidently predicted three years before his death; on the other hand, one or two works, then improbably marked for ultimate survival—*Nostromo* among them—are gradually moving into their high and rightful place. In the case of Thomas Hardy, death makes less for readjustment, since he deliberately chose to end his novel-writing with *Jude the Obscure* in 1895.[7] But although we have had over thirty years in which to study Hardy the novelist, the instance is an excellent one to make the point: Our criticism of Hardy is far from final.

But what do we mean by saying that good criticism is "a fiction about a fiction?" We mean, obviously, that it is something other than analysis, weighing, judgment. It is a penetration of the author's purpose, and a power of weaving anew the spell which his story cast originally over the author. For the first and most pressing attainment of the critic, it is immaterial whether or not the author criticised has conveyed that spell; it is the critic's business to comprehend its nature with an intimacy only less marvelous than the author's own. It is the critic's business to be amenable to the same magic and to make the indifferent reader amenable. The answer to the first question, "What has the artist tried to do?" is not made by any painstaking summary of the book's contents, but by a kind of emotional clairvoyance which pierces the cloudy crystallization and reveals the tear, the drop of attar, the petal of almond, the slow discoloration of a

[7] *The Well Beloved,* published in 1897, is an earlier work.

spreading stain for which an embodiment has been sought, on which the cunning of art has been expended, which forms the thread, as slender as a hair and perhaps brittle, perhaps broken, for the sequence of words, the procession of images, the illusion of vital curve and quenchless movement.

The critic must embrace the author's intention, and it is not likely that he can do this except he himself be in some degree a fictioner. The old taunt, that a critic is one who has failed as a writer, is perfectly true; the only thing to be said against it is that it is perhaps a little hasty, and therefore a little unkind. Fictional creativeness is not seldom the matter of a term, like other creative powers. An impulse to fertility arises, is exercised in some form of productiveness, and dies. In the physical world this is well understood; but the chapter of the emotions tells a variant story. Emotion like quintessential sex, is with us from earliest childhood, enduring usually until death or extreme old age, and its productive period may be almost equally lifelong; it does not so often become sterile as vary its function. The emotion which has produced for a number of years works of fiction is wholly dependent on some unknown source of fertilization—as a woman, sometimes, upon a particular man, a man upon a particular woman. But then a shadowy and incomprehensible bereavement takes place, and the works of fiction can no longer be birthed. Yet perhaps other works, and possibly of even more value in the individual instance, may still be produced. An indifferently good novelist has been changed into a commanding critic, just as a drone at a certain age may be transformed into a queen bee; and the very means of the alteration may be the same, special feeding, superior nourishment.

The point is worth a little emphasis because the rôle of the critic is so commonly misunderstood. "A critic is one who has failed as a writer"—very true; only we have to recognize that the causes of that failure may be entirely beyond the critic's control; we have to recognize that the preliminary failure was an indispensable preparation for the critical career; and we acknowledge that good critics are so much rarer than good writers of fiction that even in any probable exchange we are the gainers. Nothing against nature is involved in the production by one and the same person, alternately or simultaneously, of sound critical work and excellent novels, although the better the novels, the less likely we are to find a necessary breadth and receptivity in the criticism; the more valuable the criticism, the less vitality is probable in the fiction. A single paternity is the rule; of twins, one is quite likely to be a weakling.

"What has the artist tried to do?" But the critic has another question with which, if his author is yet alive and it is not too late, it is his duty to deal: "What ought the artist to try to do?" The answer may be privately given, but there may be an important reason for giving it publicly, since its clear statement is part of that divination of the author's gift and accomplishment which the critic is engaged in passing on to the author's readers. It will be readily perceived that a critic needs the best manners in the world; for if circumstances require him to answer openly the question about an artist's proper ground, the statement and exposition must be strictly impersonal throughout. Even so, it may be heartily resented, but the resentment is conceivably a better tribute to the truth of the declaration than even those moving letters of acknowledgment and gratitude which are the critic's viaticum. Of open vindication he can, of course, have almost never any.

If the facts were examined, and if the discovered truth could be enforced, we should have a decenter proportion of good critics, a lesser number of deformed novelists. It happens with rarest infrequency that a writer's self-critical powers put him on the proper track. Such an instance, notable in our era, has been George Bernard Shaw, who began by producing four novels and triumphantly shifted to the writing of plays. Does any one doubt the fate of Mr. Shaw as a continuing novelist? Then let him study the rôle enacted by Mr. H. G. Wells, whose brilliant critical gifts have been denied their highest fulfillment and their proper recognition by his insistence on continuing to write a species of work that could be styled a novel.

Since all great fiction is a critique of the emotions, criticism must press these questions: "What has the artist tried to do? What ought he to try to do?" to avoid becoming a mere commentator at second-hand. That is the principal peril of attempted criticism, the twice-remove from realities of feeling. The ideal of criticism has very generally been an ideal of detachment, even aloofness; of circumspection, of an almost purely objective study. Such indeed is the proper temper in which to approach and undertake examinations like those comprised in Mr.

Lubbock's *The Craft of Fiction.* There he gives us an anatomy of fiction prized so highly because most critical attempts are mere massage. But though fiction not clad in flesh and blood is less than nothing, flesh and blood cannot exist without the firmness of bone. Lubbock goes to the bone.

The great critic enters the subject at, or very near, the precise genetic origin of the work, which becomes to him, for his initial purposes, his own problem in creation. The inspiring reflection or imaginative vision from which the fiction sprang is not hidden from him; the emotion it seeks to convey is his, fully. Every problem of development is under his eye. If malformation has taken place, he is able to discern what the perfectly-formed issue would be. His purpose is not to find fault, nor is his temper ever that of fault-finding. It is analytical, expository, constructive and as surely creative as the fictioner's own. It may touch upon defects, but it dwells upon excellences, both those actually present and those properly to be imagined. "What has the artist tried to do?" That is all-important. "What ought he try to do?" This occasionally enters. Then the question of art: "What are the means by which he has tried to do it?" Their proper appreciation should serve simply as an illustration of all the general problems of artistic method. "How far has he succeeded in doing it?" The answer to this last question is least important of all, is incidental, may in many an instance be omitted as irrelevant.

For the critic cares less for what has been than for what is to be written.

Little, with profit, can be said further on the subject of morality. It is nonsense to protest the current morality of a book which obviously shocks many readers. So far as the critic is concerned, morality must mean considerations far removed from temporary codes; and perhaps some of the unceasing confusion could be abated if we were to use the word "indecent" for the currently immoral and reserve "immoral" for the larger, timeless tendencies with which a critic may have to reckon. What, in this view and in the critical province, is "immoral"? The first answer must be: anything that promotes meanness and smallness of the human spirit. Possibly this first answer is, with proper subdividing, nearly the whole answer. But rebelliousness, for example, is not immoral. Rebellion may take an indecent form, that is, a form violative of the current morality; but in itself it is a reach toward human freedoms, and largeness of spirit. It can be foolish, misguided, wicked, insane—what you please. There is nothing in it essentially subversive of timeless morality. On the other hand, utter and irreproachable decency may be profoundly immoral; immoral because smug, because hypocritical, because contracting. We all know the difference between the shrinking lie and the audacious lie; one is at times tempted to believe it a greater difference than that between the lie and the truth. At any rate, we may be sure that there are literal, evasive, guarded truths in statement which are morally beneath the lie of intention and boldness.

The question of decency in literature is of only passing importance; it is unlikely that future indecency in print will surpass indecencies published and long since forgotten. The question of morality stands outside time and is always serious when raised for cause. As has been indicated, Shakespeare's *The Merchant of Venice* is a most immoral masterpiece, though decent enough. And there is a certain immorality attached to work which employs the method of caricature, or extreme example, and which will plainly be taken as representative. Thus, although James Joyce's *Ulysses* is frankly and continuously indecent, it is not immoral in this sense—and probably not in any sense—for no one could possibly take its characters as typical or general; they are not so intended (one thing) and will not anywhere be so received (quite another, and a more important, matter). But whatever the intention of the author of *Elmer Gantry,* he could not but expect his portrait of a clergyman-evangelist to be received as fairly representative of a class; therefore he risked the charge of immorality in this respect—nothing to do with his book's decency, which is tolerable. A defense of intention, like a plea of ignorance of the law, cannot excuse; for the reason that the mind of the reader is a factor from the start; and the author, who has constantly and demonstrably conformed in all other respects to reader-capacity, obviously knew what he was about in this respect.

The determinations of morality require keen and just perception; they cannot always be made at once; they are often over the heads of the multitude; and there is no way of giving them practical effect except as we learn to retain and discard literary heritages. Determinations of current morality, or decency, are not nearly so difficult as some people make them out to be—nor so simple as others assume. But a large part of the situations involving decency are due to the indiscriminate publication and circulation of doubtfully decent fiction; the proper remedy lies here, and not in impromptu, amateur and partisan censorships. Publishers—who, as a class of business men, are about a half century behind other business—insist on printing indecent books in editions of regular size for promiscuous sale. They confuse decency and morality (in common with the rest of us). Some of them will be heard arguing that for a book to be merely "frank" cannot be indecent; but this is nonsense. Whatever the merits or demerits of James Branch Cabell's *Jurgen,* the author understood with perfect clearness how to take advantage of this confusion of ideas, and, his tongue in his cheek, he wrote certain passages that were bound to be acquitted of indecency, since literally they were decent. It is worth noting that at no other spots in the book is there anything to suggest that the work is addressed to the literal-minded reader.

After the prosecution of *The Brook Kerith* in London, Mr. George Moore took the sensible course of allowing his new books to be published only for advance subscribers. The editions were limited, the price was made high, and while neither Mr. Moore nor his publishers possessed the chance of "best-seller" profits, both were assured of a handsome profit and a surcease from trouble. No other course should be pursued with books where decency is in serious question. It is easy enough to limit such a book to a single edition, printed from type, of one thousand copies, the type to be distributed. The announcement of such an edition at such a price is amply sufficient to sell it out; the author need not have Mr. Moore's reputation for the success of the enterprise, the very terms of which will announce the nature of the work and stir to activity its proper public.

This is not artful subterfuge. These books have a right to be published. Due care, however, must be exercised to see that they go into proper hands. Commercial greed and a false and stupid assertion of "liberty" and the "right of free speech" are to blame for book censorships. But to broadcast indecency is bad business, quite as bad as the retaliatory actions it provokes.

On art, as we have seen, there is no final word; on taste there is no light except that of interior wisdom. But it is necessary, in closing this footnote on a philosophy of fiction, to dwell a little on the root of fiction, the root of the very soul of humankind. All our psychology has been directed along rationalistic lines and has depended on ratiocinatory systems for so long as to make the task of a new method seem extraordinarily difficult. Practically all our valuable knowledge of the emotions is "unscientific," and will remain so until the conception of a scientific process has been transformed. Nowadays there is much talk of the humanization of knowledge, in the effort to bridge a widening gulf between the knowledge that has been arrived at by acceptable process and has been formally organized and that other, vaster knowledge which men and women really live by. But the knowledge of humanization is the only Archimedean lever of world societies. *That* knowledge has had amazingly different embodiments throughout history—Francis of Assisi, Napoleon, George Washington Plunkitt of Tammany Hall, Brigham Young of Salt Lake City, Florence Nightingale and dozens of incredibly jostling figures press forward with varying but convincing claims to its accurate possession. And the knowledge of humanization, so far as it can be got into writing, still exists for us almost entirely in fiction—in the drama, in novels, in some poetry. Its secret evidently resides in a certain kind and degree of vitality, not necessarily a physical vitality, although that is a most important auxiliary and adjunct. We know nothing about it, really, except that it exists, and that it can be recognized when embodied.

In short, only the knowledge purveyed in fiction is sufficiently humanized as a whole. The old, the immemorial world of man, that existed before he began his long quest of "truth," still surrounds him. It has its distortions—postures from which he peers outside; it has its lies, for souls are as easily upset as stomachs. But it is a world he can live in, not a scientific Mars whose air he cannot breathe. Often he affects to despise it, talks of moving to a richer and better-ordered neighborhood, and remains where he is, viewing those other regions from afar.

Here in his own place, going everywhere perfectly because never leaving it, we find him.

INDEX

Adam Bede, rôle of deity in, 85
Æschylus, plot solution by deity in, 35
Arlen, Michael, *The Green Hat,* plot, 76
Art, as means of communication of emotion, 6
  definition, 8, 345
  development, 6
  emotion in relation to, 94
  fiction as, 4, 5
  form *vs.* function, 333
  literary *vs.* art of emotions, 94
  morality in relation to, 346
  taste in relation to, 348
Austen, Jane, characterization, 80
  creed, 87
  Emma, 72-80
    characterization, 80
    extracts, 122
    modernity, 72
    plot, 73
    viewpoint, 77, 79
  life, 72
  Northanger Abbey, 74
  Persuasion, 138-148
    action, 146
    dialogue, 141
    opening, 140
    reasons for selection for study, 106
    restricted society, 145
    shortcomings, 141-146
    story of, 138
  plot in, 73, 76
  sense of feminine values, 77, 79, 119
Author omniscience, 59

Balzac, Honoré de, modern realism, 82
Bennett, Arnold, *Clayhanger,* extract, 55
  life, 149
  Old Wives' Tale, 148-161
Bennett, Arnold—*Cont'd*
    extract, 96
    germ of, 184
    opening, 150
    prophetic quality, 137, 160
    reasons for selection for study, 136
    story of, 150-156
    style, 159
    subject, 157, 160
  Riceyman Steps, advertisement, 100
    extract, 123
Black Stream, extract, 108
Bojer, Johan, *The Great Hunger,* 244-258
    beginning, 245
    Christian ideal, 252
    contrasted with *Moby Dick,* 251
    deus ex machina, 256
    narrators, 256
    reasons for selection for study, 245
    story, 245-251
    technique, 253
Book reviewing, criticism *vs.,* 349
Bridge of San Luis Rey, plot, 227
Brontë, Emily, as prophet, 230
  life, 284
  Wuthering Heights, 284-299
    beginning, 286
    compared with *Moby Dick,* 296
    realism, 299
    reasons for selection for study, 283
    story, 286-294
    transcendental aspect, 295-298

Cather, Willa, *Death Comes for the Archbishop,* extract, 4
  life, 185
  A Lost Lady, 184-196
    narrators, 190, 193

Willa—*Cont'd*
ns for selection for study,
7
, 185-190
ct, 190-193
The Professor's House, as narrative, 132
extract, 121
Chance, complexity of, 162
Character, novel of, history, 57-89
Austen, 72-80
Balzac, 84
Defoe, 63-67
Dickens, 83
early, 57
Eliot, 85
Fielding, 71
Flaubert, 84
Prevost, 68-71
Richardson, 67-71
Sterne, 71
summary of development, 88
morality, 85
study in method, 136-225
Austen's *Persuasion,* 138-148
Bennett's *Old Wives' Tale,* 148-161
Cather's *A Lost Lady,* 184-196
Conrad's *Nostromo,* 161-184
laboratory study, 196-225
See also Fantasy, Prophecy, Sentimentality.
Characterization, Austen, Jane, 72-80
Defoe, Daniel, 64-67
Dickens, Charles, 83
direct *vs.* indirect, 59, 80
early fiction, 57
Euripides, 57
flat *vs.* round, 83, 304
Fielding, Henry, 71
Hutchinson, A. S. M., 61
romantic novel, 53
speech by character, narrative differentiated from, 134
Chesterton, Gilbert K., detective stories, 47
Circular Staircase, plot, 46
Oracle of the Dog, plot, 226
Clarissa, Prevost's *Manon Lescaut* in comparison with, 67-71
Clayhanger, extract, 55
Coincidence, use of, 51
Colby, Nathalie Sedgwick, ***Black Stream,*** extract, 108
Collins, Wilkie, mystery stories, 47
Conjecture, development, 3, 11
Conrad Joseph, *Chance,* complexity of, 162
chronology, inversion in, 161
life, 163
narrator devices, 162
Nostromo, 161-184
background, 164
beginning, 166
chronology, 182
germ of, 164
reality of, 179
reasons for selection for study, 137
story, 167-178
subject, 166
toil of writing, 178
on truth in relation to fiction, 31
A Personal Record, extract, 237
revaluation, 349
suspended situation in, 163
The Rescue, suspended situation in, 163
Youth, extract, 4
Cookery, direct appeal of, 6
Creeds, novelists', 87
Criticism, as penetration of author's purpose, 350
book reviewing *vs.*, 349
critic, as writer who has failed, 351
function, 99
definition, 345
ideal, 353
peril of, 353
requisites, 348
taste in relation to, 348

Death Comes for the Archbishop, extract, 4
Decency, morality *vs.*, 355-358
Defoe, Daniel, creed, 87
Moll Flanders, characterization in, 64
Deity, detective as substitute, 44
rôle, Christianity as affecting, 40

Deity—*Cont'd*
earliest fiction, 32
Eliot, 85
Greek drama, 34, 35
Hardy, 38
Hawthorne, 86
Jewish fiction, 34
Shakespeare, 42
substitutes for, 43, 44
Detective story, *deus ex machina* in, 44-47
plot, 32, 44
Deus ex Machina. *See* Deity.
Devil's Garden, plot, 48
Dialogue, Austen, Jane, 141
Dickens, Charles, characteristics, 83
Doomdorf Mystery, plot, 47
Dostoevski, Fedor Mikhailovich, as prophet, 230
creed, 88

Eliot, George, *Adam Bede*, rôle of deity, 85
creed, 88
Elmer Gantry, immorality, 356
Emma. *See* Austen, Jane.
Emotion, activity essential to, 93
art in relation to, 6, 94
communication, means, 6, 10
through fiction, 4, 10
creation of, direct, 10
development, 3, 10
human relationship as basis, 93
importance in life, 94
intensity, cause, 92
meaning *vs.* in fiction, 97
verities of, use by novelist, 94
Euripides, characterization, 58
Hardy, compared with, 38
plot solution by deity in, 35-38
Experience, definition, 30

Fact, definition, 1, 20
fiction in relation to, 20
See also Fiction, Truth.
Fantasy, prophecy, distinguished from, 229
Sterne's *Tristram Shandy*, 71
Fiction, approach, proper, 95
to inner truth through, 18
as art, 4, 5

Fiction—*Cont'd*
basis, rational, 22-25
definition, 1, 8
enjoyment of, 5
fact in relation to, 20-25
finite. *See* Character, novel of
history, 32-89
character novel, 57-89
early, 32
fantasy, 71
Greek, 34-38
Hardy, 38
Jewish, 34
plot in, ancient style, 32-40
prophecy, 86
realism, 44
rise of rational faculty, 37
romanticism, 52-57
sentimentality, 67-71
Shakespeare, 41
synopsis, 88
human relationships, 17, 90-97
mind of reader, 98-135
knowledge of humanization in, 359
life differentiated from, 19
material of, 90-135
method, character novel, 136-225
plot in the ancient style, 226-281
prophecy, 282-344
philosophy of, definition, 5
purpose, 4, 10
root of, 358
rules, 5
truth, indistinguishable from, 1
in relation to, 31
types, character novel, 57-89; 136-225
plot in the ancient style, 32-40; 226-281
prophecy, 86; 282-344
vehicle, 4, 346
See also Fact, Truth.
Fielding, Henry, *Tom Jones*, 71
Flaubert, Gustave, *Madame Bovary*, extract, 122
style, 84
Forster, E. M., *A Passage to India*, 315-325
extract, 19

Forster, E. M.—*Cont'd*
impression left by, 316
compared with Mayo's *Mother India,* 324
reasons for selection for study, 283
story, 316-322
subject, 323
Franklin Winslow Kane, extract, 124

Genius, evidence of, 348
Gothic novel, rise, 44
Great Hunger. See Bojer, Johan.
Green Hat, plot, 76

Hamilton, Clayton, *A Manual of the Art of Fiction,* extract, 20, 22
Hardy, Thomas, compared with Euripides, 38
revaluation, 350
Hawthorne, Nathaniel, *The Scarlet Letter,* deity in, 86
Hergesheimer, Joseph, *Java Head,* criticism, 96
Hichens, Robert, *The Unearthly,* extract, 121
Hildegarde, extract, 15
Human relationships as material of fiction, 90-98. *See also* Reader.
emotion as basis, 93
intensity of emotion, 92
reasons for, 91
respect for nature of material, 94
Hutchinson, A. S. M., *If Winter Comes,* characterization, 61

If Winter Comes, characterization, 61
Imagination, development, 11
in mysticism, 13
in philosophy, 14
lack of, widespread, 12, 14
mind of the race as regards, 104
Indecent books, publication, 355
Insincerity, intentional, use of, 94
Ivanhoe, characterization, 53

Java Head, criticism, 96
Joyce, James, *Ulysses,* emotion, 97
morality, 356
stream of consciousness method, 109

Knowledge of humanization, 358

Laboratory studies, *Sangre de Cristo,* 325-344
extracts, 341
form, 339
narrator, 335-339
origin and choice of subject, 325-332
subject, 332
The Strain Runs Out, 196-225
appeal of subject, 203-208
narrators, 208-212
origin and choice of subject, 197-203
outline, 208-221
subject, 204
treatment, 222-225
A Wink toward Heaven, 258-280
appeal of subject, 260
origin and choice of subject, 258-260
outline, 261-270
treatment, 270-280
Lawrence, D. H., as prophet, 230
Mornings in Mexico, extract, 91
Lewis, Sinclair, *Elmer Gantry,* immorality, 356
Life, elements, 90
emotion in, 94
fiction differentiated from, 19
for novelist's purpose, definition, 90
intensity, importance, 92
time, place in, 91
truths of, used by, 94
See also Emotion, Human Relationships.
Lost Lady. See Cather, Willa.

Madam Bovary, extract, 122
Manon Lescaut, Richardson's *Clarissa* compared with, 67-71
Mayo, Katharine, *Mother India,*

Mayo, Katharine—*Cont'd*
compared with Forster's *A Passage to India,* 324
Maxwell, W. B., *The Devil's Garden,* plot, 48
Melville, Herman, as prophet, 230
creed, 88
life, 233
Moby Dick, 228-244
animism, 235, 238, 244, 251
beginning, 239
coherent method lacking, 235
compared with *The Great Hunger,* 251
compared with *Wuthering Heights,* 206
dramatic soliloquy, 235
narrator, 238
plot, 234
reality, 240
reasons for selection for study, 232
spiritual theme, 237
story, 239-243
Memory, as foe of realism, 110
development, 2, 11
reader's, writer's appeal to, 104
Merchant of Venice. See Shakespeare, William
Mind, development, 26
See also Reader, mind of.
Moby Dick. See Melville, Herman.
Moll Flanders, characterization, 64
Morality, art in relation to, 346
decency *vs.,* 355-358
taste, in relation to, 348
Morals, definition, 346
Mornings in Mexico, extract, 91
Mother India, compared with Forster's *A Passage to India,* 324
Music, communication of emotion through, 8
material, respect for nature of, 97
Mysticism, imagination as basis, 13

Narration, principal character as narrator, 63
Narration—*Cont'd*
speech by a character differentiated from, 134
story presentation by means of, 132
Northanger Abbey, characteristics, 74
Norris, Kathleen, *Hildegarde,* extract, 15
Nostromo. See Conrad, Joseph.
Novel. *See* Character, Plot.

Old Wives' Tale. See Bennett, Arnold.
Oracle of the Dog, plot, 226

Painting, communication of emotion through, 7
Passage to India. See Forster, E. M.
Personal Record, extract, 237
Persuasion. See Austen, Jane.
Philosophy, approach to inner truth through, 17
imagination in, 14
Photography, fiction not, 95
Plot, ancient style, artistic requirement, 51
coincidence, 51
definition, 74
function, 50
history, 32-42
conscience as substitute for deity, 48
decline, 37-42
detective as substitute for deity, 32, 44-47
earliest, 32
Greek, 34
Hebrew, 34
romantic novel, 52-56
synopsis of development, 88
reality, effect of, 102
short fiction, examples, 226
study in method, 226-281
Bojer's *The Great Hunger,* 244-258
laboratory study of *A Wink Toward Heaven,* 258-281
Melville's *Moby Dick,* 228-244

Plot—*Cont'd*
use of, tests, 51
See also Deity, Reason.
Poe, Edgar Allan, detective stories, 44
Point of view, shifting, 134
Post, Melville Davisson, *The Doomdorf Mystery,* plot, 47, 226
Prevost, Abbé, creed, 87
Manon Lescaut, compared with Richardson's *Clarissa,* 67-71
Professor's House. See Cather, Willa.
Prophecy, history, 86
characters, 231
definition, 86, 228
fantasy distinguished from, 229
prophets, examples, 137, 160, 229
study in method, 282-344
Brontë's *Wuthering Heights,* 284-299
Forster's *A Passage to India,* 315-325
laboratory study of *Saugre de Cristo,* 325-344
Tolstoy's *War and Peace,* 300-314
transcendental realists, examples, 232
Proust, Marcel, stream of consciousness method, 109
Swann's Way, extract, 273
Psychology, approach to inner truth through, 17
fiction not, 95

Reader, mind of, 98-135
author's need of comprehension of, 99
imagination, 104
importance of relationship with, 98
point of view, 134
reality, 100-127
recognition by, 104-106
re-creation of novel by, 99
realism and reality, confused by, 106
sequence, requirement, 127-131
See also Reality, Recognition.
Realism, advantages and disadvantages, 109
Arnold Bennett, 160
as substitute for deity, 43
danger of, 107
definition, 107
memory as foe of, 110
method, 107
modern, Balzac, 82
reality achieved by, 111
reality differentiated from, 106
stream of consciousness method, 108
Reality, 100-127
achieved by realism, 111
coercions of life imitated for effect of, 102
determinations of, 110
feminine, 112-127
vs. masculine, 116, 119
fictional, forms, 110
plausibility *vs.* probability, 101
reader's mind as guide, 103
reader's requirement of, 100
realism differentiated from, 106
recognition as basis, 14, 104
refinements, 100
See also Recognition.
Reason, definition, 26
deity *vs.,* 38
development, 27, 37
Recognition, definition, 104, 105
feminine, 112-127
memory of traditional knowledge, as, 105
primary, 106
reader's, importance, 104
sexual, 112
types, 110
See also Reality.
Religion, approach to inner truth through, 16
imagination in, 13
Rescue, suspended situation, 163
Riceyman Steps. See Bennett, Arnold.
Richardson, Samuel, *Clarissa,* compared with Prevost's *Manon Lescaut,* 67-71
Rinehart, Mary Roberts, *The Circular Staircase,* 46

INDEX

Romanticism, as substitute for deity, 43
  definition, 52
  growth of, 44
  romantic novel, 52-56

Scarlet Letter, deity in, 86
Scenes, story presentation by means of, 131
Science, definition, 2
Scott, Sir Walter, *Ivanhoe,* characterization, 53
Sculpture, communication of emotion through, 6
Sedgwick, Anne Douglas, appeal to, communication of emotion through, 10
  development, 2, 11
  Franklin Winslow Kane, extract, 124
  Tante, extract, 9
Sensation. *See* Emotion, Memory.
Sentimentality, Dickens, Charles, 83
  finite novel, 67-71
Sequence, 127-131
  chronological, 127
  definition, 127
  difficulties for writer, 130
  importance, 127
Serials, sequence, chronological, 127
  suspense, 129
Shakespeare, William, *The Merchant of Venice,* morality, 356
  plot, 41
  reason *vs* deity in, 41
Sincerity, importance, 94
Sterne, Laurence, *Tristram Shandy,* fantasy in, 71
Story, method of telling, narrative, 132
  scenic, 131
Style, place in fiction, 84
Swann's Way, extract, 273
Tante, extract, 9

Taste, definition, 347
Time, place in living, 91
Title, selection, time for, 203
Tolstoy, Leo, *War and Peace,* 300-314
  author's intrusion, 308
  characters, 306
  faults, 305
  Napoleon as motif, 311
  reasons for selection for study, 283
  story, 300-305
  subject, 308
  transcendental viewpoint, 312
Tom Jones, characteristics, 71
Transcendental realism. *See* Prophecy.
Tristram Shandy, fantasy in, 71
Truth, definition, 1, 20
  fiction in relation to, Conrad's description, 31
  fiction indistinguishable from, 1
  inner, approaches to, 16
  of feeling, novelists' use, 94
  of man's own nature, approaches to, 16
  See also Fact, Fiction.

Unearthly, extract, 121

War and Peace. See Tolstoy, Leo.
Wilder, Thornton, *The Bridge of San Luis Rey,* plot, 227
Wish to believe, development, 2
Women, misunderstanding of, by man, 114
  recognitions, 112-127
  verification of sensations *vs.* thought, by, 113
Written word, appeal of, indirect, 8
  as vehicle of fiction, 4
Wuthering Heights. See Brontë, Emily.

Youth, extract, 4

ESSAYS AND BELLES LETTRES

THE PEAL OF BELLS

By ROBERT LYND. An attractive volume of informal essays, their themes varied and treated in a fanciful, humorous manner with a real philosophy and sympathy underlying. $2.00.

THE MONEY BOX

By ROBERT LYND. Spontaneous and free essays which treat the most commonplace of everyday subjects in a manner by no means commonplace. $2.50.

CHAUCER'S NUNS and Other Essays

By SISTER M. MADELEVA. Four essays displaying a vitality of material and a delightful vivacity of treatment. $1.50.

PEARL: A Study in Spiritual Dryness

By SISTER M. MADELEVA. An interpretation of the famous old English poem by an unknown writer of the fourteenth century. $2.00.

CAPTAINS AND KINGS

By ANDRÉ MAUROIS. A discussion of leadership in dialogue form, written with all the wit and brilliance that characterizes the author's "Ariel." Translated by J. Lewis May. $1.50.

GREAT COMPANIONS

By EDITH WYATT. Essays on a miscellany of topics, marked by a freshness and briskness and showing a delightful intimacy and sound critical judgment. $2.00.

D. APPLETON AND COMPANY

NEW YORK LONDON

LITERARY STUDIES AND ESSAYS

DE SENECTUTE
By FREDERIC HARRISON

The first essay gives the title, very fittingly, to the last book of this grand old Victorian, recently dead at the age of ninety-two. These essays cover personal recollections besides a variety of literary topics.

SKETCHES FROM A LIBRARY WINDOW
By BASIL ANDERTON

A genuine booklover's talks on the many subjects which attract his fancy and interest. Some are critical and appreciative, others touch on curiosities. All open charming vistas in the world of books.

THE POETIC PROCESSION
By J. F. ROXBURGH

Reviews the course which English poetry has run from the time of Queen Elizabeth down to the present day, pointing out how the poets of each age reflect the times in which they lived.

ROBERT BROWNING: The Poet and the Man
By FRANCES M. SIM

An intensive study of the most significant portion of Browning's life, that in which his earlier successful poems were written, and in which the love story of Browning and Elizabeth Barrett developed.

TENNYSON: A Modern Portrait
By HUGH I'ANSON FAUSSET

A brilliant character analysis of the great Victorian poet. It is largely a study of the man through his work, but intimate personal touches are combined with literary appreciation.

DANTE: The Man and the Poet
By MARY BRADFORD WHITING

A life of Dante for the general reader, describing the events which influenced his early writings and shaped his career, and providing an illuminating study of his great "Divine Comedy."

D. APPLETON AND COMPANY

New York **London**